W9-DEC-914

Your World in Miniature
A Guide to Making
Small-Scale Rooms and Scenes

YOUR WORLD IN MINIATURE

A Guide to Making Small-Scale Rooms and Scenes

Betsey B. Creekmore

and

Betsey Creekmore

LINE DRAWINGS BY
Betty Lynn Jasper

DOUBLEDAY & COMPANY, INC.
GARDEN CITY, NEW YORK
1976

Library of Congress Cataloging in Publication Data

Creekmore, Betsey Beeler.
   Your world in miniature.

   Bibliography: p. 183.
   Includes index.
    1. Dollhouses.   2. Doll furniture.   I. Creekmore,
Betsey, joint author.   II. Title.
TT175.3.C73   745.59'23
ISBN 0-385-06521-3
Library of Congress Catalog Card Number 73-83622

Acknowledgments

The authors are grateful to the following persons for their assistance with the preparation of this book: Louise Condit, Metropolitan Museum of Art, New York; Sally Kington, The London Museum, The Barbican, London; J. E. Schaap and J. B. Braaksma, The Royal Netherlands Embassy, Washington, D.C.; G. H. Dorr III, Phoenix Art Museum, Phoenix; James Fordham, The Victoria and Albert Museum, Bethnal Green, London; Leonie von Wilckens, Germanisches Nationalmuseum, Nuremberg; Victor J. Danilov, The Museum of Science and Industry, Chicago; Charles C. Cunningham, The Art Institute of Chicago; William Ross McNabb, Dulin Gallery of Art, Knoxville.

The Weaver's House described in the text is the property of the College of Home Economics, Department of Crafts and Interior Design, The University of Tennessee, Knoxville. The Hall of Statuary, The Sidewalk Art Show, and the oriental room titled The Culture of the Yellow Race are the property of the Dulin Gallery of Art.

The following miniature scenes, as described in the text, were displayed at the annual meeting of Zone IX, The Garden Club of America: The Garden Club Plant Sale; Mid-City Mini-Park; Suburban Garden in a Fifteen Gallon Aquarium; Conservation; and Tabletop Centerpiece Garden.

Contents

I	Through the Wrong End of the Telescope	1
II	Seven Wonders of the Little World	7
III	Displaying Miniatures in Full-size Furniture	25
IV	Miniature Rooms That Preserve the Present	46
V	Period Rooms That Recapture the Past	68
VI	Flower Arrangements for Miniature Rooms	91
VII	How Miniature Gardens Grow	112
VIII	Portable Scenes and Shops	140
IX	To Build a Mountain	165
X	Under the Christmas Tree	173
	Sources of Supply	199
	Selected Bibliography	201
	Index	203

Your World in Miniature
A Guide to Making
Small-Scale Rooms and Scenes

I

Through the Wrong End of the Telescope

By definition, a miniature is "a small-scale copy of a full-size object." Each of us deals daily with miniatures so familiar that we fail to identify them as such—a watch, for example, is a working model of a clock, and a miniature moving picture fills the screen whenever a television set is turned on. The snapshots we hoard are small-scale landscapes and group portraits; the coins we spend are decorated with tiny sculptures in bas-relief. Every deck of playing cards includes miniature paintings of medieval kings, queens, knaves, and court jesters, while the pieces of a chess set are little sculptured busts or figurines. Each time we mail a letter we stamp it with a miniature engraving. Furthermore, in the interest of compact storage, ever-proliferating public records and newspaper files now are preserved in miniature form on microfilm.

The one thing all these miniatures have in common is that they are proportionately smaller than the originals they copy; how *much* smaller is a matter of scale. Scale is the relative size of a model in comparison to the dimensions of the object it represents. When, for instance, we say that a tiny vase is scaled one inch to one foot, we mean that this inch-high miniature is modeled after an actual vase that is twelve inches tall.

Sometimes the process of making things to scale is reversed: A precision-measured miniature is made first to serve as the prototype for a full-size object. Model houses, towns, and contoured landscapes are indispensable tools-of-the-trade for architects, real estate developers, and regional planners. Testing laboratories experiment with working models of complicated machinery or simulate the stress of flight on model aircraft in miniature wind tunnels. Patent applications are accompanied by scale drawings and models of new inventions.

When and where the first miniature was made we do not know, but in all primitive societies small objects have been shaped, and magical powers have been attributed to them. The charms and fetishes of voodoo are but the most recently forged links in an unbroken chain that reaches back for thousands of years; on every continent archeological digs have yielded small, crude human or animal figures made of clay, bone, stone, wood, or metal.

The ancient Egyptians, believing that their dead could take into the afterlife anything that was buried with them, made clay models of everyday articles and placed them in tombs; the more important the personage, the more elaborate his tomb furnishings would be. Not only his house, its furniture, and his favorite foods were included in miniature, but also his family and his servants. Nor did the model makers stop there. They added the pleasure barge in which he had traveled on the Nile, the litter in which he had been borne on the shoulders of husky slaves, the shops he had owned or patronized, and the gardens that had given him pleasure. In the airless pyramids and tombs of arid Egypt these brightly painted clay models were perfectly preserved for thousands of years; they have shown a way of life in miniature to archeologists who unearthed them in the twentieth century.

In the Orient's even older civilizations home shrines traditionally have held small-size copies of temple statuary. Relatively few of us could identify the ancient deities of India or name the seven Japanese immortals, but every Occidental recognizes the seated Buddha—from ivory and gold statuettes in museums, brass incense burners in import shops, or jade bracelet charms in jewelers' showcases.

Christianity, too, has its miniature religious symbols: the cross and the crucifix, the Madonna, the Christmas crèche. In the Middle Ages small statues of patron saints were venerated talismans, and (in spite of the Vatican's disclaimer) St. Christopher medals still are carried by travelers.

Through the centuries miniatures have served as models for the making of full-size objects. Since the halcyon days of Grecian civilization sculptors have shaped their masterpieces first in clay, correcting the imperfections of these small statuettes in malleable substance before undertaking life-size marble statues. Noble patrons of the arts used to expect that a small model of a projected *chef-d'oeuvre* would be offered for approval before the work was actually under way, and in modern times it has become customary for sculptors to compete for important commissions by submitting models of the statuary they plan. In the days when The London Museum was located in Kensington Palace, a scale model of the Albert Memorial sat in a window overlooking the huge monument; the lovely little replica is made of gold and richly decorated with enamel. It was approved by Queen Victoria before the Memorial was begun, and she kept the model (as she kept every memento of Prince Albert) until her death.

For frescoes so large that they covered whole walls or entire ceilings, Renaissance artists made small preliminary color drawings that were called cartoons, and cartoons also served as directions to the workmen who fitted chips of colored and gilded stone together in marvelous mosaics. Instructions for making the unbelievably intricate motifs of tapestries were given to weavers in the form of cartoons that were drawings in color on cloth and looked like miniature tapestries.

Master builders of the late Middle Ages drew no blueprints for their glorious Gothic churches, for the very good reason that carpenters and stonemasons could not read. Instead, they made scale models of each building at various stages of its construction, and the models were carried to the site for on-the-spot reference. In the National Museum at Munich a large hall is devoted to the display of such small skeletal structures.

The Maximilian Museum in Augsburg exhibits a comprehensive collection of miniature armor, hand weapons, and early artillery pieces that look like toys but served a deadly serious purpose. Through the use of these working models, inventors demonstrated new and improved weapons of war to royal patrons; approved models then guided armorers, iron founders, and gunsmiths in the making of arms and armament.

Before the Industrial Revolution of the nineteenth century, manufacturing was literally done by hand and was under the control of powerful craft guilds. Apprentice pieces of furniture—usually small-scale carved or inlaid cabinets and chests—were made by apprentice cabinetmakers to demonstrate that they had fully mastered their craft and were entitled to membership in its guild. Sample pieces, on the other hand, were small replicas of a master cabinetmaker's work, from which his customers could order full-size furniture. Because these samples could much more easily be transported than bulky, heavy furnishings, new styles often made their way from one country to another, or across the Atlantic, in miniature form.

During the eighteenth century fashion dolls brought the latest modes from London and Paris to Boston, Philadelphia, Baltimore, and Charleston. Famous mantuamakers charged a pretty penny for these jointed wooden dolls wearing the newest of panniered gowns with stylish plumed hats perched atop their elaborate coiffures, and colonial ladies considered them well worth the price. Better than any description or sketch, the dolls' clothes established the proper depth of a décolletage, the draping of an overskirt, the width of a brim, or the placement of a powdered curl.

There are other miniatures that claim historical importance not as working models but as works of art. We think of the Dark Ages as a time when learning and the arts were in abeyance, but out of this darkness came a special form of art-in-miniature—the illuminated manuscript. A monk might spend his lifetime in the scriptorium laboriously copying letter after letter of long Latin words he did not comprehend. To lighten the tedium of this endless task, artistic scribes began to enlarge and ornament the capital letter at the beginning of each chapter. From simple ink-black curlicues the venturesome progressed to gold-leaf scrolls and tiny paintings in rainbow colors; portraits could be framed by letter O's, or grapevines bearing bunches of ripe fruit might clamber up and over M's. As time went on, white parchment borders virtually disappeared beneath marvelous panels in which flowers bloomed, birds soared, and animals disported. Then breviaries and Books of Hours were illustrated, to the greater glory of God, with miniature scenes in glowing colors where biblical characters were garbed in the clothing of the late Middle Ages.

In the mannered eighteenth century, artists in Italy and France were busily producing miniature landscapes on enameled snuff-box lids, and leisured ladies occupied their time with découpage which involved the coloring, cutting, and pasting of printed motifs on trays and boxes to create miniature pastoral scenes. Portrait painters in Europe and America were following a trend toward miniaturization when they perfected a far more famous art form: the miniature portrait on ivory. Not everyone could afford these beautiful but costly little paintings, so a less-expensive substitute for them was found in silhouettes; amateur and professional artists deftly cut miniature profile portraits, with scissors, from black paper and mounted them on white.

Aside from any religious, practical, or artistic significance they might possess, little things have always appealed to adults because of their delicacy and charm. As a case in point, Alexander III of Russia—that giant of a Czar—kept a collection of tiny glass and porcelain animals in a locked drawer of his imperial desk. Furthermore, Napoleon is reputed to have determined his strategy before important battles by deploying miniature cavalry and cannon on a table top. Although this story may be apocryphal, it is undeniably true that military-minded men have often joined their sons in fighting sham battles with lead soldiers and toy artillery.

For centuries ship models were made by sailors on long voyages and by ship fanciers at home; today, exciting sea battles in the movies are fought with model ships, on an ocean the size of a small swimming pool that is churned into waves by machine. Late in the nineteenth century trains supplanted ships as the most miniaturized form of travel, and in the early nineteen-hundreds the electric train became the most exciting working model of all time for railroad buffs of all ages. In recent years boys have delighted in erector sets that teach the basic principles of bridge and building construction, and in model kits containing precut plastic or balsa-wood parts for automobiles and airplanes. Budding aeronautical and mechanical engineers move on from these juvenile exercises to making elaborate models from scratch.

Many modern women profess themselves totally uninterested in miniatures yet collect bracelet charms or cherish cameos that are miniature profile portraits carved in layered stone or shell. Most girls (and their mothers) still are fascinated by miniature household furnishings and dolls—which are, of course, small-scale representations of babies, children, and adults. Frances Hodgson Burnett, in an article for the April, 1915, issue of the *Ladies' Home Journal,* described once and for all the allure of these diminutive things:

> . . . I was walking through a village and saw a small shop whose window presented objects before which I paused transfixed. There were a small Japanese tea-table, and six small chairs made of bamboo. On the table was a tiny Japanese tea-set of green-ware, the tea-pot with a wicker handle. And around the tea sat a small Japanese family, composed of a mamma, a papa, and three unextinguishably beautiful Japanese babies, all in dazzling kimonos and with shaved heads except the mamma, who wore fans in her hair. It was impossible to pass them by.
>
> "I will go in and buy them," I said in that sneakingly specious manner in which we always make plausible excuses for our weaknesses. "I can give them to some child."
>
> The unadorned truth was I did not want to give them to "some child." I wanted them for myself because they were so human and delicious and tiny and quaint . . .

The acquisitive instinct is strong in all of us, but space is at a premium in the twentieth century's functional houses and high-rise apartments. It is therefore hardly surprising that statistics show the most popular present-day collectors' items to be small in size—coins, stamps, and miniatures, in that order. Many an ardent miniature collector embarked upon this hobby quite by accident because a little silver tea set or a minute chair with petit-point upholstery would fit into the corner of carry-on luggage for the plane trip home. Buying a tiny porcelain plate here and an inch-high brass candlestick there is habit-forming, so the travel souvenirs quickly fill a hanging shelf. Sooner or later the shelf becomes crowded, and the miniatures are moved into a cabinet; then the cabinet overflows. Reluctantly, a few little things are weeded out—not to be given away or discarded, but to be carefully wrapped in tissue paper and packed in cardboard storage boxes. By now, however, the habit is too strong to break; one goes right on acquiring miniatures because they are completely and utterly irresistible.

The mere collecting of little objects would be a selfish hobby, and miniaturists are too gregarious a group to be content with gloating over tiny treasures in solitude. The question is, what *can* one do with a miniature collection, other than dust it? While the collection is growing it can be displayed to advantage in attractive pieces of furniture to interest family and friends. Eventually, following the example set by miniaturists in the past, one can create delightful small-scale rooms and scenes that can be used in many ways. Period rooms recapture the past as museum displays or serve as valuable teaching aids that capture the attention of a child and linger in his memory. Miniature scenes can arrest and preserve the quirks of the present fleeting moment for instant amusement and for future edification.

Becoming a practicing miniaturist means cultivating a seeing eye, a sense of scale, and a steady hand. It presupposes ingenuity and a sense of humor, for half the fun of making diminutive displays lies in using small everyday objects in unusual ways. Seeing a miniature rug in a patterned washcloth, or a miniature flowerpot in the cap of the toothpaste tube, one begins to understand the joys of looking at the world through the wrong end of the telescope.

II

Seven Wonders
of the Little World

Throughout recorded history, miniatures have been made and cherished. Of course, it is primarily because they *were* cherished that so many have survived the vicissitudes of time and war, but their very smallness and uselessness have helped to make survival possible. Full-size household articles wear out and are discarded—plates chip and glasses crack, saucepans leak and skillets lose their handles, even the sturdiest furniture eventually succumbs—while scale models of these vanished things remain in mint condition. Belatedly recognizing their historic and sociological merit as well as their charm, museums all over the world have begun to acquire collections of miniatures that attract both serious scholars and excited children. For adult collectors of small-scale objects, these museum displays have a very important additional value; they prove beyond the shadow of a doubt that miniatures are far more interesting and effective when arranged in rooms and scenes than when they are merely grouped by type and period in glass cases.

Such a multitude of little things are on view in so many widely separated cities that years could be spent happily in visiting them; to catalogue and describe them all would require more than one lifetime. Certain displays stand out, however, because their techniques are worthy of imitation or their ideas are capable of expansion, and seven of these have been selected to represent the many wonders of the little world. Four of the seven are composite wonders—types of rooms or scenes rather than specific examples—while the remaining three wonderful displays are complete within themselves. As a group they illustrate such practical yet imaginative ways of combining miniatures in small-scale rooms and portable scenes that one or more of the procedures is sure to appeal to today's collector.

I - Miniature Mountains of Semi-precious Stone

The rough-hewn pyramidal mountain peaks of Europe and Asia stand guard over richly colored buried treasures—among them amethyst, lapis lazuli, topaz, garnet, rose quartz—that sometimes are unearthed in the form of jagged, cone-shaped chunks. In eastern Europe, during the Byzantine Era, polished semi-precious cabochons were set in heavy gold jewelry while flat chips were fitted into colorful mosaic designs, but it was not until the time of the western Renaissance that a use was found for the large triangular masses.

Renaissance philosophers saw these rough pyramids of semi-precious stone as miniature mountains, and it was as mountain peaks that the translucent, glowing cones became coveted objects of art. Every crystalline peak differed from all the others in size, shape, and color, so each was given a specially designed mounting. Then gold- and silversmiths further embellished the shining pinnacles with miniatures made of precious metals. Historians think that the originator of this unique art form was Wentzel Jamnitzer, who was born in 1508 at Vienna and enrolled in the goldsmith's guild at Nuremberg in 1534. Among his contemporaries, the imaginative design and delicate precision of his work earned for him the title of "the German Cellini."

Indeed, some of the elaborate footed stands that Jamnitzer devised for his decorated mountains were strongly reminiscent of a Cellini saltcellar; but only the smallest of the stone pyramids could be balanced on such slender-stemmed compotes. Wider, heavier masses were given architectural bases whose designs derived from ancient Rome: square entablatures borne on the heads of sturdy silver caryatids, or circular architraves supported by bronze columns.

Each conical mass was distinctive in the position of its peaks and planes and suggested its own ornamentation to the artist who studied it. Slender peaks could be crowned with tiny onion-domed churches in imitation of the actual churches that perch so precariously on alpine crags. Castle towers and battlements could balance on overhanging cliffs, exactly as full-size castles cling to the palisades beside the Rhine. Miniature knights on horseback might ride along narrow horizontal ledges, while burdened peasants toiled up steep slopes, past grazing sheep and groves of silver-filigree trees. The height of these decorations varied, of course, with the size of the mineral masses they adorned, but most of the churches and castles were less than two inches tall. The trees, animals, and human figures were no larger than bracelet charms.

So costly were these sumptuous ornaments that only the very wealthy could afford them, and they often were presented by one prince to another, or by king to queen. From the castles of Austria, Hungary, Russia, Germany, and Italy have come marvelous examples of miniature mountain scenes that are now in various museums. The collection of Vienna's Kunsthistorisches Museum is so extensive that it fills a large display hall. Here the semi-precious specimens range in height from a mere four or five inches to a towering two or three feet.

The most unusual of these pieces is one whose coloring has inspired a theme of ornamentation that is singularly appropriate, but macabre. The mineral specimen is both wide and deep; at its base, where the stone is thickest, it has the deep rich red of glowing coals. Thin, translucent ridges and slender spires rise from this mass of embers, and light turns them into scarlet, orange, and brimstone-yellow flames. At the heart of this fiery inferno a smiling Satan brandishes his pitchfork over a pit where damned souls writhe in torment.

In soothing contrast to this diabolical display is a small crystalline peak on a stand shaped like the scallop shell that was the badge worn by medieval pilgrims on their way to worship at miraculous shrines. Here the only ornament is a tiny golden church whose elongated steeple points hopefully to heaven.

II - Germany's Portable Rooms and Scenes

No one knows precisely when small carved wooden miniatures were first arranged together in a portable scene. It well might have happened during the Dark Ages when some patient lay brother whittled a few pairs of animals and fitted them into a boxlike Noah's Ark. By the early sixteenth century, at any rate, carved wooden "hunts" were favorite gifts for German princelings; these included hunters on horseback, hounds, and gamekeepers, to say nothing of stags, boars, foxes, wolves, and rabbits. At about the same time, miniature poultry yards were being made for little girls of noble birth; they contained ducks, geese, chickens, swans, and peacocks molded of wax and covered with feathers, individually applied.

From the sixteenth through the eighteenth centuries the city of Nuremberg was the acknowledged center of toymaking, and it was here that the world-famous Nuremberg kitchens originated. These were topless, three-sided oblong wooden boxes, crammed with every kitchen necessity and every known convenience; they antedate by some three hundred years the twentieth century's vaunted educational toys, yet they were made (and used) as teaching devices. With them, little girls imitated in play the work of the adult household and learned by doing without getting underfoot.

"Nuremberg kitchen" came to be a descriptive name, identifying the type of toy rather than its place of manufacture. Portable kitchens were produced in Augsburg, Ulm, Basel, and Zurich, to name but a few of many toymaking cities, and teaching toys were also made for boys: updated versions of the earlier hunts, and portable stables complete with hide-covered wooden horses, tack, and vehicles. A little later there were portable shops: butcher and apothecary shops for boys, milliner's and draper's establishments for girls, toy stalls and basket booths for children of both sexes. All these early portables varied in scale according to the whim of the toymaker. Some of the shops and kitchens were small enough to be balanced on the palm of a child's hand, while others were so large that they were doll (rather than dollhouse) size.

There was no toy factory as such, but every kitchen and shop was a co-operative effort. Each type of miniature object was turned out as a sideline by craft-guild members who made similar full-size articles: Miniature furniture was produced by cabinetmakers; kitchen utensils by tin- and coppersmiths; bowls, pitchers, and jugs by potters.

In the eighteenth century toymakers in the cities were forced to meet stiff competition from the wood carvers of Thuringia and the Tyrol, whose toys were crude but much cheaper than those collectively made by guild members. City toyshops therefore added new types of rooms and scenes to their shelves. Instead of a single shop, they displayed street fairs; in addition to the ever-popular kitchens, they offered parlors. Some of the new shops and rooms even had hinged wooden cases that folded up for carrying or storage. The more imaginative toymakers also began to produce miniature scenes that illustrated Bible stories, historical events, or folk legends.

Where are they now, those thousands of little rooms and scenes? Although most of them were quite literally loved to pieces long ago, a surprising number have found their way into museums and locating them there is easy—the toy collection is invariably five flights up at the very top of the stairs. Understandably, Nuremberg's Germanisches Museum and Augsburg's Maximilian Museum are generously supplied with early kitchens and shops. The National Museum in Munich and the Historisches Museum der Stadt Wien in Vienna have shops and rooms; so does the Nordiska Museet in Stockholm. In Zurich, the famous toy-manufacturing firm of Franz Carl Weber, founded in 1881, has opened its own museum of antique toys in which fine eighteenth- and early-nineteenth-century rooms and shops have been selected to serve as the precursors of the company's own products. The most interesting and inclusive display of single shops, street fairs, and story-illustration scenes can, however, be seen in Basel, at the Schweitzerisches Museum für Volkskunde.

In London, an enormous collection of British-made and imported shops and scenes is on display at the Bethnal Green branch of the Victoria and Albert Museum. English peddler dolls of the eighteenth and nineteenth centuries are a delightful change from the customary shops in boxes and fairs on boards. Most of these female peddlers carry their wares on large trays supported by neck straps, and additional items are pinned to their voluminous skirts. The dolls themselves are small, averaging from eight to twelve inches in height, and their stock consists of an amazing variety of "notions"—pincushions, scent bottles, scissors, knives, and toys—all infinitesimal in size.

In the United States, there are predictably fine examples of rooms and shops at New York's Metropolitan Museum of Art and Washington's Smithsonian Institution, and a fine collection of early toys is shown at the Denver Art Museum.

Every Nuremberg kitchen, wherever it is on display, features a bewildering array of cooking utensils. Around the walls hang long-handled skillets and saucepans, fish poachers and pudding molds, colanders and ladles, and so on and on. In addition to the pots and pans there are washtubs and wringers. Pewter and/or pottery plates are lined up on a plate rail, and shelves are crowded with bowls, platters, cream jugs, mugs, and covered soup tureens. Above the cooking hearth with its grill and roasting spit, a wide chimney hood is placed to draw off smoke and fumes.

Milliners' shops also follow a set pattern: Background shelves hold tiny bolts of silks and velvets, rolls of ribbon and lace, and baskets of curled plumes. In the foreground, elaborately coiffed mannikin heads display becoming wide-brimmed hats, sensible bonnets, and flower-trimmed chip straws; sometimes the shopkeeper in her black silk apron stands behind the counter, conferring with a modishly dressed customer. Butcher shops resemble each other in a rather alarming way, with gory carcasses hanging from the eaves outside the little building, and realistic cuts of meat arranged below draped strings of sausages in the window. A wooden butcher's block centers the sawdust-covered floor, and here the aproned proprietor, cleaver in hand, is plying his trade.

In Basel's Schweitzerisches Museum für Volkskunde, an amazingly colorful and detailed nineteenth-century street fair is made on a wide wooden board, grooved and painted to resemble paving stones. Along one side of this road is a series of shops, each in its own brightly awninged booth, and customers—children and adults—are examining the wares of the balloon man, the toy stall, the basket booth, and the sweetshop.

Even more fascinating is this museum's series of storybook scenes. One of the most interesting illustrates the famous children's classic by Heinrich Hoffman, *King Nutcracker and Poor Reinhold,* on which the delightful *Nutcracker* ballet is based. A little boy is shown asleep in his tumbledown bed beneath a patched and threadbare coverlet. On the opposite side of the room is the Christmas tree of which he is dreaming, laden with sweets and surrounded by toys. The poverty of the room and its furnishings is in startling contrast to the festive tree and the wealth of marvelous playthings.

Among the miniature treasures in London's Bethnal Green Museum is a very old and very beautiful room with carved wood paneling, leaded windowpanes, and simple furniture. This serves as the setting for a scene that some call an historic event, but others declare to be a legend; it shows Martin Luther, in black scholar's garb, about to light the candles on the first Christmas tree while Frau

Luther and the children look on in astonishment. As the story goes, Dr. Luther was walking alone among the bare-branched trees at the edge of the forest on a clear, cold Christmas Eve. Suddenly, he was struck by the beauty of a little fir tree, bravely testifying by its bright green foliage that life was everlasting—its branches, outlined against the darkening sky, seemed to be tipped with twinkling stars. As a lesson for his children, he took the little fir tree home and placed it on a table, adding a candle at the end of each branch to simulate a star.

III - The Christmas Putz at Old Salem

According to another well-loved legend, it was St. Francis of Assisi who assembled the first Nativity Scene, in the early thirteenth century. The truth of the matter is that the good saint merely popularized a Christmas custom that had been in existence for eight hundred years or more; Nativity scenes had been described as early as A.D. 400 by St. John Chrysostom and St. Gregory Thaumaturgus. It was, however, during the lifetime of St. Francis, and in response to his urging, that churches began to stress the observance of Christmas, and to use seasonal displays that were life-size statues of the Holy Family, kneeling shepherds, and Wise Men bearing gifts.

Soon the nobles of Italy and southern France were commissioning small-scale models of these figures for their villas and châteaux. The simple manger gradually grew into an outdoor scene that might contain hundreds of persons—all in contemporary dress—wending their way on foot, in carts, or on horseback to pay homage to the Infant Jesus. Not only the ox, the ass, and the lambs of the church scene were reproduced in miniature, but also all the beasts of the forest and the birds beloved of St. Francis. Especially in Italy, the crèche came to contain a myriad of tiny objects that were offered as gifts to the Christ Child: jeweled crowns and scepters, beribboned lutes and mandolins, fruits, vegetables, meats and fishes, loaves of bread, and bottles of wine.

In northern Europe, table-top-size Nativity scenes were cherished possessions of poor families as well as rich, for there the figures were carved and painted by members of the household. Because December weather was severe, the wooden stable was depicted against a snowy background. In Germanic countries, the secular carvings of people in contemporary dress were soon separated from the sacred scene in a special display called a *putz*. (The name comes from the German verb *putzen*, which means "to decorate.") After the introduction of the Christmas tree at the time of the Reformation, the *putz* was arranged around the base of the table tree, in a snowy landscape made of a linen sheet strewn with wisps of white wool. The *putz* often included trees and buildings as well as animals and people; a woodcutter bent beneath the weight of a bundle of firewood, and a horse-drawn sled loaded with sacks of grain or kegs of beer were favorite motifs of the Thuringian wood carvers.

Each group of colonists coming to America brought the beloved customs of some European homeland, and early German settlers clung to the idea of the candle-lighted Christmas tree with a *putz* beneath its branches. This was true in Salem, North Carolina—a congregation town that was founded in 1766 by members of the Moravian Church—where the *putz* has always been a featured Christmas decoration.

In the midst of the modern city of Winston-Salem is the historic area of Old Salem, with its many original eighteenth-century buildings, centering around the church square. On one side of the square stands the Single Brothers' House, which was built in 1769 as a home and workshop for the unmarried men and boys of the Moravian community. In the deep arched cellars of this house (once storage rooms where smoked hams hung from iron hooks, and rows of barrels held sauerkraut, apples, or beer) a men's committee of the Home Moravian Church annually sets up the traditional Christmas scene that actually is a dual display: a huge *putz,* and a large and reverent representation of the Nativity. The men of the *putz* committee bring many talents to the task of designing, constructing, assembling, dismantling, and storing these two impressive displays that are open to the public only during the month of December.

In a long narrow tunnel of a room, a raised platform holds the entire town of Salem as it appeared in the years between 1830 and 1860. The platform is approximately twenty-two feet long and nine feet wide, and the scale of this tremendous *putz* is one-eighth inch to the foot; this means that the carved human figures are a mere three-quarters of an inch tall. Like the town itself, the *putz* centers around the Home Church; faint recorded organ music seems to be coming from within it, and at intervals there is a silvery chime from the tower clock. The season is winter, and the time is early evening. White marble dust covers streets and rooftops with a snowy blanket, and the yellow lamplight streaming from the windows of the tiny buildings is provided by model-railway bulbs wired into transformers below the platform. Leafless trees (made of fine wires) mingle their snow-encrusted branches along the streets where workmen are trudging home, heavily laden wagons are headed for the farm barns at the edge of town, a happy family is enjoying an outing in a horse-drawn sleigh. At the far end of the platform, snow-tipped cornshocks stand in neat rows, and a bridge across a narrow stream leads to the tall grist mill with its silently turning water wheel.

Since 1950 an organization called Old Salem, Inc. has been acquiring, renovating, and opening to the public the ancient buildings of this historic area. Whenever another house is purchased and restored, the restoration is duly recorded in miniature for the *putz*. More than fifty structures now are shown, ranging in size from the columned Main Hall of Salem College for Women (founded in 1772) to small side-street cottages built in German fashion of squared logs. Each house is a faithful scale copy of a large original, but the barns, corncribs, and outhouses of the *putz* no longer exist in actuality.

Following the German custom of separating the secular from the religious, the Nativity Scene is presented in another cellar, so small and dim that it might be a cave, or a cave stable. Dramatic lighting is an essential feature of this display. As a guide in eighteenth-century Moravian costume begins to read the Christmas story from the Gospel According to St. Luke, the hillside town of Bethlehem is spotlighted at the end of the cavernous chamber. Its buildings are no larger than those of the Salem *putz,* and because they are so small they appear to be seen from a great distance. The spotlight then shifts to a group of shepherds tending their sheep on a rocky hillside in the middle distance; the scale here is larger, about one inch to the foot. The angel that appears above this pastoral scene in the glow of a second spotlight is a little larger than the earthbound shepherds. On the right, and closer to the spectators, a many-pointed Moravian (Advent) star suddenly shines in the darkness; below the star, bathed in its light, is the large cave stable in which the Holy Family is surrounded by cattle, sheep, and kneeling shepherds. Finally, Wise Men (still larger figures, in a scale of two inches to the foot) are floodlighted in the left foreground; their faces are turned toward the starlit stable. Scale is used here not as a means of indicating perspective but as emphasis—the figures grow larger as the story approaches its climax.

When the reading ends, the lights come on again in sequence as the soft strains of *Oh, Little Town of Bethlehem* sound in the darkened cellar.

IV - The Cabinet Houses of Holland

During the sixteenth century, Europe's wealthy nobles were spending fortunes on impressive "art cabinets" whose shelves were crowded with miniature hunts, clockwork toys, and tiny valuable *objets d'art* of the sort first made for elaborate Italian Nativity scenes. Soon someone was inspired to place a Nuremberg-type kitchen and a model stable in an art cabinet, and to add other miniature rooms; from such a cabinet evolved the first dollhouse of record, which was built in 1558 for the little daughter of Duke Albrecht V of Bavaria. The finished toy was so elegant and so unusual that the delighted Duke immediately claimed it for himself and placed it in his art collection; a detailed inventory of Duke Albrecht's possessions, made in 1598, describes the cabinet house as a many-windowed palace four stories tall, containing such luxurious appurtenances as a ballroom, a bathroom, a chapel, and a zoological garden. The fame of Duke Albrecht's treasure inspired the toymakers of Augsburg, Ulm, and Nuremberg to reproduce tall city houses in miniature and to furnish them completely in the prevailing mode.

It was in the Netherlands, however, that the craze for displaying costly household miniatures in handsome cabinets reached an all-time high during the seven-teenth and eighteenth centuries. The typical cabinet was a massive piece of furni-ture, five or six feet wide and seven or eight feet high. Its deep shelves were raised on sturdy legs, and enclosed by carved or painted doors; the shelves were divided into rooms filled with replicas of furnishings that were scaled about one inch to ten. These miniatures were definitely not toys, but were status symbols. The use of silver in place of baser metals for chandeliers and fireplace tools might be defended on the grounds that silver was easier to mold in miniature than iron or brass, but it was obviously for show alone that pots and pans, buckets, washtubs, and chamberpots were also made of silver.

It was a point of pride with the wealthy burghers who commissioned such cabi-net houses to have them include everything a well-appointed Dutch household would contain—the mousetrap in the kitchen, the baby's rattle in the nursery, even the chair with the broken leg in the attic. As the demand for household miniatures increased, the celebrated silversmiths of Schoonhoven redoubled their efforts. Cabinetmakers produced more and finer small pieces of furniture, glass blowers created incredibly tiny stemmed wine glasses and delicate decanters, and the famous potters at Delft turned out thousands of pieces of miniature crockery decorated in the prevailing fashion with blue-and-white oriental motifs.

No full-size seventeenth-century Dutch house remains absolutely unchanged today, but several cabinet houses have survived intact. These now serve as primary source material for eminent historians and sociologists, who study them to find out what life was like in Holland's Golden Century. For this reason, Dutch museums are proud of their cabinet houses and display them prominently; every general museum has at least one, but particularly fine examples are in Utrecht's Centraal Museum, The Hague's Gemeentemuseum, and Amsterdam's Rijksmuseum.

The Utrecht House (c. 1680) is one of the oldest and handsomest of all the cabinets. Its fifteen rooms include a drawing room with walls and ceiling painted by the celebrated muralist, de Moucheron; there is also an art chamber, on whose walls hang miniature landscapes and portraits signed by famous Dutch painters of the period. This house claims the doubtful distinction of being the only Dutch display cabinet ever burglarized; in 1831, discriminating thieves stole its drawing room chandelier and silver fire irons, a set of forks and spoons, a tortoise-shell cabinet, and an amber chest inlaid with ivory and gold. Fortunately, the burglars did not damage the garden—definitely French in feeling—that is tucked away in a corner of the lowest shelf. Here there are pear trees espaliered on low walls, dwarf orange trees in planters, marble statuary, and a latticed summerhouse. Typically Dutch, though, is the undersized bowling green where a game of nine-pins is set up. Time seems to have stood still in this garden, and American visitors expect a miniature Rip van Winkle to appear at any moment.

Although the Utrecht specimen is older, a house in The Hague's Gemeentemuseum is the best documented of all Dutch curio cabinets. On April 10, 1743, Sara Ploos van Amstel attended an auction in Amsterdam, where she bought three curio cabinets complete with furnishings; two of the three dated from the previous century, for they had been sold once before, in 1700. Sara was a woman who kept meticulous records. She promptly inventoried the furnishings of the cabinets she had bought, and then commissioned a fine walnut cabinet-on-a-chest-of-drawers to house their combined contents. As she arranged her cabinet, refurbishing the old furniture with upholstery and hangings which she made herself, she ordered new pieces to complete her collection and kept careful account of their cost. In one of the seventeenth-century cabinets there had been a small "china room," in which miniature Chinese porcelain was displayed on shelves in arched alcoves. (From the day the first blue-and-white Nanking ware arrived in Holland in 1603, no Dutch housewife could be content without at least one cabinet filled with it.) Mme. Ploos van Amstel ordered her cabinetmaker to incorporate this room into the new house, greatly enlarging the display space to accommodate her other porcelain miniatures.

Alongside the Ploos van Amstel house in the Gemeentemuseum, a full-size wall of shelves (from a patrician house in The Hague) holds a fine collection of Chinese porcelain, mirroring in larger scale the arrangement of Sara's expanded china room. The full-size pieces on display are genuine and rare, but most of Sara's "Chinese" miniatures were locally made, of delft pottery or milkglass, and merely painted with blue-and-white oriental designs.

On the lower floor of the Ploos van Amstel house is a lying-in room, where the recently confined lady of the house is receiving a caller who has come to see the new baby. This entire scene is an interesting bit of social history perfectly preserved, for lying-in rooms have long since vanished from Dutch homes. Because a lying-in chamber was a reception room as well as a bedroom and nursery, its furnishings were expected to be elaborate and costly. Here the wall covering, bed curtains, and coverlet are of rose-colored watered silk, and the wicker cradle is covered with a crewel-embroidered spread. The dressing table is crowded with silver toilet articles, and beside it stands a charming replica of Sara's curio cabinet itself; the miniature's shelves are neatly stacked with folded sheets, pillowcases, and baby clothes. The center table is lavishly set for tea, with the kettle just coming to a boil beside it on a small portable stove. Presiding at the tea table is the baby's proud grandmother, who is wearing an elaborate tea gown with a collar and wide sleeve ruffles of fine lace; she has completed her costume with a pair of pearl earrings. The new mother is looking rather pale and wan. She reclines in an easy chair, attired in a blue silk negligee, a close-fitting white cap, and a white shoulder cape to ward off drafts. The stout elderly visitor is dressed for the street in bonnet, gloves, and a fitted velvet jacket. The baby, in the arms of the aproned nurse, wears a lace cap, a tight bodice, and skirts as voluminous as an adult's.

In Amsterdam's Rijksmuseum, a tall cabinet house stands beside its own portrait, which was painted by Jacob Appel about 1700. The museum's official booklet, printed in 1967, asserts that this house belonged originally to a lady named Petronella Oortman Brandt; then the booklet adds the tantalizing statement that the house "used to be associated with the Czar Peter the Great, but there is no foundation for this claim." A persistent legend still insists that Czar Peter, who spent some time studying navigation in Holland as a young man, was so captivated by the Dutch cabinet houses that he ordered an elaborate one for himself, at an estimated cost of twenty thousand florins. Returning to Russia before the house was finished, Peter is said to have directed his Dutch resident agent, Christoffel van Brants, to supervise the cabinet's completion and send it on to him. When after five years the work was finally done, the cost had greatly exceeded the agreed-upon amount. Perhaps Peter, concerned now with larger affairs, had lost interest in little things; perhaps he simply rebelled at what he considered an exorbitant price. For whatever reason, he is supposed to have rejected the cabinet sight unseen.

No other cabinet house had its portrait painted, and possibly it was the painting that gave rise to the legend. After all, if the cabinet had been going to an imperial palace in far-off Russia, it seems logical to suppose that its Dutch designer would have wanted a portrait of his masterpiece as a souvenir. Conceivably, on the other hand, the portrait might have been painted for Peter, to be sent to him for approval (along with a request for payment) before the valuable cabinet was dispatched on its long journey. Disregarding the portrait, the myth may simply have arisen as a result of confusing the name of Czar Peter's Dutch agent, van Brants, with the surname of Petronella's husband, which was Brandt. Although there is a difference in spelling, the pronunciation of the two names would be almost the same.

There is always the possibility that Czar Peter did order a number of miniatures in the course of his youthful travels, and that he actually received them. The Hermitage Museum in Leningrad has on display a series of miniature rooms furnished in solid gold that are labeled as seventeenth-century French.

In its own right, the Brandt house is grand enough to be a royal residence, with walls, ceilings, and chimney breasts painted by such celebrated Dutch artists as Nicolaas Piemont and Jan Voorhout. The silver brazier, kettle, and urn on a bedroom table are signed by Christiaan Waarenburg, a famous Amsterdam silversmith, and the Rijksmuseum proudly displays a similar full-size urn by the same maker. An additional point of interest is the miniature curio cabinet in this curio cabinet: In a room whose walls are entirely covered with flame-stitch embroidery, a black-and-gold lacquered Chinese chest holds a collection of minuscule shells.

The most attractive room, however, is the "best kitchen" with its tiled walls, marble floor, and ceiling painting of a *tromp-l'oeil* octagonal dome. A built-in cupboard runs the length of one wall, and holds an astounding collection of fine china and glassware—part of the housewife's dowry—that includes rummers, flute glasses, cruets and vases, tea canisters, covered jars, and patterned plates. The "best kitchen," another unusual feature of Dutch houses in the Golden Century, was not for cooking but was rather a showplace where the housewife's close women friends were entertained.

V - Queen Mary's Dolls' House

Meanwhile, across the narrow Channel, the cabinet houses esteemed by Dutch adults had turned into English "baby houses" that were made for children and meant for play. In the last decade of the seventeenth century, daughterless Queen Anne presented to her goddaughter, Ann Sharp, a baby house that contains nine rooms and an attic, and is inhabited by a large family of little dolls. Its kitchen features food rather than utensils, with a plum pudding boiling in a copper kettle above the fire, and a suckling pig roasting on the spit; there is more food on the sideboard in the dining hall—a roasted fowl, and the inevitable leg of mutton.

During the eighteenth century, English baby houses were designed by architects and often were modeled after actual manor houses, inside and out. The plans for these miniature manors were carefully drawn to a typically British scale —one inch to the foot—that has since become the internationally recognized size for dollhouse furniture.

In 1924 Queen Mary of England received as a gift from the British people a royal residence so remarkable for its beauty and its mechanical perfection that it immediately became the world's most famous miniature house. Although it is called Queen Mary's Dolls' House, it contains no dolls—and was never a toy. The idea behind the construction of this imposing edifice was to produce a model twentieth-century home, complete in every artistic detail and containing every convenience and comfort yet devised; it was also foreseen that the house could be exhibited to the delighted public for the benefit of the Queen's favorite charities.

A dolls' house may seem an unlikely object to have been presented by admiring subjects to so dignified and stately a sovereign, yet no gift could have been more appreciated. The Queen's predilection for miniatures was well known. In 1879 Princess Mary of Teck (the future wife of King George V) received an elaborate dolls' house for her twelfth birthday; its commercially made furnishings appropriately and prophetically included a tiny Bible and an even smaller *History of England*. Her enjoyment of this house inspired her lifelong hobby of miniature collecting. She gave to the Victoria and Albert Museum many royally beautiful rooms, among them a kitchen with all its utensils made of solid gold, and a drawing room furnished entirely with delicately carved ivory. Queen Mary never could resist buying antique dolls' houses and locating proper period furniture for them; some she gave to small relatives, while others were donated to the Victoria and Albert. The Queen's splendid rooms and antique dolls' houses now are part of the wonderful toy collection at the Bethnal Green Museum, in London.

To build and furnish a miniature house worthy of so discriminating a collector was no mean undertaking. Sir Edwin Lutyens, a distinguished architect who had planned the city of New Delhi and had built many imposing English country houses, was chosen to design a mansion in the classical tradition of ancient Rome, with overtones of Renaissance Italy; many stately homes of England are similar in style.

The wooden facade and roof of the house, grooved and painted to resemble stone and slate, form a separate outer shell that can be vertically raised by means of an electric motor to reveal the entire interior. The house has electric lighting and an elevator, but it boasts even more interesting mechanical features: functional door locks; hot and cold running water; an electric vacuum cleaner and an electric iron that actually work when plugged into baseboard sockets. Its stone foundation hides two deep drawers that pull out to reveal a delightful garden on the east front, and a garage on the west. The garage, which fascinates masculine visitors of all ages, contains a fleet of 1934 model cars—a seven-passenger Rolls-Royce limousine, two Daimlers (one a shooting brake), a Lanchester, a Vauxhall, and a Sunbeam open touring car—plus a grease rack and a gasoline pump. In addition, the garage finds room for a motorcycle with sidecar, a fire engine, two perambulators, a bicycle, and a cleaning cart.

Not only the cars, but also the furniture, the silver, the china and crystal, the clocks, the coal range, and the plumbing fixtures were produced especially for the house by prestigious British manufacturing firms. Linens, carpets, upholstery materials, and draperies were specially woven in selected English textile mills. As if this were not wonder enough, the arts as well as the artistry of England are represented. Renowned Royal Academicians of the 1920s were asked to paint miniature landscapes, portraits, or murals for the entrance hall, the drawing room, the sovereigns' bedrooms, the dining room, and the library which is the most remarkable of all the rooms. Here musical scores by contemporary British composers fill fifty inch-square volumes, and more than seven hundred prints, water colors, and drawings are stored in large cabinets; but the library's greatest treasures are the many unpublished, handwritten mini-manuscripts by England's illustrious novelists and poets that have been bound in leather and ranged upon the shelves.

Because this is a royal house, it contains a strong room where replicas of some of the British crown jewels are stored. But since it is also a family's home, it has a day nursery well stocked with toys: a model railroad, a dollhouse, a puppet theater, and a wind-up phonograph that actually plays its one and only record, *God Save the King*.

Many years ago Queen Mary's Dolls' House was placed on permanent display at Windsor Castle. The house, with its facade raised above it, stands in the center of a large room and is completely surrounded by plate glass. This most famous of all miniature marvels is also the most frequently visited. In summer, long lines of expectant viewers form outside the building and inch forward to the special entrance where tickets are sold; inside, the line moves two abreast around the house in its glass enclosure—no loitering, please—and then the visitors find themselves in a corridor lined with glass cases of dolls. Only minutes have been spent in the presence of a wonder that should be savored slowly over a period of several days.

VI - The Thorne Rooms

During the nineteen-thirties and -forties, an extensive and exciting series of miniature period rooms was produced by Mrs. James Ward Thorne of Chicago, Illinois.

From early childhood Mrs. Thorne had felt the fascination of small furniture and accessories. Graduating from dollhouse decorating, she progressed to collecting eighteenth-century "sample" furniture and apprentice pieces; then as an adult traveler, she searched the antique shops of several continents for old and unusual miniatures. By 1930 she had assembled a large collection of antique pieces one-twelfth actual size, and a selection of fabrics woven or printed in extremely small designs; she then decided that these treasures could most effectively be displayed in a series of rooms built to the same scale as the miniatures—one inch to one foot.

Having seen how small, shallow dioramas in museums were built into the walls at adult eye level, Mrs. Thorne adapted this idea to her purpose. In so doing, she invented an entirely new technique of concealed indirect lighting for her recessed rooms: the light came from outside, through windowpanes and open doors, as daylight comes into full-size houses. Like most great inspirations, the idea was a simple one. Instead of recessing a single three-sided box into the wall, Mrs. Thorne used two—a smaller oblong that was the actual room, fitted inside a larger box that contained the sources of illumination. Since it was possible to see through the openings that admitted the light, it obviously was necessary to extend some decoration to the outer shell. Mrs. Thorne therefore arranged street scenes or garden areas outside the windows, to be glimpsed through their glass. As she elaborated and perfected this technique, tantalizing segments of hallways and corners of adjoining rooms appeared beyond archways or through open doors.

With the mechanics of her displays established, Mrs. Thorne embarked upon a program of intensive research that reinforced her already considerable knowledge of history and architecture. Having decided that no less than twenty-eight rooms would be required to hold all the fine pieces of her collection, she was fortunate to find, in Chicago, a master woodcraftsman who could construct a double-walled shell for each room. Working from Mrs. Thorne's own rough sketches, and using photographs of extant walls, floors, and ceilings as guides, he produced the amazingly exact paneling, decorative sculpture, and intricate trim that make these rooms so remarkable.

Relying on past experience as a dollhouse interior decorator, Mrs. Thorne herself painted woodwork, stained floors, made curtains and carpets, and reupholstered chairs and sofas before placing the furniture and bric-a-brac in their charming settings. For the final finishing touches in many rooms, she resorted to ingenious subterfuge. She painted round wooden toothpicks white, and used them as candles; she cut up old petit-point handbags to make area rugs; for doughnuts to fill a glass jar, she painted the tiniest of toy automobile tires brown, and sugared them with baking soda.

Even though her collection was extensive, there were gaps in the furnishings for some rooms; to complete these scenes, she commissioned small-scale copies of selected museum pieces. The new reproductions mingled so happily with her genuine antiques that it often was impossible to tell one from the other, and she filed this knowledge away for future reference. After the rooms were finished, a group of rare oriental *objets d'art* remained unused. Mrs. Thorne ordered a miniature glass showcase, lighted from above, in which to display them.

The twenty-eight rooms and one vitrine were completed in time to be displayed at Chicago's Century of Progress Exposition in 1933 and '34. Five years later, they traveled west to San Francisco for the Golden Gate International Exposition; when this fair closed in 1939, the twenty-nine displays were purchased by the International Business Machines Corporation, and shipped all the way across the continent to the New York World's Fair of 1940. Then, as part of IBM's traveling art collection, the rooms were sent on a tour of museums throughout the country that lasted for several years.

Meanwhile, Mrs. Thorne had begun upon a far more ambitious undertaking. At this time the best endowed American museums were buying full-size European rooms, dismantling them, and shipping them across the Atlantic to be reassembled and exhibited. Period rooms added enormously to a museum's prestige, but for most institutions their cost in money and display space was prohibitive. Mrs. Thorne agreed to construct for the Art Institute of Chicago a series of miniature rooms that would trace the development of styles in architecture and interior design, in England and France, from 1500 to 1925. Twenty-nine historically correct interiors were designed by noted architects; fine furniture pieces in museums, French châteaux, and English manor houses were copied in one-inch-to-the-foot scale by Mrs. Thorne's orders. Textiles and carpets were woven and embroidered, sewn and draped by the Needlework Guild of Chicago under her personal supervision. The twenty-nine rooms were first exhibited at the Art Institute in 1937; then they were sent to join the earlier group of scenes at the San Francisco and New York fairs.

While these peripatetic "Thorne Rooms" were everywhere being acclaimed as a new art form, Mrs. Thorne was hard at work upon a third and final series. The thirty-seven new interiors provided a doll's-eye-view of American history from 1675 to 1940, and no area of a household went unrepresented—the series embraced entrance halls, drawing rooms, bedrooms, dining rooms, and kitchens. Fourteen were composite scenes, typical of areas and eras but copying no specific house. The remaining twenty-three were scale reproductions of actual rooms in historic American homes, including such gems as the West Parlor of Mount Vernon, the entrance hall of Andrew Jackson's Hermitage, and the parlor of the reconstructed New York City house that was the childhood home of Theodore Roosevelt. In 1942, the American Rooms were presented to the Art Institute of Chicago, where they joined the European series in a specially designed exhibition area.

In 1962, the first group of rooms was at last allowed to retire from traveling when IBM presented a large part of this series to The Phoenix Art Museum, in Arizona. Mrs. Thorne selected and refurbished sixteen of her favorite scenes, to be displayed there as a memorial to her daughter-in-law. Two oriental rooms from the first series—one Chinese and one Japanese—were given to the Art Institute of Chicago, where they were added to the European displays. A final group of nine scenes remaining in the possession of IBM was presented to the Dulin Gallery of Art in Knoxville, Tennessee, where these early Thorne Rooms are now on view.

As she worked on first one type of scene and then another, Mrs. Thorne's ideas did not remain static. There is a discernible progression from the early, unretouched Thorne Rooms at Knoxville's Dulin Gallery, through the European and American Series at Chicago's Art Institute, to the sixteen revised interiors at The Phoenix Art Museum. The original twenty-eight rooms (now divided between Phoenix and Knoxville) had consumed most of her own collection, but in completing these interiors she had learned that fine copies of museum pieces had a delicacy seldom found in genuine antiques.

There is a Victorian parlor in Knoxville, and a Victorian drawing room in Chicago. Both are authentic representations of the same period and have the same basic furnishings, but there their resemblance ends. The furniture in the parlor is from an elegant English dollhouse of the nineteenth century. Although the room is generously proportioned, every inch of space is filled; its colors are muted and dark. There is an upholstered "parlor set": a sofa, lady's and gentleman's chairs to flank the round center table, and several occasional chairs. In addition, the room contains a mirrored console, a towering desk, several tables, a tiered bookshelf, an *étagère*, Rogers groups on marble pedestals, and a padded ottoman. For lighting, there are kerosene table lamps and a large gas chandelier with glass shades and crystal prisms. This room looks lived-in. There is a comfortable clutter of ornaments on tables, desk, and *étagère;* an umbrella stand bristles with canes and *parapluies,* and a magazine rack holds a copy of the *London Times.*

The drawing room is a far more elegant and spacious apartment. Its chandelier is smaller and less heavy; the upholstered pieces are not so numerous, and there is no table in the center of the room; the ornaments are fewer and finer, and include the crowning period touch of a painting displayed on a gilded easel. Tomato-red carpet and draperies are bright against green walls with white Gothic molding, and the lighting is much stronger.

There is a marked contrast between the sturdy toy furniture of the parlor and the equally ornate but better-executed reproductions in the drawing room. The chief difference between the rooms is, however, a matter of overall impression. The drawing room is perfect, while the parlor is fallible and human.

VII - Madurodam

Madurodam, the Netherlands' smallest city, is undoubtedly the world's largest miniature display—the visitor's pathway through the town is two miles long! It is located on the main highway between Holland's capital, The Hague, and the famous seaside resort of Scheveningen, and is open each year from April to October; the story of its development is very nearly as interesting as Madurodam itself.

Young George Maduro of Willemstad, Curaçao, was a student at the University of Leyden when Holland was invaded by Hitler's troops in May 1940. As a reserve lieutenant in the Dutch Hussars, he reported at once to his regiment and displayed such exceptional courage during the invasion that he was awarded the Willemsorde, a coveted military decoration for bravery. George Maduro never knew of this honor, for he had been captured and imprisoned in the Nazi concentration camp at Dachau, where he died in 1945. After the war his parents, Mr. and Mrs. J. M. L. Maduro of Willemstad, were anxious to establish a lasting memorial to their only son. They hit upon the idea of building, in the country for which he had sacrificed his life, a typical Dutch city in miniature that could be visited and enjoyed by children and adults, and they selected a well-known architect, S. J. Bouma, to plan the model. This was not to be a reproduction of a specific city, but was to incorporate the outstanding features of many Dutch towns, large and small; some of the landmark buildings chosen now exist only in memory and in Madurodam, for they were destroyed during World War II.

Mr. Bouma began by bestowing upon his town a fictitious history, dating from the building of a castle in the year A.D. 1000 at the forks of the imaginary River Maduro. A walled medieval settlement, with a church and a few shops, grew up around the castle and was called Madurodam. The town prospered, and by 1600 it had outgrown its walls and was spreading out over the nearby farmland dotted with windmills and crisscrossed by drainage canals. Other canals provided easy transportation within the town, and tall brick buildings were erected along these canals to house people and shops. Inspired by such affluence, the burghers decreed the building of a center of government and a university; new banks and businesses, churches (Catholic and Protestant) and charitable foundations followed. Finally, in modern times, Madurodam became a center of industry and transportation, with a harbor, a railroad station, an airport, and excellent superhighways serving its many factories.

Every phase of this typically Dutch history is visible in Madurodam, from its castle (a copy of one built on the Island of Voorne in the year 1000) to its modern industrial plants. At the heart of the city is a scale model of The Hague's Binnenhof, which contains the Houses of Parliament and is the Netherlands' center of government. Madurodam's college buildings duplicate those of Leyden University where George Maduro lived and studied, while the tall canal-side houses reproduce the famous Jordaan Quarter of Amsterdam; the Protestant church is a copy of, and a memorial to, the Grote Kerk and Lange Jan Tower at Middelburg, both destroyed during the war.

With capital provided by Mr. and Mrs. Maduro, the building of the town began in 1950; as the work progressed, many businesses and industries offered to contribute models of their own establishments. Madurodam was officially opened by its Mayoress, Princess Beatrix, on July 2, 1952. Since then, it has been visited by more than sixteen million persons, and all profits from its operation have been distributed to Dutch charities.

The paths along which visitors stroll are actually the city's streets, flanked by waist-high buildings; at intervals, there are arching bridges only two steps long to span the placid canals. Everything moves that should be moving. Trains streak down the tracks, slow down, and pause at the railroad station; ships sail in and out of the harbor; sightseeing boats glide through the canals; trucks, cars, and buses speed along the belt highway at the edge of town. And there are sounds to remember: the chiming of church bells; the striking of the Binnenhof's clock; the stirring martial music of a brass band; the tinkling tunes of a barrel organ. At night, the city sparkles under the light of forty-six thousand tiny electric bulbs.

Looking down on this marvelous spectacle from the terrace-restaurant is like seeing Holland from a low-flying airplane. Madurodam is the ultimate in miniaturization—an entire mechanized city, one-twenty-fifth actual size.

III

Displaying Miniatures in Full-size Furniture

When one of our unknown European forebears—prodded, no doubt, by a tidy wife—came up with the outlandish idea of arranging his hoard of seashells on a special set of shelves, he unwittingly invented what has come to be called the curio cabinet. Since then, display cabinets have appeared in many guises, but their purpose has remained the same: to provide a showplace for collections of small treasures.

As early as the sixteenth century, handsome "art cabinets" were considered ideal repositories for articles of great interest or value: medals, jewels, miniature art objects, and, in particular, the little clockwork curiosities that were so much in vogue. An especially fine example of this type of display piece still exists, and can be seen at the University of Uppsala. The elaborate cabinet, made in 1637 and presented by the city of Augsburg to King Gustavus Adolphus of Sweden, numbers among its riches a mechanical dancing couple, a tiny peep show, and a falconry perfectly reproduced in miniature.

Some art cabinets took the form of houses, as did the one made in 1558 for Albrecht V of Bavaria that contained not only kitchens, halls, and sleeping apartments but such esoteric extras as an armor room and a zoological garden. Although the Duke insisted that this marvel had been ordered for his little daughter, he gave it a place of honor in his own art collection. The Dutch cabinet houses of the seventeenth century continued the tradition established by Duke Albrecht; they, too, were intended to impress and astonish adults. Many Dutch houses offer further insight into the custom of displaying collections since they contain miniature models of their period's typical shell or medal cabinets which were tall, narrow chests with many shallow shelves or drawers.

In due time, lacquered tea or spice chests imported from the Orient served to house ivory and jade miniatures brought from India, China, and Japan. The late eighteenth century's cherished oriental porcelains often were exhibited in glass-fronted cabinets of Chinese Chippendale design, or arranged on hanging shelves with latticed sides. Eighteenth-century French vitrines that held collections of enameled snuffboxes were destined to be revived in the early twentieth century as glass-topped tables with shallow wells, in which apostle spoons lay on a background of black velvet. The pyramid-shaped *étagères* of the Empire Period, with their bibelots from Egypt, Italy, and Greece, were followed in the mid-nineteen-hundreds by corner "whatnots" whose triangular shelves were cluttered with little Victorian boxes and figurines.

All these types of display pieces are very much at home in our eclectic era. The *étagères* of all sorts that are fashionable accents in today's traditional or contemporary rooms seem made to order for displaying collections of minute animals, tiny china dolls, antique banks, porcelain figurines, mechanical toys, or music boxes. Lead soldiers could be drawn up in battle array on these tiers, or arranged in marching columns on the treads of seldom-used library steps. For prominence and ease of viewing, little silver or ivory miniatures often are grouped on hanging shelves. When such a collection outgrows its shelf space, it well might be transferred to a vitrine; seen from above in a glass-topped end or coffee table, the diminutive things will seem even more precious and will be better protected.

Other, larger pieces of furniture offer excellent housing for specialized collections. A secretary-bookcase is the obvious home for Sebastian-type literary figurines, with each famous character displayed in front of the book that was his "birthplace." Miniature portrait busts of authors beside their famous works, and composers with their biographies belong here too. The breakfront can accommodate a little more than valuable china, antique silver, or rare books. The appeal of a dainty Haviland teacup is enhanced if a miniature porcelain tea set is displayed beside it; a miniature silver service draws attention to a Georgian coffeepot; tiny books reinforce the importance of choice volumes. Because the translucency and sparkle of glass miniatures appear to best advantage in sunlight these fragile treasures often are arrayed on window shelves, but a safer place for them is a lighted breakfront or glass-shelved curio cabinet. An electrified display cabinet also is the happiest of homes for very small silver, ivory, or porcelain pieces whose fine detailing needs direct lighting to be appreciated. Secretaries, breakfronts, and display cabinets have the further advantage of glass doors that provide transparent dust protection for all these little things that are so hard to clean.

Collectors of miniature furniture consider it axiomatic that any small-scale piece worth keeping is worthy of display. Interior decorators delight in using the largest of eighteenth-century sample chests as chair-side tables in elegant traditional rooms. Taking a leaf from their book, one might make much of antique doll furniture by substituting a pedestal dining table for the coffee table before a Victorian loveseat in the living room, or placing a doll dresser beside a bedroom's slipper chair. A single tiny sample piece—perhaps an apothecary's cabinet with its multitude of minute drawers, or an inlaid *bombé* chest—will attain its deserved importance if it is displayed at eye level on a simple wall bracket. Because a triangular whatnot shelf is shaped like the corner of a miniature room, it is an eminently suitable location for a piece or two of inherited Victorian dollhouse furniture. A hanging corner shelf is even better for this purpose than a tiered stand, for it places the corner grouping on view at eye level.

In this country, very few families continue to live in the same house year after year, generation after generation. With each move, a ruthless weeding out of possessions takes place, and this process of elimination applies especially to outgrown toys that have no immediate practical use and therefore seem expendable. Books and games, skates and tricycles, are sent off to the Goodwill Industries without a qualm, but rare indeed is the woman who can bear to part with a dollhouse! Faced with the fact that there is positively no space for it on the moving van, she may bow to the inevitable and leave the bulky house behind—but not until she has tucked the best of its tissue-wrapped furniture into the corners of a carton of linens. All too often, the miniatures are then merely transferred from the moving carton to a cardboard box, and left to languish on a storage room shelf.

For many miniaturists, the hobby of making and decorating small-scale rooms begins as an attempt to find suitable housing for just such a set of dispossessed dollhouse furnishings. In the course of their specialized house hunting, they often discover anew what collectors have known since the sixteenth century: The shelves of a full-size cabinet can shelter several miniature rooms.

Frances Hodgson Burnett was the sort of collector who kept giving away the contents of her display cabinet for the sheer pleasure of buying and arranging other little things. She divided the two shelves in the lower section of a massive Jacobean court cupboard into four rooms: a drawing room hung with pale green brocade, a dining room with leather-upholstered chairs, a kitchen where plaster-of-paris vegetables and fruits outnumbered pots and pans, and a combination bedroom and nursery with a baby in a china bathtub. When children were brought to call, she knelt on cushions before the opened cupboard, explaining all its wonders, while grown-up visitors waited and the tea grew cold. She said of this cupboard with its hidden miniature rooms:

> I have built houses and furnished them; I have made gardens in
> various countries and revelled in them; I have written quite a number
> of things; but I do not think that anything I have ever done has been
> more amusing and satisfying to me.

Most Dutch cabinet houses of the seventeenth and eighteenth centuries were handsome pieces of furniture in their own right, with solid doors that added an element of suspense and surprise to the ceremony of viewing their built-in rooms. When the doors were flung open, the shelves and their contents were suddenly revealed in all their glory. When closed, such a house might be mistaken for the linen cabinet or garderobe it so closely resembled. This idea is still a good one and can be applied to any piece of furniture whose exterior is attractive and whose interior has been, or can be, fitted with shelves. An ancient armoire, or an early-day pie safe with pierced tin doors, would make a superb display cabinet; but a late-Victorian wardrobe or a McKinley-period linen press could also serve. An antique corner cupboard might be made to earn its space, or a lacquered bar-cabinet be given a new role to play.

In any cupboard or cabinet, miniature furniture will practically disappear when placed against untreated wood, so each room's walls obviously will require some sort of decorative treatment. Cloth, self-stick plastic, wallpaper, or paint could be used, but should not, of course, be applied directly to the interior of a fine piece of furniture. Measure carefully the back and side walls of a shelf space, and cut thin cardboard to fit over them. Then paint or paper the cardboard to your heart's content before setting it in place and be sure to carry the paint or paper around the front edge of the cardboard side walls. Solid-color wall covering can be obtained even more easily by cutting colored blotters or sheets of poster board to fit the back and sides of the shelf and attaching them to the wood at the corners with double-stick Scotch tape.

One has only to look at a built-in bookcase with a seeing eye to realize that it is divided into ready-made miniature rooms. If it is a sectional piece, its dividers probably are placed at twenty-four-, thirty-, or thirty-six-inch intervals. Each shelf will very likely measure ten or eleven inches in depth, but the distance between the shelves may vary from eight to twenty inches. A room thirty-six feet long but only ten feet wide would be out of proportion in an actual house unless it were an entrance hall, a jalousied Florida room, or an enclosed porch—and the same holds true of rooms in miniature. A thirty-six-inch shelf section can, however, be partitioned with plywood into a large room and a smaller one, such as a bedroom and bath, a living room and hall, or a kitchen and pantry. A floor space measuring eleven by twenty-four inches adapts much better for a room scaled one inch to the foot—a living room, dining room, bedroom, or period kitchen.

Horizontally, a miniature room should follow its scale exactly, but its vertical dimension must be increased for visual proportion. A bookshelf section is essentially a box with an open front; if this opening is twenty-four inches long but only eight inches high, the ceiling of the enclosed room will appear to be pressing down upon the furniture. As a general rule, the walls of a miniature room should be at least one and one-fourth times as high as literally required by scale, but if the room's furniture is massive and includes tall pieces such as bookcases, or if a large chandelier will be hung from the ceiling, one and a half times the scale height will not be too much. In order to attain the desired ceiling height, one shelf may have to be removed from the bookcase.

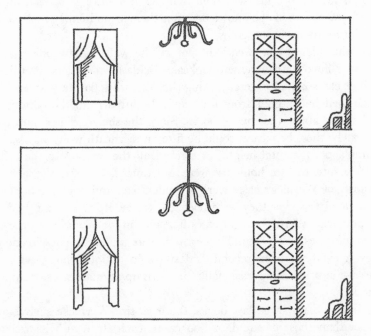

Built-in bookshelves are not the only ones that can be converted into tiers of miniature rooms. Relatively inexpensive unfinished bookcases can be found in department stores and do-it-yourself shops, and since these often come with adjustable shelves, any desirable ceiling height can easily be obtained. Budget furniture departments and secondhand stores sometimes offer small wooden cases with four or five shelves, in twenty-four-inch width. At first glance such a bookcase might be rejected as too low, because the rooms it eventually contained could only be seen by sitting on a footstool in front of it. If, however, the bookcase is placed on top of a three- or four-drawer chest of the same width, its shelves will be elevated to viewing level; and if bookcase and chest are painted in a bright accent color or attractively antiqued, the makeshift cabinet becomes a conversation piece of furniture.

Visitors often are seized by an uncontrollable urge to reach into a miniature room and pick up an especially appealing tiny object for closer scrutiny, not realizing that in so doing they may knock over half the furnishings with a slight movement of a hand or the flick of a sleeve. To avoid the embarrassment of having to say "please do not touch" (and ostensibly to protect the scenes from dust), a whole built-in or free-standing tier of rooms can be covered with a single sheet of thin glass (or Plexiglas) held in place with mirror clips.

No matter how tight its transparent shield fits, a miniature room's furniture eventually will be covered with a fine film of dust. When this occurs, slip the sheet of glass out of its clips and engage in a bout of house cleaning. Use very small camel's hair artist's brushes with long handles for dusting wooden and uphol-stered surfaces, secure in the knowledge that these same homely tools are used to clean miniature rooms in museums.

Around the turn of the twentieth century the walls of law offices and home libraries were lined with patented bookcases made by the Globe-Wernicke Com-pany. These cases actually were stacking shelves with separate wooden bases and tops; each shelf had a glass front that could be lifted from the bottom and slid back to balance above the row of books. Since the shelves, bases, and tops were sold separately, these bookcases could be fitted underneath windows, used in pairs beside fireplaces at mantel height, or stacked all the way up to the ceiling. Al-though those intended for home use were sometimes made of dark mahogany, the vast majority of Wernicke cases were of golden oak, and once the brief popular-ity of this wood was over they were relegated to the attic. Because they were ex-tremely practical, Wernicke legal cases lingered on for years in attorneys' offices and school libraries, but eventually they, too, were replaced. These sectional cases have now moved up from secondhand stores to antique shops, with a corre-sponding rise in price, but occasionally they turn up at estate sales or storage com-pany auctions.

Being intended for large law books, the legal-size Wernicke shelves are taller and deeper than those of standard bookcases; each shelf with its wood-framed glass window front is a perfect showcase for one or more miniature rooms. By an interesting coincidence, some of the earliest dollhouses made in Germany are composed of stacking shelves on separate base stands; the seventeenth-century houses in the Germanisches Museum at Nuremberg and the National Museum at Munich look very much like glassless Wernicke cases with ornamental rooflines added. These large houses stand nearly seven feet tall, but they can be moved with ease by lifting off their floors, one by one. A sectional Wernicke case or a bookcase-on-a-chest has a special advantage for these times in portability—when you move, you *can* take it with you.

A golden oak Wernicke bookcase could be bleached, stained, painted, or an-tiqued to make it more compatible with other furniture, and with very little addi-tional effort, it can be transformed into a "lacquered" cabinet or a "campaign chest." For the oriental look, paint the cases with mandarin red, deep blue, or black "lacquer" made by stirring one tablespoonful of clear varnish into a half-pint of flat enamel, and add large, ornate corner brasses. Paint a campaign chest light tan, maroon, or pumpkin, and finish each shelf with plain brass corners and handles.

Without some form of lighting, rooms and scenes arranged in cabinets and bookcases lose much of their impact. Naturally, no one is about to bore holes in a fine pie safe or an antique secretary to admit electric wires, but small spotlights or intensor lamps can be focused on the shelves from outside. In The Hague's Gemeentemuseum, the magnificent Ploos van Amstel house is lighted in a surprisingly easy and unobtrusive manner with strings of very small bulbs placed along the right and left front edges of the cabinet; each bulb is covered with a shallow, translucent shield. In similar fashion, lighting the rooms in a built-in bookcase can be done with a string of Christmas grain-of-wheat bulbs (replaceable, of course) shielded with sections cut from a plastic ice-cube tray.

Unless some member of the family is truly qualified to splice the string of tiny bulbs and install them, it is wise to call in outside help. Faced with a problem so totally different from those he deals with every day, the average electrician is apt to shrug disgustedly and let it be known that miniature lighting is beneath his notice. Fortunately, most large electrical retailers, and many public-power compa-

WIRE BROUGHT
THROUGH HOLE

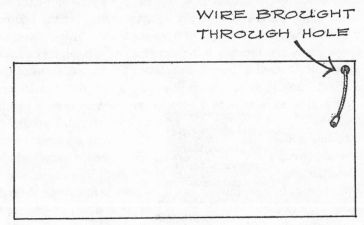

CORD ATTACHED WITH ELECTRICIANS'
BRADS SUPPORTED WITH LARGE CUP
HOOK.

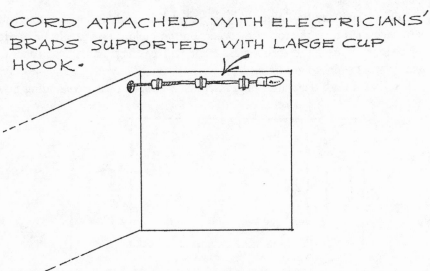

nies, have resident lighting experts who are available for free consultation, and any expert worth his watts will consider this type of problem a challenge. Instead of Christmas lights, he may suggest the use of electric train lights with a transformer hidden in the cabinet below the bookshelves; in this case, a special switch controlling all the shelf lights can also be concealed behind the cabinet doors. The Swedish firm of Linde now makes illuminated chandeliers for the type of dollhouse that is wired to a transformer, and one of these ceiling fixtures could be substituted for concealed side lighting in a bookcase room.

Unfinished or secondhand bookcases should have holes drilled for wiring before their wood is stained or painted, and this can be done by anyone who knows how to use an electric drill with a $\frac{3}{8}''$ bit. An inexpensive device for lighting each room can be put together of one socket from a set of indoor Christmas lights (which is the right size to hold a frosted $7\frac{1}{2}$-watt night-light bulb), a length of insulated flex, and a plug. Obviously, the outside of the bookcase will look neater if all the wires are brought in from the backs of the shelves, but light must not shine directly into the eyes of the viewer, so a bulb cannot be left to dangle on the rear wall. It should, instead, be placed at the upper front of the shelf, and beamed back into the room. To do this invisibly, let the electric cord enter through a hole as near as possible to the top of one back corner, and be brought forward along the angle where the wall and ceiling meet; the cord should be secured to ceiling and wall at intervals with electricians' brads, which are insulated double-pointed tacks. To support the bulb itself, a large cuphook can be screwed into the ceiling at the front edge of the shelf. The easiest way to hide this bulb, and to direct its light inward, is with a strip of molding wide enough to cover the outer edge of the ceiling shelf and to extend down at least $\frac{1}{4}''$ below the bulb.

Wernicke cases can be lighted in this way, with cords brought through the back of each shelf near the top of a corner, but no molding strips will be needed. The wooden frame of the shelf's glass front will be deep enough to conceal a Christmas tree or night-light bulb.

A shelf that is both deep and long, in either a built-in or a freestanding book-

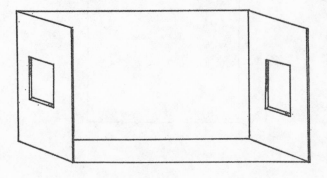

case, can be given indirect lighting with a simplified version of the method developed by Mrs. James Ward Thorne. Mrs. Thorne's rooms were double-shelled—in other words, she placed a box containing a scene inside a larger box that held wiring equipment and permitted light to enter the inner room through windows or open doors. To obtain this effect easily, one begins by making a three-sided screen of plywood or heavy cardboard as tall and as deep as the shelf, but 4″ narrower. Put the screen together with finishing nails. Its three panels will serve as the room's walls, while the shelves above and below will provide a ceiling and a floor; there will be a 2″ space between each side panel of the screen and the nearest end of the shelf, to hold the lights.

Cut window or door openings in both side panels of the screen. Cover the outside of the window apertures with the sort of thin clear plastic used in wallet windows—available at hobby shops among the leather-work supplies. Then, on the inside, add window sash made by painting a section of a latticed plastic berry box.

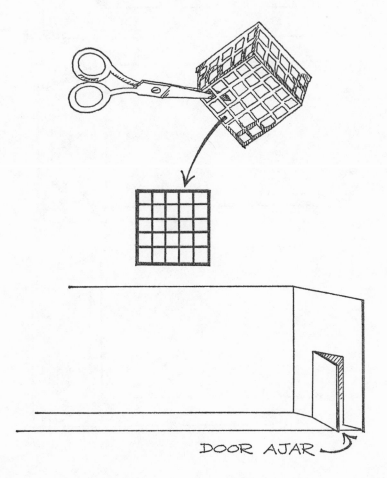

DOOR AJAR

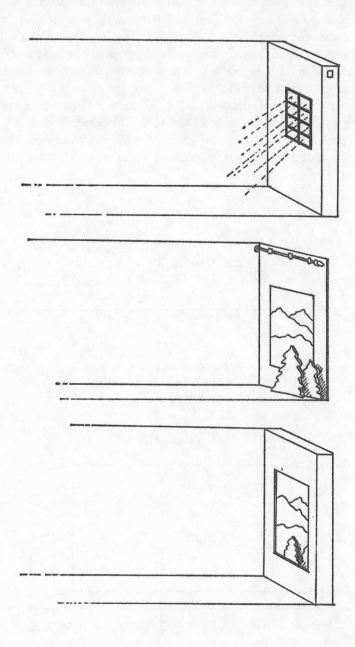

Balsa wood is a miniaturist's best friend. Balsa strips of various widths and thicknesses are sold in toy and hobby shops where kits for airplane and ship models are displayed; some strips are so thin and pliant that they could be shaped with scissors, and even the thickest piece can be cut or carved with a paring knife or a razor blade. Doors and doorframes are easy to make from this marvelous material which, because it is real wood, can be waxed or stained as well as painted to deepen or disguise its natural pale beige color. For paneled doors, mount thin balsa squares or oblongs on the thicker flat rectangular door shape, beveling their edges with an emery board. Narrower balsa strips will do for framing, but more decorative doorframes can be made of ½"-wide molding strips from a builder's supply company. Round-headed brass nails make good plain doorknobs and, for closed doors, hinges are really unnecessary. If you feel you must hinge the door, search among the jewelry-box and purse-top hardware in a hobby shop for the tiniest of metal hinges that come with pin-size brass nails for attaching them. If you go to all the trouble of hinging the door, leave it slightly ajar, but swing it open in such a way that only a glimpse of the shelf beyond the doorway will be visible.

In a freestanding bookcase drill a hole at each end of the shelf back, near the top, and bring the wires through. Place the light bulbs near the middle of the compartment's ceiling, supporting them with large cuphooks. For a built-in shelf, the wires must be brought up from the cabinet below, through a hole drilled at each end of the shelf floor; the bulb should be held in an upright position by a cuphook screwed into the shelf's end wall.

Slip the screen into the shelf temporarily and check the position of the bulbs to be sure light comes through each opening without showing its source; then mark the area on the wall of the shelf that can be seen through each window or door. Remove the screen to allow more working room, and arrange a "view" in each marked space. This could be a street scene, a garden, or merely a side view of the house next door. An interesting effect can be achieved by gluing a large scenic postcard to the end wall of the shelf, and cementing one or two miniature evergreen trees to the shelf floor between this scene and a window, in the interests of perspective.

Papering or painting the inner walls of the room will be much easier to do before the screen is placed inside the shelf. Once this decorating is complete, coat the upper and lower edges of the screen's three panels with liquid cement, wait fifteen seconds, and carefully ease the walls into position. Then close off the lighting compartment at each end of the shelf. This can be done with a wide strip of decorative molding or picture framing hinged to the edge of the ceiling shelf to permit a change of light bulbs.

In the Thorne Rooms and their shelf copies, windows and doors are actual openings, but it would be the height of impracticality to insist that this be true of every miniature room. Cutting holes in a fine piece of furniture would be no less than desecration and, unless one follows the box-in-a-box technique, the walls of a bookcase shelf must also be accepted as solid. In most early Dutch cabinet houses, the problem of ventilation was ignored completely, and there were no win-

PLASTIC
BERRY BOX
BOTTOM   PURSE MIRRORS.

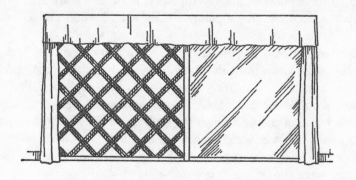

dows at all. The casual viewer is not even aware of their absence; perhaps sub-consciously one assumes that they are on the missing wall at the front of the house. In cabinets of a later date, windows were indicated with perspective paint-ings framed as windows, with painted or frosted glass panes, or with closed draperies.

Drawn draperies are still a favorite substitute for windows on a solid wall, but there are other forms of camouflage. A very effective picture window can be made by pasting a picture of a landscape or a street scene to the wall of a room, and covering it with a sheet of thin clear plastic. Travel magazine illustrations are excellent for these distance views, as are giant scenic postcards. The sill of the paper-plus-plastic window can be made of a narrow strip of balsa wood, while the window's top and side edges may simply be hidden behind a valance and draperies. Double-hung or side-hinged windows can be made of mirror. Tiny oblong mirrored tiles cut from a strip of shelf edging, or 1"-square blocks cut from a mirror-tiled placemat or trivet, are ideal for windowpanes, but mir-ror shelf edging and placemats are not always obtainable. One large or two small rectangular purse mirrors, attached to the wall with liquid cement, will serve the purpose, and will not be instantly recognizable if their reflective sur-faces are crisscrossed with sash strips made of painted latticed sections cut from a plastic berry box. These lattice patterns are not all alike. Some have square holes, some oblongs, and some diamonds—these last make splendid panes of "leaded" glass.

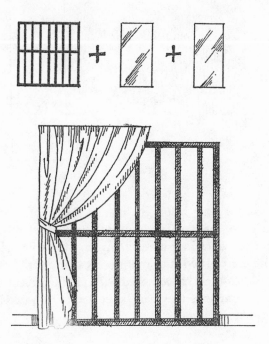

A fireplace is a natural center of interest for a traditional, contemporary, or rustic miniature room. The wooden mantels (some stained brown and others painted white) that are sold in toyshops as dollhouse accessories could be used "as is" in a traditional setting, or faced with marble. This is not so difficult as it sounds, for the very thin "marble" wall tiles sold in do-it-yourself centers actually are molded of plastic so thin that it can be cut with a razor blade. Tiny square or oblong tiles are sold in hobby shops for mosaic work, and these are perfect in size for facing fireplace openings or building brick hearths. Among the newer dollhouse furnishings are simple plastic fireplaces with built-in lighting: A tiny bulb hidden by stacked logs is powered by penlight batteries.

It is perfectly possible to make a mantelpiece from scratch beginning with a cardboard box lid of appropriate size and depth. Cut off one long narrow rim. Then cut an opening on this side for the fireplace. Add a facing of wood or stone to the simple cardboard base. A paneled mantel is easily made of balsa applied with white glue to the cardboard box lid. By grooving ¼″-thick balsa strips with the tines of a fork, one can simulate the fluted pilasters of an Adam

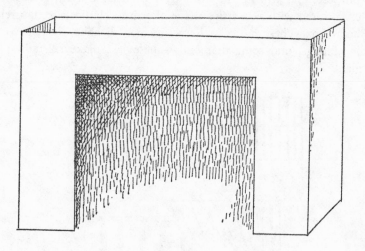

mantel. To add a carved swag below the mantel shelf, glue on a curved floral garland cut from a paper doily. After an overall coat of white paint, the paper motifs will appear as carvings in low relief. Among the trimmings in a needlework shop are miniature plastic fruits and flowers that are flat on the back and pierced for sewing. When these are attached with plastic cement to a plain mantel to form a swagged garland, they can be coated with wood-brown paint to imitate a Grinling Gibbons carving.

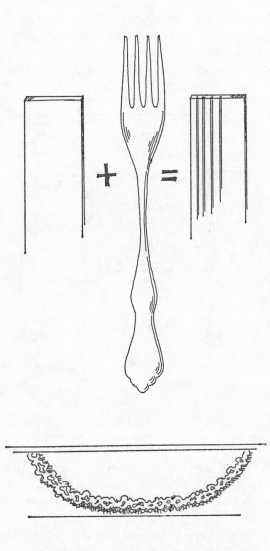

A fieldstone fireplace for a rustic room will require only a small amount of gravel (from your own driveway or from a pet shop). Lay a cardboard mantel flat, with its open back down, on a pad of newspaper. Pour some white glue into a saucer, and dredge each gravel in this cement substitute before placing it on

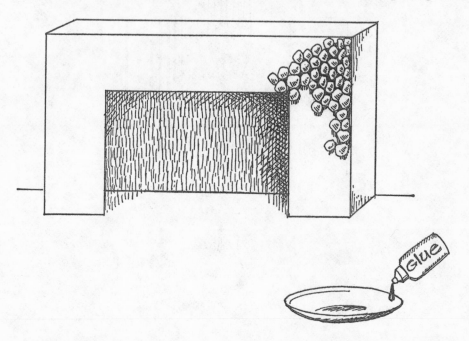

the cardboard. Fit the pebbles close together, covering the cardboard entirely, and let the mantel remain undisturbed for several hours to allow the glue to become completely dry. Then lift the mantel and turn it over; any stones that were not properly seated will fall off, but they can quickly be redipped in glue and replaced.

A freestanding fireplace for the center of a contemporary room is made like a fieldstone mantel, on a cardboard core. Very few of our "modern" ideas are really new, and this type of fireplace looks like the hooded hearth in a seventeenth-century Nuremberg kitchen. You will need the lid of an oblong box and the bottom portion of a small cardboard cube for the wood-burning firebox. Cut two wide fireplace openings on opposite sides of the square box, and glue this box (bottom up) on top of the larger box lid which becomes the hearth. When the glue is completely dry, face the hearth and the firebox with tiny brick-shaped tiles or with gravel. A metal funnel from the kitchen drawer will make a perfect chimney hood to carry off the smoke; camouflage its shiny tin with a coat of rub-on copper finish that comes in a tube or a small jar and is sold at paint stores.

If the miniature room is to have wall-to-wall carpeting, the floor of the shelf

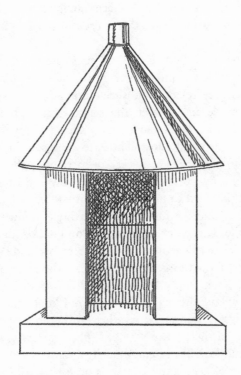

will require no treatment at all; if the floor will be almost entirely covered by a room-size rug, staining the exposed edges of flooring, or painting them dark brown, will suffice. Otherwise, a floor of planking, parquetry, marble, or vinyl must be laid. Hardwood flooring can be imitated easily with narrow strips of wood-grain self-stick plastic tape. This tape comes on a roll, in light tan or dark brown, and needs only to be cut to the proper length and pressed in place. It is not nearly so effective, however, as the "random width" flooring that can be made from pressed-wood self-stick panels. Be sure to buy the very cheapest wall panels at a discount house because these are much thinner than pressed wood of better quality. To cut such a panel in strips, mark the width of a miniature board at each end of the panel and draw a line between the marks with a ball-point pen. Using a yardstick as a guide, groove the surface of the pressed wood deeply along the ink line with a razor blade; then bend the panel at the groove and it will snap in two.

The effect of parquetry is most easily obtained with 6"×6" pressed-wood parquet tiles from a floor covering center, but perfectionists will not be satisfied with their too-large, too-coarse patterns. The alternative lies in fitting together tiny squares and oblongs of thin wood veneer and gluing them in place. Narrow rolls of veneering, in various light and dark woods, are made for wood-inlay work and for repairing veneered furniture. Occasionally these rolls are available at paint stores and do-it-yourself centers, and usually can be obtained at a friendly furniture refinishing shop.

For tile floors, there are thin, cheap self-stick plastic wall panels grooved in very small squares or oblongs and colored to resemble popular patterns of tiling. Again, perfectionists may reject these sheets that are so easy to cut and apply because the "plaster" joints between the slightly raised tiles are too wide for miniature flooring. Mosaic tiles from a hobby shop will give a more realistic appearance, with very little extra effort. These, too, are sold in sheets, on a backing of coarse cloth mesh, and it is not necessary to remove the mesh before gluing the tiles to the floor. By cutting between the rows of tiles with scissors, the 12"×12" sheets can be sized to any room. For two-tone effects or geometric designs, these tiles can be pulled off their cloth backing and glued individually.

Marble floors, either in solid color or in light and dark squares, can be made of thin self-stick marbleized wall tiles cut with a razor blade. Sometimes 4"×4" vinyl wall tiles are patterned in geometric designs; these are good possibilities for miniature "mosaic" floors. Only the most artistic and dedicated craftsman will want to attempt an inlaid circular design cut from linoleum tiles of two or more solid colors with a jigsaw, and glued together on the floor. The easiest of all patterned floors is made of the backs of "poker" playing cards, which are patterned in blue and white, and look like miniature delft tiles.

Usually the ceiling of a miniature room is little noticed, and needs only to be given two thin coats of white latex paint, which will have the textured look of plaster. For a molded plaster medallion to surround the top of a chandelier, use the center portion of a small lace paper doily, pasting it in the middle of the ceiling before the white latex paint is applied. The paper will appear as a raised design after the paint has dried. Heavy twisted cord glued in the crevices where ceiling and side walls meet, and then given two thin coats of white latex paint, will look like plaster rope molding. For plain wood molding, a ¼"-wide strip of thin balsa will do, but for a more decorative effect, use a narrow strip of gold-paper découpage trim which, when painted, will look like carved wood.

The slanted beamed ceiling of an A-frame or split-level house should be made of lightweight balsa strips glued to a heavy cardboard backing that has been carefully cut to fit within the shelf walls when angled downward from front to back. Cut beams of proper length from square balsa dowels, and attach them to the wood-strip ceiling with liquid cement—spread the colorless cement on one side of a square dowel, and wait ten seconds before pressing it down upon the stripping. The pale balsa strips and dowels can be made to look like redwood planks and beams by brushing them with liquid oxblood shoe polish. To set the finished ceiling in place, mark the location of its lower edge, in pencil, on the shelf's rear wall. Then cover the edges of the cardboard and the ends of the balsa strips with epoxy or household cement; wait ten seconds and fit the lower edge of

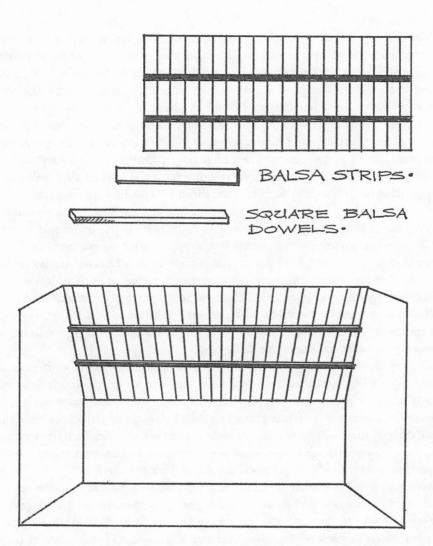

BALSA STRIPS.

SQUARE BALSA DOWELS.

the ceiling on its mark. Lift the rest of the ceiling into position and press hard against the side and top edges to wedge them in place. Support the center of the slanted roof for a few minutes and then tap along the edges very lightly with a tack hammer to ensure a tight bond.

Plain paneled walls for such a room can be made of wood-grained self-stick plastic, wood veneering, or stained flat balsa strips, applied vertically with liquid cement. For the painted wainscoting or dado of a more formal interior, use a wide balsa strip, applying it horizontally and finishing its upper edge with a narrow molding. Make this molding of a thin ¼″-wide balsa strip, or of a ¼″ gilded paper strip with beaded edges of the sort sold in art shops as framing for découpage designs.

The best type of paint for miniature woodwork is semi-gloss enamel; for larger wall surfaces, flat paint is preferable. In either case, watch out for brush marks! Enamel should be used sparingly, without thinning. It is advisable to thin flat paint drastically with turpentine, and to plan on at least three coats for complete coverage. Latex paint has the appearance of plaster on a wall, as it does on a ceiling, but this homogenized paint is extremely thick as it comes from the can, and brush marks that would be unnoticeable in a full-size room will appear in a miniature setting as deep grooves and high ridges. Ordinary tap water will thin white latex paint, and vegetable food coloring from the kitchen shelf will tint it any pastel shade; for richer, deeper colors, stir in water-soluble poster paint.

Contact plastic is the best wall covering for miniature rooms. It has several advantages over the wallpaper it so closely resembles. Its paper backing is marked off in one-inch squares, which makes it a simple matter to measure and cut a piece of exactly the right size; it comes in a wide range of colors, and in several patterns that are really miniature wallpaper motifs; once its backing is removed, it is extremely thin and pliable and can be fitted into corners without tearing; it will stick to painted or varnished surfaces and can be pulled off without damaging the finish; it can be bought by the yard, and is available everywhere in housewares departments and variety stores.

Good-quality wallpaper is so thick that it is difficult to apply with paste in minute quantities, and textured papers are out of scale in miniature interiors. Ready-pasted papers usually are thinner and more pliant, and have only to be brushed with water before being hung; in solid colors, pin stripes, or very tiny floral designs, these will be usable. Gift-wrap paper often is sprinkled with minute bouquets, or covered with small-scale repeated motifs. This thin paper can be applied to walls with library paste slightly thinned with water.

Scenic wallpaper is lovely in a full- or small-size dining room, and the sample books at a decorator's shop show scene designs in a reduced scale that is perfect for miniature walls. Beg for a few pages from an out-of-date book—you may even be given an entire book of discontinued patterns. This paper is thick, and it is important that its designs be trimmed and fitted together perfectly for best results. For this reason, it is wise to measure each wall and cut a thin sheet of poster board to cover it exactly. Lay the three pieces of cardboard flat, and place larger sections of scenic paper over them, adjusting the paper until the design is correctly carried from one segment of the cardboard to the next. Trim the paper to fit the poster board and attach it with library paste slightly thinned with water; weight the three sections with books, to keep the paper smooth as it dries. Then brush the back of each piece of poster board with white glue, and press it carefully against its corresponding wooden wall.

With its walls papered, its floors laid, and its architectural features present in fireplace, windows, and doors, the shell of the miniature room is now complete. At this stage, it is a small-scale version of the unfurnished rooms that one encounters in looking at apartments for rent or houses for sale. Basically it is attractive, but it will not come alive until it is furnished.

A miniature scene is frequently compared to a stage, which also has a missing front wall. But this simile is not really apt; in order that actors may be heard as well as seen, the sofas and chairs in a stage setting are arbitrarily—often awkwardly—faced forward, toward the audience. In an actual room, the furniture is not all turned in one direction, nor is it lined up stiffly around the walls. Desks and sofas sometimes are turned sideways, so that they protrude into the center space; armchairs are pulled away from the wall completely, and may be placed at right angles to sofas in order to create pleasant conversation groupings. Occasional chairs and tables cluster like satellites around the major furniture pieces.

The best guide to the placement of a miniature room's furnishings will be a photograph of a full-size room, which will clearly demonstrate how the arrangement of furniture is governed by fixed features such as picture windows or built-in bookshelves. Furthermore, the pictured room will have a "missing wall," and will be seen as a rectangular floor space framed by back and side walls—no matter how wide its lens angle, a camera cannot see the wall and furniture to its immediate right and left.

IV

Miniature Rooms That Preserve the Present

A contemporary miniature room is like a three-dimensional candid snapshot that captures and preserves the fleeting present moment.

The twentieth century was only two decades old when the British people set out to typify it in a gift for their Queen, and this aspect of preservation was uppermost in the minds of the planners of Queen Mary's Dolls' House. The official booklet on the house explains that its lofty and laudable purpose was

> . . . to present a model of a house of the 20th century which should be fitted up with perfect fidelity, down to the smallest details, so as to represent as closely and minutely as possible a genuine and complete example of a domestic interior with all the household arrangements characteristic of the daily life of the time. . . .

Fifty years later the apartments that were then traditional in styling do not seem out of date: the eighteenth-century formality of the throne room's gilded furniture and pedimented marble fireplace is no less impressive; the dining room with its massive buffet and "Grinling Gibbons" carvings still reflects the late seventeenth century; the king's bedroom is unalterably Chinese Chippendale. The "ultra-modern" marble bathrooms, however, seem hopelessly outmoded even though their tiny taps still emit droplets of hot and cold water, and the mammoth coal range in the kitchen has become a monument to inconvenience. The single electric drop lights in all the "modern" rooms are as much period pieces as are the vintage automobiles in the garage.

On the other hand, the Dutch cabinet houses that were designed merely to be admired and enjoyed in their own times have unintentionally preserved an authentic picture of daily life in the seventeenth century. Lying-in rooms and best kitchens were included in these cabinets as a matter of course, because it would have been unthinkable to omit them; seventeenth-century burghers who marveled at their accuracy would have hooted with scorn at the suggestion that these miniatures might long outlast their full-size prototypes.

Sara Ploos van Amstel was a practical (though not a penurious) woman, as her detailed records of expenditures prove. At a time when other owners of curio cabinets were having all new furniture and accessories made to order at great expense, Sara was buying old cabinets at auction, and lifting their rooms out bodily to fit them into her new cabinet house. Nor did she hesitate to alter the furnishings she had bought in order to make them conform to her tastes and plans; she re-covered the walls of a lying-in room with rose-colored watered silk, made new hangings and coverlets for beds and cradles, reupholstered a day bed with flame-stitch embroidery, and re-dressed a number of dolls in up-to-date fashions. These alterations were not undertaken purely for the sake of economy since she paid a high price for such handsome new furnishings as a tall case clock and a fine brass hanging lantern for the entrance hall. The point is that Sara was willing to expend time and talent, as well as money, on her cabinet, which was for her not merely a showpiece but an enjoyable continuing hobby.

Buying what is available, and altering some pieces if necessary, is still an excellent method of furnishing a contemporary room. This is an ideal time to be acquiring miniature furniture by the roomful or by the piece, for the shelves of toyshops hold a fascinating array of dollhouse-size chairs and tables, beds and chests. The very best contemporary upholstered furnishings and the finest mahogany pieces in traditional styling are those made in Colombia, South America, to the specifications of American importers. The Swedish firm of Linde also is outstanding among the manufacturers of contemporary wooden pieces; Linde chairs and tables have the simple sturdiness of full-size Swedish modern furniture. The American firm of Shackman offers a large line of wooden miniatures in early-American and Victorian designs. These actually are made in Japan, and although there is great variation in their styling, all the pieces seem to be made of the same light wood and stained alike in an uninspiring cross between yellow maple and fruitwood tan. The Hall Company's traditional and modern wooden miniatures are made in the United States, but are very slightly larger than the standard scale of one inch to the foot. If all the pieces in a room are Hall miniatures, they go together admirably, but a Hall chair towers over a Shackman chest or a Linde table.

It is maddening to spend weeks searching for a wooden chair of particular styling, find it at last, and discover upon taking it home that it is taller than the rest of a roomful of carefully collected furniture. The first thought is to shorten the piece by sawing off the bottoms of its legs, but in most cases this would merely make the chair look chunky. It is better to shorten turned chair legs from the top, and this is not as difficult as it sounds since wooden miniatures are put together

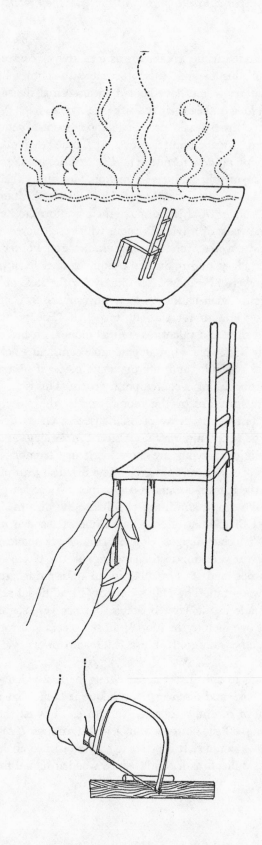

with glue. Submerge the chair for five minutes in a bowl of hot water and then move the legs gently back and forth until they pull away from the softened glue. Measure and mark the amount of wood to be removed from each leg. Lay a leg flat on a breadboard and use a small keyhole saw with a fine-toothed blade to do the cutting. Replace the legs with liquid household cement.

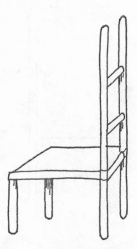

Sometimes it is better to change the legs of a chair or table instead of shortening them—in some rare but happy cases, a piece that is too short can exchange extremities with another piece that is too tall. Much modern-day furniture is made with plain square legs for which dowels of appropriate size can be used. Wooden golf tees make marvelous tapered table legs, and one tee mounted point up on a metal faucet washer can become a simple pedestal for a chair-side table.

A wooden miniature that is too tall by only a sixteenth of an inch may still throw a whole room out of kilter, but for such a trifling correction major surgery

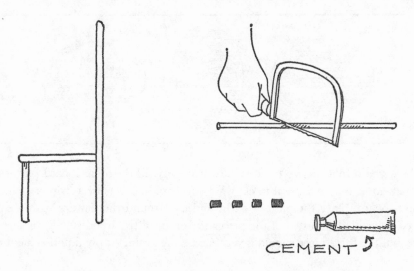

CEMENT

will not be required. Shorten the bottom of each leg with a fingernail file and smooth the outer edges with the back of an emery board.

Legs that are too short can always be exchanged for longer ones, but it is sometimes possible to extend them unobtrusively. A bulbous leg, for instance, can be lengthened with a round or oval wooden bead glued to its tip. Straight

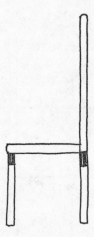

or tapered legs should be removed by soaking in hot water, and lengthened from the top with sections cut from a round or square dowel that is slightly larger than the top of a leg. Beds are much easier to elevate than chairs or tables, because the lengthened legs can hide behind the skirts of a conveniently long spread or dust ruffle.

Occasionally, the legs of a table may be to your liking, while its top is thick and clumsy or of undesirable shape. Paper-thin maple, oak, walnut, or mahogany veneering is sold in wide or narrow rolls for repairing veneered furniture. For a table-top project you will not need a whole roll, but an obliging refinishing shop

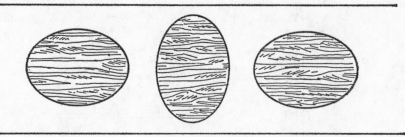

will sell you a foot or two of your chosen variety. Make a cardboard pattern for the new table top, and use it to cut three pieces of veneer: lay a strip of veneer on a breadboard, place the pattern on it, and cut around the pattern with a single-edged razor blade. In two of the pieces the grain of the wood should run lengthwise, but the third piece should be cut across the grain. Apply liquid cement with

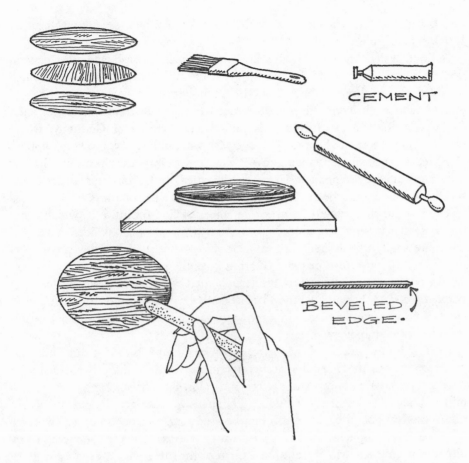

CEMENT

BEVELED
EDGE.

a small paintbrush to put these three layers together like a sandwich, with the crosswise piece in the middle. Lay the laminated top on the breadboard and go over it with a rolling pin to press out any excess cement; wipe oozed glue off the edges with a soft cloth moistened with nail-polish remover. Leave the laminated table top on the breadboard overnight, weighting it with heavy books to prevent buckling as the cement dries. Then bevel the sharp upper edges with the smooth side of an emery board, and attach the legs with liquid cement.

The close of World War II marked the beginning of the Plastics Period. Plastic was hailed as the ultimate replacement for wood, metal, glass, and leather, and for a time the only miniature furniture available was stamped out of this cheap new substance. It was instantly obvious, however, that man-made plastic was only an imitation of, and a poor substitute for, most genuine materials; wooden furniture—full and mini-size—returned by popular demand. As plastics have been improved, they have proven to be both versatile and practical, and although many miniaturists profess an aversion to this substance in any form, the best plastic is preferable to other materials of poor quality for small-scale furnishings. After all, a plastic table should no more be taboo in a twentieth-century miniature living room than a silver washtub in the kitchen of a seventeenth-century Dutch cabinet house.

Antique dealers know very well that "one generation's trash is another generation's treasure." Fifty years ago, cheap dollhouse furniture was made of painted or gilded pot metal rather than of wood, and filigree metal Tootsie Toys that sold for ten cents each in the nineteen-twenties have now become collector's items. Today, metal dollhouse furniture is rarely made outside of Germany, where tubular-framed sofas and pedestal chairs, with vinyl upholstery, are very popular. Fifty years hence plastic as we know it may have disappeared entirely, having been supplanted by some material not yet invented, and plastic miniatures of the nineteen-seventies may be avidly sought by discriminating collectors.

The best molded miniatures are scale copies of fine furniture in which every detail is meticulously reproduced—lids raise, drawers open, padded seats and backs are neatly upholstered with satin or velvet—but smooth, shiny plastic permeated with mud-brown or ivory coloring lacks the texture and graining of polished wood and is an obvious counterfeit. Painted plastic *does,* however, look like painted wood. A brightly enameled plastic Parsons table or an antiqued plastic chest of drawers can be placed in a contemporary miniature room without hesitation and without apology.

Be their framework wood or plastic, many of the upholstered chairs and sofas made today are sound in styling and correct in size but are clumsily covered with thick materials of inappropriate pattern and color. Reupholstering miniature furniture is not easy, but it can be done. The first task is to get the old upholstery material off in one piece, so that it can be used as a pattern to cut a new cover from thin but opaque fabric. Fill a bowl with hot water and put the piece of furniture in it upside down. Weight the bottom of the piece with a glass ash tray to keep it submerged, and leave it in the water for five minutes to soften the uphol-

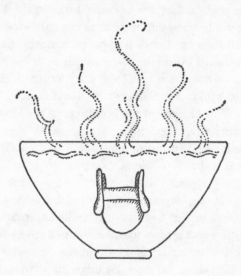

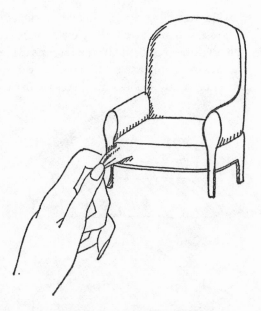

stery glue. Beginning at a corner or a straight edge, pull the material off slowly and carefully and lay it on a thick pad of paper toweling. Pin the edges of the

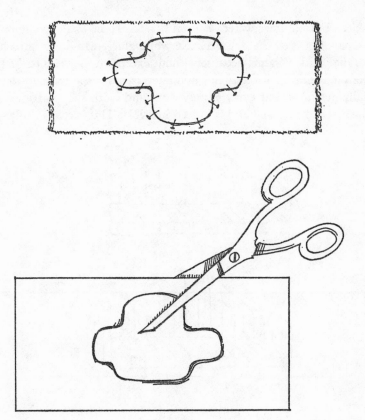

cloth to the paper, to avoid wrinkling and shrinkage during the drying period. Then place the old upholstery material on the new fabric and cut around it, allowing an extra ¼″ on all sides to be turned back for a neat edge.

It probably will be necessary to replace some or all of the water-soaked padding with absorbent cotton or lamb's wool—thin foam rubber is fine for separate

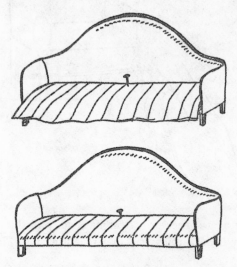

couch cushions but not for covered seats and backs. None of the common household adhesives—not even the indispensable white glue—will do for attaching the covering to the padded frame, because without exception they will strike through the material and stain it. Professional upholsterers use a special glue that is not commercially available, but every variety store and cloth shop carries a type of fabric cement that holds well and is indeed invisible. This is sold in tubes, under

various brand names, and is commonly called liquid thread. Apply a little of this thick clear substance directly from the tube to the turned-back edges of the upholstery fabric, and spread the glue smoothly with a flat wooden toothpick. Center the cover on the seat of the sofa; smooth the material toward the sides, then tuck in the crease behind the seat and carry the fabric up and over the sofa back. Finally, cover the arms. Sometimes it is necessary to slash the edges of the cloth at intervals to obtain a neat, tight fit. Press each edge down firmly with a fingertip and, if cording is needed, glue on matching crochet thread.

The seats of dining-room chairs usually are separate from the frames and are only cloth-covered rectangles of thin wood or cardboard. Remove such a seat by levering it up with the point of a nutpick, soak it in hot water, and pull off the old material. Lay the seat upside down on the wrong side of the new upholstery fabric and cut around it, adding a ¾" margin on all sides to allow for the height of the padding. Put a dot of liquid thread on the point of one corner of the cloth; pull this corner up and over the corner of the seat frame, stretch it tight, and

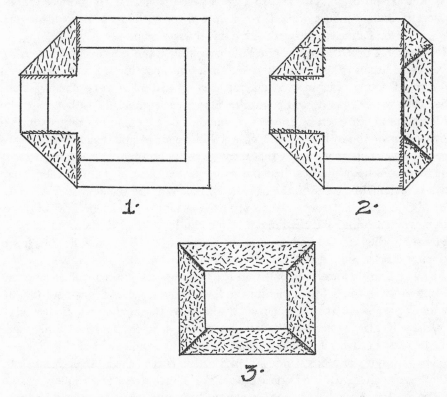

press it down. Repeat this process with the other corners and then spread glue along the four side edges of the cover. Lift the edges, one at a time, pulling them straight and pressing them down. When the fabric glue has dried turn the chair seat over and marvel at its neatly mitered corners.

Compared with reupholstering miniature furniture, making small-scale bedding seems like child's play, and indeed many little girls can and do make mattresses, sheets, pillowcases, blankets, and spreads for doll or dollhouse beds. Cut a mattress from a thin piece of foam rubber of the sort used in packing breakables for mailing, and make a box-edged ticking cover for it of any pin-striped material. Two small hemstitched or floral-patterned handkerchiefs will provide a splendid pair of sheets, and a third handkerchief can be converted into matching pillowcases. Solid-color flannel blankets can be edged at top and bottom with narrow bias binding. The bedspread may match the bedroom's draperies or take another form entirely. A quilted spread can be cut from quilted lining material, and padded trapunto work is imitated by small raised white-on-white motifs of cotton fabrics. For a room with solid-color carpeting and curtains, silk, satin, or percale in a tiny all-over floral pattern would make a luxurious spread; miniature boudoir pillows to toss on top of such a coverlet are sold in boutiques or in the notions departments of large stores, in the form of tiny lace-edged pillow sachets. Dark plaid gingham and thin dress tweed would be appropriate fabrics in more masculine rooms, while the best spread for a child's bed would be one made of cotton flannelette printed with a tiny nursery motif.

It is far more practical to design a suitable setting around furniture you already have in hand than to construct the room first, and hope to find furnishings that will fit it. If you are planning a contemporary room that is to be one-of-a-kind rather than one-of-a-series, you might decide to house it in a shadow box raised to eye level on top of a chest of drawers. A shadow box that is to be painted can be put together for you by a carpenter, of any thin wood; a cabinetmaker or a furniture refinisher could make a box that matches its supporting chest. In either case, the box should be 3″ deeper than the room you envision, to allow for lighting, and a hole should be bored in the back of the box to admit the electric wires. The pane of thin glass that covers the front of the shadow box can be held in place with narrow molding, and the same molding can be applied to the front edge of the box top, which should be hinged at the back to open like a lid. The glass front and hinged top should be added after the room is decorated.

The wall that divides the room from the lighting compartment must have an opening to admit the light—a picture window, or sliding glass doors—but it cannot be all glass or else the bulb and wires will show. If you choose a picture window, make it a large one; have an opening cut for it in the center of a plywood wall. Its glass need not be a single large piece—this could be a shallow, three-sided bay window, or a box window glazed with a curved sheet of very thin clear plastic rescued from a round corsage box. For a view from the window, use a large color picture cut from a garden or travel magazine and pasted to the back wall of the box: a suburban scene, perhaps, or a seascape. The suburban scene might show a tree trunk (made of a section of a small bark-covered limb) in the foreground, with a single branch of foliage slanting down across the outside of the

window top, and a shrub or two to tie in with the plantings in the picture. The seascape could have a low sand dune between the window and the pictured water, with a child's sand pail and shovel at one side. Shape the dune of plastic wood, which will stick to the floor of the box without additional glue, and cover the plastic wood while it still is moist with a layer of fine sand; as the wood dries, the sand will adhere to its surface.

Because sliding doors begin at the floor and extend upward almost to the ceiling, it will be easier to hide the mechanics of the exterior lighting if the glass doors are placed at one end of the room's rear wall instead of in its center. Use two panes of thin glass or clear plastic for these doors, covering half the wall opening with one panel but showing the other panel partially open; half of the second glass should be slid back to overlap half of the first, and one-fourth of the wall opening will thus be left unglazed. The easiest way to give these sliding glass panels the look of customary metal frames is by fitting silver-colored cloth tape over their edges. Half-inch-wide self-stick cloth tape is sold in rolls at variety stores, and can be narrowed with scissors before being pressed over the door rims.

This time, consider the room as part of an apartment, with a narrow balcony overlooking a city scene. First paste to the back wall of the box a giant postcard or an enlarged color photograph of your own city's skyline. Then set up a balcony parapet, placing it 1″ away from the picture for better perspective. Make a solid coping of wood brushed with antique-white latex paint for the look of concrete, or a low cinder-block wall of snap-together cubes from a child's plastic building set. For an iron railing, buy plastic parakeet ladders at a pet shop, cut them to size with a hacksaw, paint them black, and cement them on edge. Decorate the top of any balcony barrier with two or three potted plants and cover the floor with small squares of coarse red-brown sandpaper, which will look like pebbled concrete.

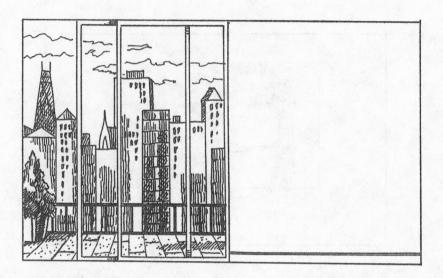

Paint the room's interior walls, or paper them with self-stick contact plastic, and add white-painted balsa woodwork. Use ½"-wide flat strips for the baseboard, and ¼" strips for ceiling molding. If the room will have wall-to-wall carpeting, this should be laid before the baseboard is attached to the wall with liquid cement.

For wall-to-wall floor covering, one thinks first of actual carpet samples, but these are so thick that the legs of miniature chairs and tables sink down into the pile as though it were quicksand. Splendid carpeting will be found in a cloth shop—hopefully on the remnant counter: solid-color velvet, velveteen, and felt; printed velveteen in small floral or geometric patterns; and solid-color terry cloth. Pale green, aqua, royal blue, or orange felt will remarkably resemble indoor-outdoor carpeting. Velveteen and velvet (in beige, gold, green, or deep maroon) will have the rich look of deep pile carpeting in living and dining areas, while dull blue, dusty rose, or sulphur-yellow terry cloth will make wonderful shag carpeting for bedrooms. Solid-color washcloths can be used as room-size rugs in bedrooms, and washcloths woven in geometric designs may be trimmed with shears to oval, round, or octagon-shaped area rugs.

For straight contemporary-style draperies that hang in simple pleats, rayon lining materials and thin nylon jersey would be more acceptable if their surfaces were not so shiny. Buy these fabrics in solid, muted colors, and turn them on the wrong (dull) side, which will look rather like antique satin. Materials for sheer glass curtains are hard to find, and stiff nylon net is *not* the answer. Many miniaturists have resorted to fine lawn handkerchiefs with hemstitched borders, but thin chiffon will be even better because it hangs so gracefully and drapes so easily with a minimum of bulk. Draperies and glass curtains that appear to hang from traverse rods should be pinch-pleated at the top. Behind each pleat, sew a link

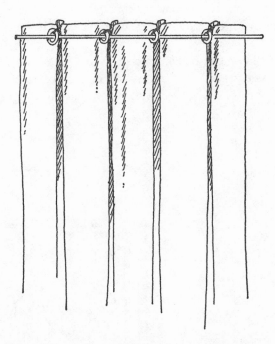

from a thin chain necklace, and thread through these rings a length of stiff wire. Support the wire on finshing nails whose heads protrude an eighth of an inch from the wall. When it is necessary to wash or replace these curtains, it will be a simple matter to lift the wire rod off its supports, and slip it out of the curtain rings.

The venetian blinds that are so excellent an alternative to glass curtains can be made with relative ease from plastic matchstick window valances. For vertically slatted blinds, it is only necessary to cut between matchsticks with scissors, and finish each side edge of the shade by turning back one matchstick and securing it with plastic cement. The end of a matchstick valance makes the top of a blind with horizontal slats. In narrowing the miniature blind, take advantage of the interwoven threads that hold the sticks together; be sure to incorporate at least two of these retaining threads in each shade, cutting off the matchsticks on either side, with tin snips. Allow ½″ of extra length for this type of shade and roll the sticks up from the bottom to reach just to the lower edge of the window; overcast the rolled sticks with thread to hold them permanently in place.

In many of today's rooms light fixtures on chains have supplanted traditional chandeliers. Among the key rings at a discount house there often are short rope chains that end in little metal lanterns with colored glass sides, or in openwork metal balls; these will make splendid chain-light fixtures. Suspend a ball or a lantern on a section of a gold-colored metal necklace chain from the ten-cent store by forcing open the jump ring that secures it to the key chain and threading this ring through the end link of the new chain. Close the ring with pliers. Affix the chain to the ceiling with the tiniest of eyebolts, or with decorative brass upholsterer's tacks.

A miniature pole lamp can be constructed from a length of black coat-hanger wire, plus four or five peaked tops from small plastic bottles of white glue. The flairing orange caps can be disguised with paint, and given light bulbs made of

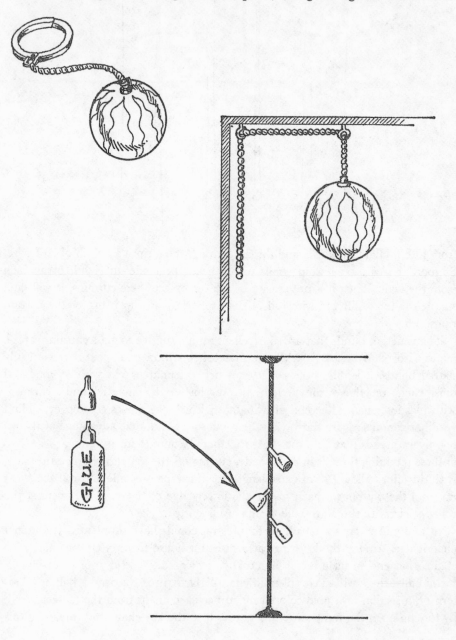

pear-shaped white corsage-pin tops. Angle the lights on the wire pole with dots of liquid solder (which comes in tubes at hardware and variety stores) and solder metal grommets for finishing plates around the ends of the pole where they meet floor and ceiling.

The combination of fireplace, hearth, and mantel makes a natural center of interest for any room, but present-day apartments and small houses seldom have functional firesides. Still, a room must have a focal point—a picture window, a bookshelf wall, a large painting above a long sofa, or a group of prints above a console stereo-television. The bookshelf wall that is so fine a feature for an up-to-date room is not difficult to construct if it is made with 1″-wide, ⅛″-thick balsa strips for shelves, side braces, and dividers. Paint these strips to match the room's other woodwork; attach the vertical shelf ends and dividers first by coating one long edge of a strip with liquid cement and pressing it against the wall. Spread liquid cement on the back and side edges of a shelf-strip and wait ten seconds before fitting it in place between its vertical supports; push it back against the wall and hold it under pressure for a minute or two until the cement has begun to grip.

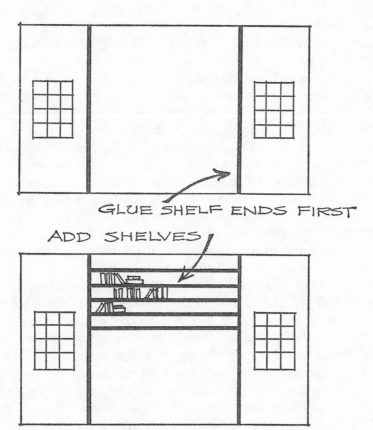

GLUE SHELF ENDS FIRST

ADD SHELVES

A set of miniature books bought at a toyshop will be an excellent nucleus for this home library, and can be augmented with volumes you make yourself. The books in such a set vary in height and thickness, but their realistically printed dust jackets cover only blocks of wood. A long strip of balsa, $\frac{1}{2}''$ wide and $\frac{1}{8}''$ thick, can be cut crosswise into a great many books that differ slightly in height; two or three of these strip segments can be put together with liquid cement to form weightier tomes. These basic book shapes may simply be painted in bright colors or covered with solid-color self-stick cloth tape, and interspersed with titled copies from the toyshop set. For greater authenticity, pictures of book jackets and/or spines, cut from publishers' catalogues, might be pasted on to title the painted or taped book blocks. In variety stores and college bookshops, narrow bright-colored plastic strips are sold as theme binders; these can be cut crosswise with shears into slender volumes that add good variation of color and texture to the wall shelves. Colored plastic notebook tabs are sold in sets and go onto the shelves instantly as slim books. For paperbacks, select a thin catalogue with a colorful color, and cut off its pages $\frac{1}{2}''$ from the folded, stapled spine; then cut this strip into $\frac{3}{4}''$ sections.

The built-in bookcase will be even more attractive if a few bibelots are scattered among the books. At a party shop, you may find glass cocktail picks with interesting colorful tops: cocks, of course, and other birds; fish, seals, and dolphins; animals or animal heads. It is almost impossible to remove these brittle shapes from their glass shafts without breaking them, but this can be done for you in a trice at a retail glass company. Provide the ornaments with bases, to enable them to stand unsupported, by attaching them with glass cement to clear glass buttons. Hunt through the silver- and gold-plated charms at a discount house for horses, lions, dogs, or elephants. In addition, look for ballet dancers, skiers, bowlers, golfers, and tennis players. Paint the animals and the ballet dancers gloss white, in imitation of porcelain, and add them to the shelves for china ornaments, but leave the sports figures untreated. Use liquid solder to mount the miniature athletes on black button bases, and then group them with tiny party-favor loving cups to turn them into trophies.

Table lamps are important appurtenances of contemporary rooms, and it now is possible to buy miniature lamps that actually light. These functional lamps often are permanently attached to the tops of hollow chests that conceal batteries to provide their electricity. Other lamps have cords leading to batteries encased in plastic capsules but, although the battery holders are not very large, they cannot hide behind a miniature sofa or masquerade as ottomans and are, therefore, difficult to disguise. At any rate, the lamps will shed their feeble light for only two or three hours before they burn out, and such evanescent illumination hardly seems worth the trouble (and expense) of constant bulb and battery replacement.

The selection of nonworking dollhouse lamps is so limited that you probably will find it more satisfactory to make these yourself, matching them to the room's decor. Tall metal or plastic candlesticks can serve as the slender bases for desk or dressing-table lamps, and china boudoir lamps can be made of decorated miniature vases or of long oval beads impaled on inverted thumbtacks to make them stand upright and steady. Fluted shades for these little lamps can be contrived from paper candy cups that come in pastel colors or in overall floral patterns. Cut the bottom out of a cup and replace it with a circle of clear wallet-window plastic, attaching the rim of the plastic circle to the fluted inner sides of the cup, ⅛″ below the cut bottom edge, with white glue. When this glue has dried thoroughly, push a straight pin with a colored head down through the center of the thin plastic. The pinhead will serve as a lamp finial, while the pin point can be dipped in liquid cement and wound with wisps of cotton to make it fit a candlestick, the hole in a bead, or the narrow neck of a vase.

Pairs of bracelet charm figurines attached with liquid solder to thick square brass or silver button bases make good lamps for living room end tables, and round, square, or swirled sample perfume bottles can be converted to chunky crystal lamps. Tall wooden lamp bases may be made from sections of round or square dowels, or built up of tiny blocks of wood. Tall ceramic lamps can be simulated with large plastic beads—round, square, or faceted—cemented together in a stack.

A drum shade for any of these larger lamps can be fashioned from a plastic pill vial shortened to appropriate height by cutting off its top with a fine-blade keyhole saw. Cover the cylinder with wide white or pale beige self-stick plastic tape and cement the solid colorless bottom of the vial to the top of the lamp base. Since the shade is opaque, a light bulb will not be needed; a finial would not show above the top of such a deep drum shade. For a wider, shallower drum shade, use the lid of a small round cardboard match holder; cover it with plastic tape and finish its edges with gold cord before mounting it upside down on a base.

Candles are much used in decorating today, but the single candlesticks sold in toyshops are too tall and too traditional for most contemporary rooms. Small bright-colored wooden beads, round or square, look exactly like miniature Danish modern candleholders. Round toothpicks are splendid candles; minus one pointed tip, a toothpick makes a very tall taper; broken in half, the pick makes a pair of medium-length candles. Paint the candles white (or any desired color) and force their cut ends down into the holes in the wooden bead holders.

Toyshops do have low, plain, three-cup silvery candleholders that are right in styling for the sideboard or table in a contemporary dining room, and slim wax matches make perfect candles for them. Cut off the head of a match with scissors, dip the cut end in white glue, and fit it into a candle cup. If the cup is too large to hold the candle steady, wrap a wisp of cotton around the glue covered match end and set it in place immediately.

Heavy brass holders with large round candles are used singly on coffee or dining tables and in pairs on modern mantels. To simulate these, find a retail electric company or a decorating shop that specializes in table lamps, and buy the shortest lamp-shade risers. The hollow portion of such a riser will be ½" tall, and when set on end will look like a handsome turned brass holder. The short threaded end of the riser can be dipped in melted candle wax to become a smooth fat candle, or merely painted in imitation of a twisted candle.

Large round candles in flat holders, the universal adornments for round coffee tables, can be concocted of large-size birthday candles and flat buttons with raised rims. Choose either a plain or a twisted candle, and cut off a short section from its base with a serrated paring knife dipped in hot water; attach the short candle to its rimmed button base with white glue. As an alternative to the button, use a birthday candleholder, removing its pointed pick with a fine-toothed keyhole saw. An elephant, a lion, or a tiger candleholder from a circus birthday-cake set will be especially effective.

Saucers from miniature tea sets make perfect ash trays for coffee or end tables, and Coalport earrings are miniature copies of the popular porcelain flower ornaments. Break off the clip back of an earring with pliers, and the metal-backed mound of tiny china flowers will need no container. Complete the coffee-table arrangement with miniature copies of current magazines, and a folded newspaper, all of which can be found among dollhouse accessories in a toyshop.

Accessories for the miniature desk are equally easy to devise. A rectangle of dark green craft paper with black photo-mount corners will look like a blotter, and a metal watchband calendar can be made to stand upright by cementing the edge of a wooden triangle to its back. Tiny round and square picture frames may be found among the silver bracelet charms at a large department store, and filled with "studio photographs" clipped from snapshots. Straight pins come in various lengths and thicknesses; the so-called banker's pins and sequin pins are shorter and thinner than the common steel variety. Cut off the heads of these pins with wire-cutter pliers and paint them, to turn them into ball-point pens or yellow pencils. Every desk should have its wastebasket, but only kitchen and bathroom miniatures seem to be sold in toyshops. Cut off the top of a slender plastic pill vial, with a keyhole saw, to make a round wastebaset 1½" tall. Paint the outside of the cylinder, or glue inside it—facing outward—a map or picture cut from the color illustrations in a catalogue. Finish the top edge of the basket with *soutache* braid, or thin gold cord.

Over the desk a painting might be placed, and other oils or prints will probably be needed on the long wall above the sofa. Toyshops sell miniature pictures in sets for dollhouse decorating; even though their subjects do not appeal to you, buy these for their frames. Replace a picture by pasting over it a commemorative postage stamp that is a miniature color engraving, a color print of a well-known work of art cut out of a museum catalogue, or a bird or flower print from an individual bridge-party tally. Miniature reproductions of famous paintings are sold as postcards in museum shops and sometimes appear on the backs of playing cards; these can be trimmed to fit thin snapshot frames from a stationery department or a variety store.

You, or an artist friend, can of course produce an originial oil and have it framed at an art shop, but a reasonable facsimile of an oil painting can be made by even the most untalented tyro. Cut a colored photograph of an ultra-modern painting from a catalogue and coat it with white glue applied in streaks with a ⚹ 1 artist's brush; the glue will dry clear and the picture will show through it, but the ridges and brush marks will look like paint laid on thickly with a palette knife.

Miniature mirrors abound in any variety store. A 5″×7″ rectangular mirror for the space above a sideboard or a mantel should be removed from its flimsy metal frame and cemented directly to the wall. A tiny round hand mirror framed in scalloped plastic becomes a dressing-table mirror for a bedroom once its handle has been cut off flush with the frame by means of a fine-toothed saw. Pairs of square or oblong unframed purse mirrors look well over pairs of side tables in a living room, while the round mirror from the lid of a small rouge compact makes a mirrored plaque beneath the centerpiece on a dining-room table. The narrow oblong mirror from the back of a pocket-comb case can serve as a full-length mirror on the back of a bathroom door or on a bedroom wall.

An item described in catalogues as a "full-length purse-size mirror" has a curved surface about 4″ long and 2½″ wide. Like all convex mirrors, it greatly reduces the size of anything it reflects, and it would make a truly amazing overmantel or wall mirror for a contemporary room. Gazing into this little looking glass, a viewer will feel that he has drunk from Alice's bottle in Wonderland, for he will see himself diminished as though he actually stood before the mirror, inside the miniature room.

In our child-centered society, the family room epitomizes this servantless split-level era and takes the place of the day nursery of yesteryear. The focal point of a miniature family room would be the omnipresent television set, which can be found among the dollhouse accessories in a toyshop, or among the pencil sharpeners in a variety store. Pencil-sharpener TV screens often are double-layered so that action appears to take place as you look at the set from different angles. Matchbox tops and Christmas cards sometimes have similar changeable scenes, and one of these could be superimposed on the front of a long, low chest to make a console entertainment unit. If the television screen is placed at one end of the chest front, the other end will be assumed to contain a stereo-phonograph, and this impression would be fortified by the presence on the chest top of a stack of tiny plastic records from a party-favor packet.

Where there are teen-agers there are cushions on the floor in front of the television. Make these cushions for the family room of felt, wide velvet ribbon, or wide decorative braid trimming; stuff them with cotton and close their seams with liquid thread. A dollhouse princess telephone should certainly keep these cushions company. Place it on the floor, adding a long extension cord of crochet thread that reaches to the wall across the room.

An up-to-the-minute bathroom or kitchen can be fitted into the corner of a bookcase shelf beside a contemporary bedroom or dining room, and it will be interesting to see how rapidly these marvels of a mechanized age become outmoded. Most inexpensive plastic bathroom sets include only a bar of soap and a pair of fringed towels along with the plumbing fixtures; more elegant and costly sets come with tall shelf-racks for towels, dressing tables, and toilet-tissue holders. To prepare a suitable setting for purchased fixtures, cover all the bathroom walls with marble cut with a razor blade from thin marbleized wall tiles, or tile only the shower stall and the lower half of each wall. Decorate the upper half of the wall with contact plastic wallpaper. For a more unusual wall covering, one might use panels of "antique" venetian mirror made by painting over mirror strips with brown water color. Carpet the floor with a thin solid-color washcloth, cutting it with scissors to fit around the tub, lavatory, and toilet; first attach the fixtures to the floor with white glue and then spread more glue over the whole floor before pressing the terry-cloth carpeting down smoothly. Make a matching window- and shower-curtain set of thin plastic material, sewing on curtain rings removed from a dime-store chain necklace. If no dressing table came with the set, build in a long one by bridging small painted plastic chests with a counter top of marble wall tile. On the dressing table place a box of facial tissues, a hand mirror, a comb and brush (all of which are sold as dollhouse accessories), and perfume bottles made of large colored glass beads with small clear bead stoppers held on by slender sequin pins. A pole towel rack, constructed of a painted piece of coat-hanger wire with metal grommets for finishing plates, might have small brass curtain rings for towel holders; attach all these metal fittings to each other, as well as to the floor and ceiling, with liquid solder. Alternatively, use tiny lion-head ring pulls (for jewel-box drawers) as towel holders, soldering them directly to the bathroom wall.

Good plastic dollhouse kitchen sets contain cabinets as well as major appliances, and sometimes include washing machines and clothes dryers along with stoves, refrigerators, sinks, and dishwashers. To personalize such a set, put milk, eggs, and vegetables in the refrigerator; line up canned goods on wall-cabinet shelves and stack cooking utensils and mixing bowls in base cabinets; place dish towels, carving knives, and mixing spoons in drawers; and don't forget a box of soap flakes in the cabinet below the sink. All these miniatures can be found in toy and party shops. Add a vacuum cleaner in one corner; a toaster, a radio, and a blender on the counter top; a telephone on the wall. Radios and telephones are often found among the accessories for fashion dolls, and small appliances among dollhouse accessories. Finally, make a grocery bag of brown paper and white glue, and fill it with leftover staples and fresh foods, with a stalk of celery sticking up out of the top.

Because you are the person who arranged its furniture and devised its accessories, it will be difficult for you to see small imperfections in a miniature room. A
good way to check the placement of furnishings as you work is by using a trick
well known to artists: Turn your back on the room and look at its reflection in a
hand mirror. For some unknown reason, reversing the image of the scene will enable the eye to discern previously unnoticed minor faults that can easily be cor-
rected: a table may need to be moved a mere quarter of an inch away from the
arm of a chair, or a lamp may be so tall that it obscures a vital portion of the
painting on the wall behind it. When you decide at last that a contemporary
room is finished, take a picture of it. If it is in perfect scale and balance, the photograph will show what appears to be an actual interior rather than a miniature
room.

V

Period Rooms That Recapture the Past

History is no more (and no less) than the story of people, and if this lengthy narrative is to be interesting and understandable to us, it is important that we know how people lived as well as who they were and what they did.

Early in the twentieth century, house museums came into being in the United States as a means of preserving historic homes that were endangered by the rapid growth of cities; when these houses were carefully restored and refurnished in the styles of their proper periods, they provided remarkable insight into the lives and labors of preceding generations. In response to rising public interest in the nation's past, the curators of general museums brought out of storage the pioneer tools and furnishings to which they had been giving only custodial care. To supply a European background for America's cultural heritage, the directors of art museums dreamed of importing the shells of ancient rooms and filling them with period furniture and paintings, but most museums' budgets and buildings were too small to permit such extravagant acquisitions.

A tremendous breakthrough occurred in 1937 when the Art Institute of Chicago first placed on display twenty-nine period rooms *in miniature:* Mrs. James Ward Thorne's English and French interiors that delineated major changes in architecture and demonstrated trends in decorating from 1500 to 1925. This series created such a stir in museum circles that in 1942 the Art Institute added Mrs. Thorne's "American Rooms in Miniature." A house museum was able to exemplify the American way of life in only one time and city, but these thirty-seven new interiors spanned the years from 1675 to 1940, and covered the entire continent. The 1962 edition of the Art Institute's descriptive booklet had this high praise for miniature rooms:

Models such as these . . . are in many ways superior to the so-called "period room" for presenting a complete picture of a type or style in its entirety. They offer a flexibility of lighting, setting and furnishings, which the actual period room with its demands of piece by piece authenticity, its spatial requirements, and the exigencies of lighting and accessibility, can never approach. Supplemented by displays of original objects and furniture, they would seem to offer an ideal solution of the hitherto unsolved problem of an adequate three-dimensional demonstration of the arts of decoration in the public museums.

Mrs. Thorne's European and American interiors were in no sense amateur productions; they were made especially for the Art Institute, and were the culmination of many years' research and experimentation. In an earlier and more eclectic group of rooms Mrs. Thorne had tested and proven her methods of decoration and lighting and had used antique miniatures from her own collection. While these early scenes were in production she herself had done most of the needlework and had put the finishing touches of paper and paint on walls and woodwork, but to make the sixty-six rooms of the European and American series rapidly (and to museum standards) she obviously needed the help of many experts. Even though she supervised and correlated all their efforts she must have missed the pleasure of personal involvement in each stage of a room's gradual development.

The first group of her rooms had sustained considerable minor damage during its eighteen years on the road by the time IBM decided, in 1962, to retire this traveling exhibit and place it in storage. Sixteen of the rooms were released, upon request, to Mrs. Thorne for restoration and presentation to The Phoenix Art Museum. Aided by only one craftsman she completely renovated and redecorated them, adding recently acquired antique furniture and *objets d'art*. The completed scenes now in the Phoenix museum represented a talent that had come full circle—from do-it-yourself to have-it-done to do-it-yourself—and had matured along the way. They are even more beautiful than when they first were made, and they have a look of human habitation that is lacking in the self-consciously precise rooms of the European and American series.

The European rooms are the ones in which architecture is most painstakingly presented. Every detail is perfectly accurate and perfectly executed, and in miniature scale, the total effect is perfectly overwhelming! In the European series and the Phoenix group there are several "matching pairs" of rooms: Louis XV libraries, Louis XVI dining rooms, Louis XVI salons, and Adam dining rooms. In each case, the Phoenix rooms' architectural details have been de-emphasized in favor of the lovely antique furniture and accessories, and this difference in emphasis is especially apparent in the Adam dining rooms. The raised plaster designs of the two ceilings are identical; below both cornices there are plaster medallions and swags, and the walls of both rooms are ornamented with corinthian pilasters. But the ceiling of Chicago's Adam room has a vignette painting in each raised medallion; the pilasters, the wall panels, and the cornice are busy with scrolled ornamentation and classical figure groups in high relief. The museum-reproduction furnishings here are actually more delicate and fine than the antiques of the Phoenix model, but they are subordinate to their background and overshadowed by it.

European styles arrived late in the American colonies and lingered long. Each style that crossed the Atlantic "suffered a sea change" as the colonists modified what they imitated, simplifying imported fashions to suit the needs and tastes of a pioneer society. Houses and furnishings had a disciplined look that was very pleasing and typically American.

Because their architecture and their furnishings are less pretentious, Mrs. Thorne's American interiors are more appealing than the European rooms. She was careful to show how plain as well as prosperous people lived, balancing handsome and historically significant entrance halls, drawing rooms, dining rooms, and bed chambers with a typical seventeenth-century New England kitchen, a Pennsylvania Dutch miller's house, a Shaker communal home, a Cape Cod cottage, and an adobe casa of the Southwest. Furthermore, she elected to portray the kitchens of the Governor's Mansion in Colonial Williamsburg instead of its impressive reception rooms. One of the loveliest of the American interiors is the entrance hall of the Pierce Mansion in Portsmouth, New Hampshire, which contains only three pieces of furniture: a graceful Hepplewhite settee shaped to fit the curve of the stairway that rises behind it, and a pair of small tripod tables that flank the fanlighted front door.

Very few would-be makers of period rooms have enough time to seek out large numbers of antique miniatures, or enough money to have fine scale reproductions made in quantity, and no one can hope to be more inventive and creative than Mrs. Thorne. Why bother, then, with making period interiors that cannot surpass or equal the incomparable Thorne Rooms?

In the first place, the Thorne Rooms are literally museum pieces, and are to be seen only in Chicago, Phoenix, or Knoxville, but period rooms could be valuable museum displays and teaching devices in *any* city. Secondly, the European and American series are tied to architectural and decorating trends, but there are other aspects of history to be stressed; no miniaturist needs to copy or compete with any other but only to implement his own ideas in his own way. Recapturing the spirit of a bygone era is much more difficult, but infinitely more challenging, than distilling a little of the essence of the present; it offers an opportunity to expand one's knowledge while demanding a beneficial self-discipline and an exactitude seldom required in post-scholastic endeavors. Finally, and all-importantly, making miniature period rooms is *fun!*

A period room may be defined as one that illustrates, through its furnishings and arrangement, the tastes and customs of a particular time and place. Time is

In the courtyard of Colleen Moore's Fairy Castle, the Rockabye Baby's golden cradle actually sways in a treetop, and the weeping willow sheds tears of distilled water. Plaques on the wall outside the library illustrate Aesop's fables; inside, the shelves hold inch-square books, handwritten by famous authors. PHOTOGRAPH COURTESY OF THE MUSEUM OF SCIENCE AND INDUSTRY, CHICAGO.

Mrs. James Ward Thorne found a fine new way to light a miniature room. "Sunshine" pours through the windows of her Victorian drawing room, casting shadows of the carved and fretted furniture. Gothic molding calls attention to a pair of portraits: Queen Victoria and Prince Albert, looking with approval on the wealth of bibelots. PHOTOGRAPH COURTESY OF THE ART INSTITUTE OF CHICAGO.

Mrs. Thorne's European Rooms present a history of architecture in capsule form. This English salon of the late Stuart period follows the style of Christopher Wren. Intricate fruit-and-flower carvings on the walls are copied from Grinling Gibbons, and their motifs are repeated in the molded-plaster ceiling. PHOTOGRAPH COURTESY OF THE ART INSTITUTE OF CHICAGO.

Portable shops, stocked with scale-copies of real merchandise, capture and preserve a bit of everyday life. This typical millinery shop offers all the materials required for hat-making, and its tempting finished chapeaux were the height of fashion in the 1830s. Maximilian Museum, Augsburg, Germany. PHOTOGRAPH BY BETSEY CREEKMORE

In the days when few people could read, miniature scenes served as visual teaching aids. This early example of show-and-tell represents the home of Martin Luther. The leader of the Protestant Reformation is explaining the symbolism of the first Christmas tree to his wife and children. Victoria and Albert Museum, Bethnal Green, London. PHOTOGRAPH BY BETSEY CREEKMORE

of the essence, but place is also important: Renaissance interiors, for example, were entirely different in Italy and in England.

An interest in and a knowledge of history are primary requisites to making period rooms, and anyone who is about to embark on such a project for the first time should certainly choose a familiar era to portray. There is a vast difference, however, between general and specific knowledge. Before one can reproduce in miniature a room of a certain time and place, one must be absolutely sure what such a room looked like in actuality. This means research, but of a type that has nothing to do with gray-beard scholars poring over heavy tomes in dusty book-stacks. It could involve visiting house museums and historical restorations, picking the brains of architects and interior decorators, browsing in antique shops, look-ing at furnishings and paintings in art museums.

Whether you do your firsthand research halfway around the world or just around the corner, do it with notebook in hand, and don't be shy about asking questions. By all means purchase any booklets, postcards, and color slides that are available—these will be worth their weight in traveler's checks as aids to memory.

Every American house museum represents a limited period of its own history. Curators of house museums have an unwritten rule that permits the inclusion of a few furnishings of earlier date but prohibits the use of any object that *could* not have been in the house during the specified years, and this is an excellent criterion for miniature rooms. In most actual households there are those holdovers from the not-too-distant past that are referred to as family pieces; if a wide enough gap exists between the generation that acquired them and the generation that displays them, inherited furnishings become cherished antiques. But only that lucky per-son blessed with absolute recall will be able to remember exactly what came when, and where.

Look it up? Of course, but in what book? Public libraries do not expect con-fused patrons to find their way unaided through the mystic maze of the Modified Dewey Decimal System, so bypass the card file, and go directly to the reference librarian for help. While you are at the library, pick up a slim pictorial volume on furniture styles in your chosen period. Even if you already know more than the author has to say, the pictures will be extremely helpful. Photographs in a book show real furnishings reduced to the approximate size of the miniatures with which you will be dealing. Check out a few specialized books that offer by-the-centuries surveys of such fields as window treatment, textiles and carpets, or table appointments. Finally, to become steeped in the daily life of the times, read biographies and novels of or about your selected era.

Long before all this research is complete, you will have formed a mental image of your own period room. Use graph paper to draw a plan of the three-sided scene, first blocking in the most important piece of furniture around which the room will be arranged, and then locating such immovable features as windows, doors, and fireplace. In a bedroom, for instance, the situs of the bed will govern

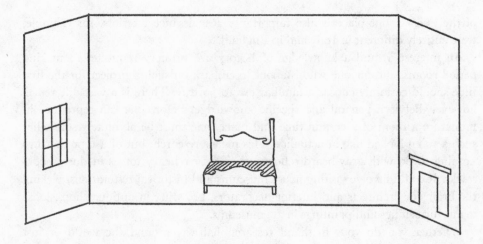

the placement of fireplace and windows as well as of all other furniture. Be sure to allow enough unbroken wallspace for chests, desks, and sofas.

If you are making this room for your own enjoyment, you probably will wish to incorporate it in a cherished piece of period furniture, or build it into a bookcase. If it is being made for a public building—a children's museum, say, or a branch library—there is an easy and economical way to recess the room into a wall at eye level. Build the room's shell by the box-in-a-box method and install the lighting in the outer box. Plan to enclose a corner of the exhibition hall by fitting heavy plywood across it; buy one 4′×8′ sheet and have a window cut to the dimensions of the *inner* box. Place this window 5′ above the floor and cover it with a pane of glass in a wooden frame; hinge the frame to the plywood at the

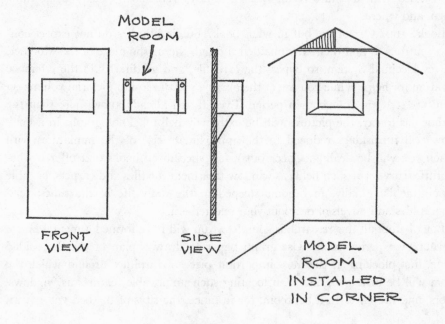

MODEL
ROOM

FRONT
VIEW

SIDE
VIEW

MODEL
ROOM
INSTALLED
IN CORNER

top to permit access to the room from the front, for cleaning. Behind this window, attach shelf brackets to the back of the plywood and secure the floor of the room to these brackets, from below, with wood screws. If there is no existing wall outlet into which the room's wiring can be plugged, have one installed; be sure that the switch controlling the lights is outside the boxed corner. When all is in readiness set the plywood with its recessed room across the corner, hinging it to the wall on one side so that it will be possible to swing the panel out and replace the light bulbs.

If, on the contrary, this room will be given to the public schools, it should be freestanding and portable. A good self-contained room can be made like a Nuremberg kitchen, with a floor and three walls but without a top or front side. The advantage of omitting the top is that the scene will require no lighting, but a transparent ceiling and front must be added. Take the exact measurements of the projected room to a builders' supply company and have the three walls cut of ¼" plywood; the floor should be of ½" thickness. If you explain what you are doing (and beg a lot), you probably will be able to have window openings cut to your specifications in one or more of the walls. If the room is to have wooden

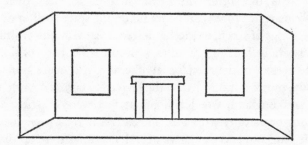

flooring, groove the plywood floor piece with a razor blade or a sharp-pointed knife in imitation of boards and stain it. Then put the three plywood wall sections together with finishing nails and attach them to the floor with plastic wood or epoxy cement. Screw drop handles to the outside of the two end walls, for convenience in carrying, and add mirror mounting clips (from a variety store) to the top and side edges of these end walls, to hold protective sheets of transparent

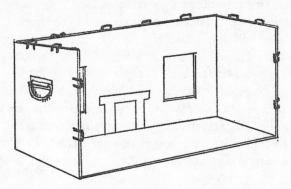

Plexiglas cut to size at a company listed under "Plastics: Retail" in the Yellow Pages. Cover the window openings with clear wallet-window plastic and add berry-box sash strips.

It is easier, and neater, to paint or paper the upper portion of a wall before installing paneling or wainscoting. In the eighteenth century, drawing-room walls were sometimes covered with watered silk or brocade; thin moiré, or brocatelle with very small raised designs, should be applied to wooden walls with liquid thread rather than with glue, which would strike through and stain it. Panels and dado should be painted before being attached to the wall with liquid cement. In France, England, and colonial America, paneled fireplace walls were often decorated with inset paintings. To achieve this effect, cut a small landscape scene from an art catalogue and paste it on the paneling above the center of the mantel. Frame it with balsa strips or balsa dowels painted to match the woodwork. In like manner, over-door paintings for seventeenth-century French or Italian rooms can be inset between a doorframe and a cornice.

In the late Middle Ages and the Renaissance, stone floors were covered with a thick layer of rushes for warmth as well as softness, and dried aromatic herbs were sprinkled over the rushes from time to time to mask their musty odor. Rushes for a Renaissance room can be found on the spice shelf at a supermarket: stiff gray-beige sprigs of rosemary, to be dusted over with bits of dull green dried dill. If the floor is to be hidden by rushes, it need not be made of simulated stone; brush the wooden floor of the room's shell liberally with white glue and apply the rosemary thickly, pressing it down with the fingers, to ensure complete coverage.

In Europe and England, wooden floors at first were left bare to show their polished planking or parquetry designs. The "ruges and carpets" mentioned in inventories of the sixteenth and early seventeenth centuries were not floor coverings, but thick Flemish tapestries that were draped over tables or spread across beds. When the colorful carpets that had been in use for centuries in the Orient and Persia were at last imported into Europe, they were small in size and were the original area rugs.

Catalogues sometimes offer 9"×12" telephone mats that are scale copies of traditional oriental carpets; if their fringe is trimmed down from 2" to ¼", these become important oriental rugs for eighteenth-century rooms. Smaller "orientals" made of flannel with printed designs are sold in toyshops, as are oval and oblong "hooked" rugs with floral centers.

Although a beautiful area rug can be salvaged from an outworn petit-point handbag, making a room-size or accent carpet of needlepoint is easy and interesting. Few of the designs already stamped and partially worked on scrim are small enough to be in scale, but plain needlepoint canvas can be bought in any needlework shop. The simplest needlepoint rug is one with a solid-color center and a contrasting solid border, but you (or an artistic friend) can draw an oriental, floral, or geometric design in color on plain canvas with felt-tipped marking pens, and work over the drawings with matching moth-proofed wool. Then the background can be filled in with a solid color. The work will go very quickly because the piece will be so small.

The wool sold for knitting or crocheting afghans is sometimes dyed in several shaded colors; pale yellow, gold, orange, and brown might appear in sequence on a single skein. Such a skein can be used to make a round rag rug of the multicolored type seen in early-American bedrooms. Begin at the center of the rug and wind the wool round and round in ever-larger flat, concentric circles, overcasting each row with white thread to the row before. In the Empire Period, round rugs with geometric designs were used on marble floors to imitate mosaics. Washcloths are sometimes patterned in sunburst or circular geometric figures, and these can be trimmed with shears to become area rugs for Empire rooms.

Drapery materials have always been the bane of miniature decorating; if they are heavy enough to look sumptuous, they are too stiff to hang properly. In the Dutch cabinet houses, where every other detail is perfect, bed curtains are bunched in clumsy folds that spoil the whole effect. This is not the fault of Dutch seamstresses, who used such small stitches that they are completely invisible, but of the stiff silk materials. In Queen Mary's Dolls' House, however, bed curtains and window draperies hang properly, in graceful pleats and folds. The difference is that these beautiful brocades were specially woven of microscopically fine silk threads. Some brocade and taffeta dress materials are thin and fine enough for miniature draperies, as are heavy chiffons. A flimsy silk scarf will drape better than an expensive length of silk crepe, and wide velvet ribbon will be more usable than velvet from the bolt, because it already is finished on both edges. For Victorian lace curtains, there is a type of wide lace edging that has a plain net center; this edging is sometimes finished on one or both sides with tiny scallops.

Although it is heresy to say so, draperies and curtains should not be hemmed. Even the most carefully turned and stitched edge is stiffer than the material itself, and this stiffness will cause the miniature drapery to ripple. Usually, the edges can be trimmed very carefully and left untreated, but if the material is one that frays badly, fringe it slightly by pulling out no more than two or three threads.

Most makers of miniature rooms would agree that the furniture for them should be the best obtainable—either authentic antiques or good reproductions. A miniaturist often decides to construct a room of a certain period as a setting for several cherished antique pieces, only to find after research that one piece is not coeval. No matter how attractive it is, an article of a later period should not be used merely because you have it; what you omit from a period room is well-nigh as important as what you include. To replace this late, lamented item and to add other missing essentials, one might write to the F.A.O. Schwarz company in New York City. This large toy store has an antiques department where, for a price, period dollhouse furniture as well as sample and apprentice pieces sometimes may be obtained. Many house and art museums have their own shops, in which good miniature reproductions of museum-quality antiques may be bought, and many mail-order catalogues offer imported reproductions. American-made miniatures of fine quality can be ordered from the Southern Craft Shop in Charleston, South Carolina, or from Chestnut Hill Studio in Churchville, New York. (See Sources of Supply, in the Appendix.)

If you have the skill and patience to make miniature reproductions yourself, you are the best qualified of craftsmen, for you alone know exactly what piece you want, and how it should look. If, on the other hand, you quail at the very thought of turning a tiny chair leg or fitting drawers into a miniature highboy, inquire at a boys' club or a senior citizens' center for the name of someone who uses the club's woodworking equipment regularly and with expertise. By this means you may find a friend who will agree to make one very simple chair or table, for a reasonable fee. You must provide not only the materials and the exact dimensions for this piece, but also a photograph to which your craftsman can refer as he works. If this first attempt pleases both of you, he may be persuaded to accept more difficult assignments.

In a room that will be moved around from place to place, it is important that the furniture not be knocked about in transit. Generous dots of white glue on the legs of chairs and tables or the bottoms of chests will secure the pieces to the floor, yet the glue will dry clear and be invisible; when it becomes necessary or desirable to remove the furniture, white glue will peel off the wood leaving the finish unharmed.

To bring the room to life once its furniture is in place, there must be accessories—the more numerous and authentic the better—but well-made accessories are rarer than beautifully finished miniature furniture. Chestnut Hill Studio's catalogue offers a large number of impossible-to-find items: sterling silver table appointments and bibelots; crystal chandeliers and sconces; brass chandeliers and fireplace fenders; handmade oriental rugs; clocks of all types; and many musical instruments. Although not so costly as genuine antiques, these are fine miniatures and are priced accordingly. Grandmother Stover dollhouse accessories are far less elegant, but are very reasonable in price. They are to be found in many toyshops, boutiques, and party shops, and include playing cards, "marble" busts, and pewter serving dishes with plastic edibles. Chrysnbon accessories, which are sold in toyshops and appear in many catalogues, run to kerosene lamps, desk and dressing-table appointments, and figurines under glass domes. These are tasteful creations mostly contrived from beads, jewelry findings, and pins.

Therein lies the solution to the problem of accessories you do not have and cannot buy. Make them yourself of readily available materials. The following suggestions are included as a possible preamble or supplement to your own ideas.

Lighting devices are perhaps the most important of period accessories. Until oil lamps came into general use in the early nineteenth century, houses were illuminated only by daylight, firelight, and candlelight. In antique shops and toy stores it is possible to find silvered or gilded candelabra and tall brass or pewter candle-sticks of proper scale, but not the unusual candleholders that some rooms require. A flat brass chamber stick, appropriate for a mid-eighteenth-century bedroom, can be put together of a ½"-wide gold sequin, a small gold bead, and a gold-filled jeweler's jump ring. Use clear household cement to center the bead over the

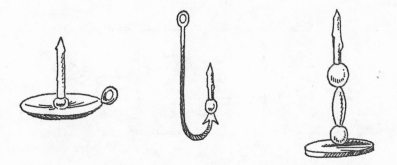

hole in the sequin cup, and cement the jump ring vertically on the edge of the sequin for a finger hold. Use a third of a white-painted round toothpick for a candle; dip its cut end in liquid cement, and press it down into the hole in the top of the bead.

In the homes of America's early settlers, wrought-iron candleholders often hung on the wall. To simulate such a holder, cover the sharp point of a fish hook with a small bead and paint this holder black; dip the end of half a wax match in liquid cement and fit it into the hole in the top of the bead. Drive a tiny black-painted headless nail into the wall and slip the ring of the fish hook holder over it. Some colonial candleholders were convertible—they could hang from a ceiling hook or be carried by a finger ring and set down upon a table. Make this sort of triple candleholder from a three-pointed fish hook and three beads; hang it from a small black cuphook in the ceiling of an early-American kitchen or place it on a candlestand in a bedroom.

A treen candleholder can be constructed of tiny round and oval wooden beads and a small flat faucet washer. Paint the washer brown or tan to match the beads and use liquid cement to cover its center hole with a round bead. Cement an oval bead on top of this round one, fitting the beads' drilled holes together; add a slightly larger round bead in the same manner, to complete the "turned" holder, and cement a toothpick candle upright in the hole of the top bead. Tall "brass" fireside or cathedral candlesticks can be made in this way of medium-size gold or gilded beads, alternating square, round, and oblong shapes on two stacked faucet washers graduated in size. For a more massive cathedral candlestick use two brass lamp-shade risers: screw one 2" riser into another and dip the threaded top of the second riser into melted paraffin to disguise it as a short fat candle.

Lanterns were not new when Diogenes used one in his search for an honest

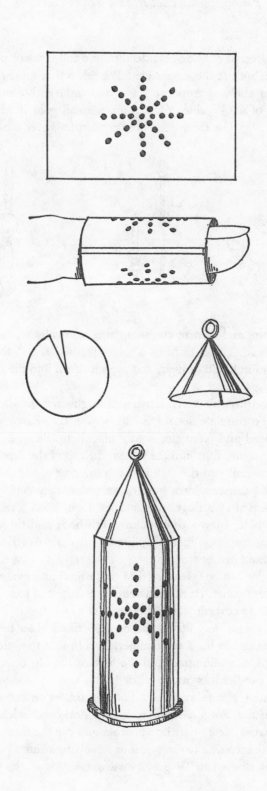

man, and their shape changed very little until their candles were replaced by kerosene containers in the nineteenth century. Silver candle-lantern bracelet charms have the look of eighteenth-century table lanterns, but so do plastic candle lanterns that are included in packages of mixed miniature party favors. Kerosene barn lanterns also are occasionally found in party-favor packets. Pierced tin candle lanterns were popular ceiling fixtures in colonial days, and can be imitated with heavy-duty aluminum foil. Cut a strip of foil 1″ wide and 3″ long and fold it in half, crosswise, to make it measure 1″×1½″. Lay the doubled rectangle flat on a breadboard and pierce the foil in concentric circles with a corsage pin to make the typical sunburst pattern of holes. Coat one end of the pierced piece lightly with liquid cement; then wrap the foil around a fingertip and press the ends together to form a cylinder. For the peaked top of the lantern, cut a doubled circle of foil, using a quarter as a pattern. Slash this circle to the center and pull one edge over the other to form a funnel shape; cement a silver jump ring on edge in the center of the peak to serve as a carrying ring. Glue the pointed top to the lantern cylinder and add a solid base made of a dime or a lighter-weight coin of silvery plastic from a set of play money.

"Brass" wall sconces can be contrived from costume jewelry and decorative trims, and the simplest sconce is made from a single metal earring back of the sort sold in hobby shops among the findings for costume jewelry. For this purpose, choose screw-type gold-colored backs with wide, shallow cups. Remove the threaded post from an earring back by cutting through it with wire-cutter pliers

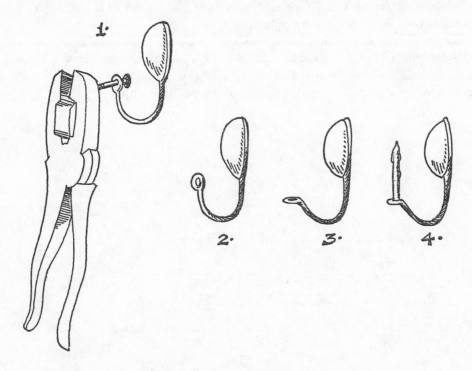

and screwing the stub of the post out of its hole. This will leave a shallow cup attached to a curved metal arm with a small hole in the end. Using the tips of needle-nose pliers, bend the tip of the arm away from the cup until the hole is at
right angles to the arm. You now have a convex brass sconce with a curved arm
ending in a candle cup. Dip the end of a headless wax match in liquid cement
and fit it into the post hole that will serve as its holder; steady the candle with a
fingertip for a moment and then prop the sconce against a book until the cement
is thoroughly dry. Use liquid solder to attach the rim of the sconce to the wall;
hold the sconce with a fingertip, applying slight pressure, for several minutes to
allow the solder to set.

Crystal chandeliers are now available in catalogues and toyshops, so it no
longer is necessary to make them of tiny beads and hair-fine wire. To convert a
purchased chandelier to gas, remove its candles and finish each arm with a small
flat silver sequin, which will look like a *bobêche*. Then center on each sequin
bobêche a translucent globe shade of a large clear or opalescent bead.

An interesting way to add artificial light to a period room is to place a small
bulb in the fireplace, hiding it behind stacked bark-covered twigs. These logs will
appear to burst into flames if jagged bits of red, pale blue, and yellow foil (from
Christmas candy wrappers) are glued between and behind them to catch the
light. In the Victorian Era, coal fires replaced burning logs. The metal grate that
held the coals can be simulated with a small curved side comb, metal or plastic,
painted black to resemble cast iron treated with stove blacking. Bits of charcoal or
black-painted gravels will do for coal, and these can be touched with red nail
polish to turn them into glowing embers.

The brass coal scuttles of Victorian parlors have been reproduced in miniature
as saccharin holders that are sold in boutiques with their own tiny shovels, but a
tall tole coal bin must be contrived. Some toothbrushes are sold in rigid plastic
cases that have slightly slanted hinged tops. Cut off the upper 2½″ of such a

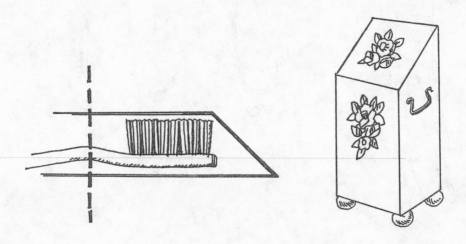

case with a hacksaw and close the bottom of the lidded box with a rectangle of cardboard. Use liquid solder to attach large metal staples, at a slant, on both sides of the box to serve as handles, and cement four tiny beads to the corners of the box bottom to raise the bin on stubby ball feet. Let the solder and cement dry overnight and then coat the entire contrivance with flat black enamel. Finally, cut out tiny flowers from small decals and apply them to the lid and front panel of the tole bin.

A firescreen is the best of finishing touches for an eighteenth-century hearthside, and this, too, can be contrived. Use the pedestal leg of a plastic table (from

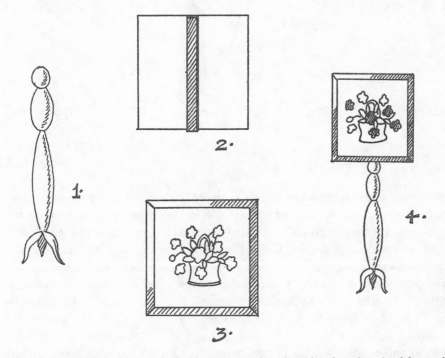

a dime-store dining-room set) for its base; paint the tripod pedestal with a mixture of brown and black enamel. Cut a square of thin balsa for the back of the screen, and cement a very small square dowel down the center of one side; paint this side of the screen brown-black. Glue to the other side of the screen a square of petit point salvaged from the top of a compact, or a motif cut out from wide embroidered braid trimming. Measure and cut 1/4″-wide strips of balsa wood to frame the screen; miter the corners of the strips and paint them brown-black. When they are dry, cement them around the rim of the screen front, covering the edges of the embroidery. Then attach the screen to its pedestal. Put a generous dot of liquid cement on the top of the pedestal and another on the bottom of the balsa dowel that centers the screen back. Wait twenty seconds before fitting the two dots together, and brace the screen in an upright position (with stacked books) overnight.

The candle shield that protected a lady's complexion from the heat of the flame, or her eyes from candle glare, was a table-top version of the firescreen. For its stand, one might use a tall candlestick of metal or plastic, and for the screen

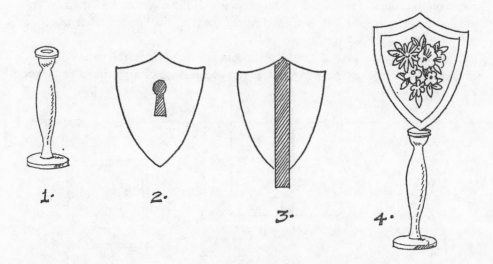

itself, a small shield-shaped key plate. Cover the back of the key plate with paper or thin balsa and cement a small square balsa dowel down its center, letting the dowel extend an ⅛″ below the point of the shield. Paint both the candlestick and the key plate dark brown. Cover the keyhole on the front of the scutcheon with a motif cut from petit point or embroidered trimming, and finish the edges of the embroidery with dark brown crochet cord applied with liquid thread. Dip the tip of the balsa dowel in liquid cement, and fit it into the cup of the candlestick. Brace the candle shield upright for several hours, until the cement has hardened.

Clocks and candlesticks for mantel decoration can be found in toyshops, but tiny figurines are harder to come by. Boutiques sometimes have Italian cocktail picks made of silvery antimony that are topped with miniature Roman statues. When these gods and senators are removed from their shafts with a hacksaw, they make perfect ornaments for a Classic Revival mantel. At Christmas time, there are exceedingly small nativity sets in which the standing figures are only one or one and a half inches tall; some of these molded plastic sets are brightly colored or gilded, while others are the yellow-beige of old ivory. Use two ivory standing Wise Men at the ends of an eighteenth-century mantel, or balance a colorful shepherd holding his crook with St. Joseph carrying his lantern on Victorian over-mantel shelf brackets. Brush two sheep, one standing and one lying down, with white latex paint to make a pair of Rockingham lambs for the mantel of a Victorian bedroom.

A doll-size round hand mirror from a variety store can be metamorphosed into a convex mirror to hang above the mantel in a room of the American Federal Period. Use a keyhole saw with a fine-toothed blade to cut off the mirror's handle ¼″ from the edge of the frame. Cover the short stub of the handle with a small brass eagle, of the spread-winged sort sold in hobby shops as purse-top trimmings, and cement twelve small beads for ornamental knobs around the frame, spacing them like the hours on the face of a clock. Then use a very small artist's brush to blend eagle, beads, and frame beneath a coating of gold-leaf paint. Finally, fit over the mirror a large curved watch crystal, a round eyeglass lens, or a small magnifying glass; cement the rim of this convex glass to the frame rather than to the mirror, to keep from blurring the reflective surface.

In an elegant Victorian parlor, a tall gold-framed pier glass often was placed between two long windows. Have a strip of thin mirror cut at a retail glass company to your specifications: 3″×7″ would be an appropriate size. Buy a cheap

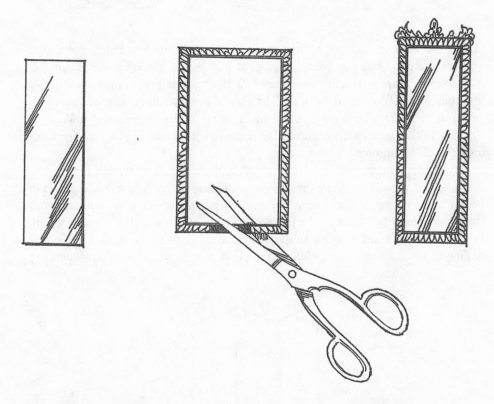

5″×7″ metal picture frame at a variety store, remove the backing and the glass, and shorten the top and bottom frame strips with tin snips to fit your mirror. For the elaborate top of such a pier glass use one large or three small filigree brass corners from a late-Victorian photograph frame found at a secondhand store;

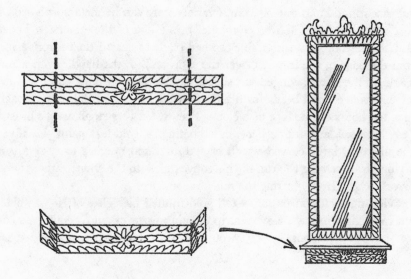

attach the trim to the top of the frame with liquid solder. Paint the frame and the pierced brass top with liquid gold leaf before inserting the mirror. A marble-topped apron usually was placed at the base of a pier mirror, and this low console can be evolved from a 6″ section of the remaining filigree brass picture frame. Make a right-angle bend in the strip 1″ from each end and cover the top of this framework with a marble slab 4¼″ long and 1¼″ wide, cut from a thin marble wall tile.

Screens were much used in the eighteenth and nineteenth centuries, for decoration and for protection from drafts, and a folding screen often adds desirable height in the corner of a miniature room. A four-panel screen can be constructed from balsa strips ⅛″ thick and 1½″ wide, put together with three pairs of tiny purse-top hinges from a hobby shop. Cement the hinges to the panels instead of nailing them on because the points of the pin-size nails would pierce through the

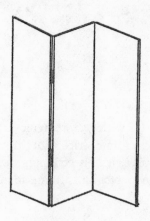

other side of the wood. To imitate the eighteenth century's favorite *chinoiserie,* paint the screen with mandarin-red enamel and decorate it with motifs cut from a sheet of small oriental-scene decals. One coat of clear shellac will keep the decals from loosening at the edges.

A three-panel hinged wooden screen sold as a dollhouse accessory can be redecorated with découpage to become a charming accent for a Regency room. Paint both sides of the screen with black semi-gloss enamel. With curve-bladed manicure scissors, cut tiny motifs from *thin* paper and paste them on the panels to make a composite design; landscapes, flower gardens, and Roman ruins were popular types of scenes, but some screens were covered with montages of playbills or

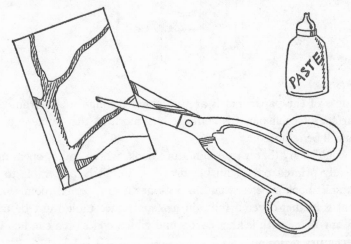

pictures of sporting events. It is better to cut all the elements of a screen design from catalogues rather than from wallpaper because the thinner the paper, the easier it is to meld with a painted background. At an art shop, buy the smallest can of clear quick-drying découpage finish, and a package of very fine sandpaper squares. Cover the whole surface of each decorated panel with a thin coat of the

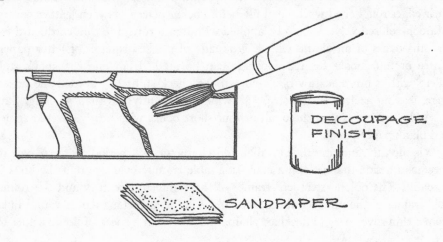

découpage finish, and let it dry overnight. Then lightly rub the glossy surface above the pasted motifs with fine sandpaper, and wipe away the dust of sanding with a soft damp cloth. In this manner, add coat after coat of the clear varnish

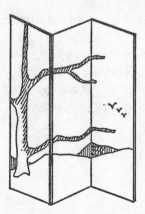

until the edges of the paper motifs are no longer distinguishable from the paint, and the surface of each panel is completely smooth to the touch—no less than seven coats will be required.

No one would deny that a true miniature book, whose covers open and whose microscopically printed pages can be turned, is infinitely preferable to a sham; still, a makeshift book is better than no book at all in a period room. The viewer assumes that a leather-covered folio on a Renaissance table must be a Book of Hours; a slim volume with leather covers and gilded edges on a candlestand in an eighteenth-century bedroom is seen as a prayer book. It is taken for granted that the thick velvet-bound tome on a Victorian parlor table is the family album, while a row of half-calf bindings in a bookcase must be the collected works of some nineteenth-century novelist. Most leather is too stiff and thick for miniature bindings, but one thin, worn brown kid glove that has lost its mate will provide several book covers. Blocks of wood of appropriate size and thickness should have their edges roughened with a nail file before being placed between leather covers. Maroon-colored velvet should be applied with liquid thread to thin cardboard for the stiff backs of an album with pages made of stacked squares of letter paper. Three or four books for the bookcase can be made from one checkbook stub filler: with a fine hacksaw blade cut off the check stubs ½″ beyond the boxed edge, leaving a cloth-bound strip ¾″ wide and slightly less than 3″ long. Saw this strip, crosswise, into three tall or four short books with neatly covered spines and blank paper pages.

It is the tiny finishing touches that add character to a period room. A pair of spectacles beside the book on a chair-side table is mute evidence that the book is readable. The oblong steel lens frames of the eighteenth century and the round gold frames of the nineteenth century can be made of rectangular or round links from a thin silver or gold necklace chain, attached with a speck of liquid solder to

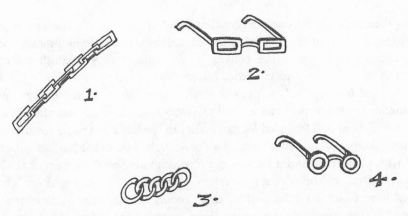

a piece of fine wire bent back in the shape of straight bows or curved earpieces. Even a monocle on a ribbon can be devised: use a paper punch to cut a round lens of stiff clear plastic from a credit-card holder; make the ribbon of black embroidery floss. To attach the ribbon, make a loop for it in the middle of a ½" length of hair-fine wire and bend the tips of the wire to extend at right angles on both sides of the flat loop; cement the tips of the wire to one edge of the monocle lens. Two round rimless lenses cemented on a nose-bridge of hair-fine wire become a pince-nez.

An early New England room should have its covered tobacco jar and its church-warden pipe, with a thin wooden skewer or a thick straw for a stem and a round or oval wooden bead bowl. No French tambour desk should be without its plume pen, and no Queen Anne writing table is complete without a quill. One-inch fluff tips, in pastel colors, are sold in small packets at hobby shops for making the centers of feather flowers; one of these will be a perfect plume pen to balance in a square silver bead inkwell. A white pigeon feather picked up in the park can be shortened and shaped with scissors into an inch-long goose quill, and a brass grommet will serve as its inkwell. Straight pins make the best of knitting needles for an eighteenth-century boudoir if they are painted white or tan in imitation of the ivory or wood of which they would have been made. Colored sewing thread can be twisted into hanks or rolled into balls to simulate knitting wool. To make it clear that the covered basket in a Victorian parlor is a sewing basket, lay a silver scissors charm beside it on the center table. The clasp of an outmoded costume jewelry necklace may provide two slender rings, one larger than the other; for a pair of embroidery hoops, paint both rings wood-tan. Cut out one motif from thin embroidered-cotton dress material, or cut off the embroidered corner of an old handkerchief; stretch this small square of material over the little metal ring and force the larger ring over the material for the outer hoop.

Playthings are interesting additions to any miniature room, and portraits of children often show the toys that were in vogue during a particular period— wooden puppets in adult clothes clutched to the bosoms of little girls, or woolly lambs on wheels pulled by little boys. Fashions in pets change also, and by consulting contemporary art one can see what breed of dog was popular in any given era. Mastiffs sleep at the feet of armored knights on medieval English tombs. Tiny spaniels frisk across the canvas in sixteenth-century Spanish paintings. Ladies of all centuries and countries sat for their portraits with their lap dogs that changed from spaniels to pugs to terriers to pekinese. Hunting dogs appear in American colonial portraits and silhouettes; huge St. Bernards and little fox terriers or Boston bulldogs vied for popularity in the late nineteenth century.

Queen Mary's Dolls' House contains not a single doll, but it has a day nursery filled with playthings, and a kitchen cat forever glaring at three mice that cower behind the bars of the wire mousetrap. Only three of the ninety-three Thorne Rooms have costumed dolls, and all three rooms are kitchens. Mrs. Thorne obviously felt that human figures would divert attention from the furnishings of her finer rooms, but she did include an occasional dog, cat, or caged bird.

It is quite true that the eye is instantly attracted to people in a miniature room. In a Dutch cabinet house, one sees first the delightful wooden dolls in seventeenth-century dress whose features are so well defined that they may have been portrait caricatures of the family that first owned the cabinet. The "Dutch dolls" often mentioned in nineteenth-century children's books are only poor relations of these elegant personages. All little wooden Dutch dolls had sticklike arms and legs, and round heads with sharp-pointed "Pinocchio" noses; two broad strokes of a paintbrush gave them hair, and their eyes and mouths were merely dots of paint. (In her childhood, Queen Victoria dressed a number of these little Dutch dolls, and they are now in The London Museum along with her two-room dollhouse.)

Similarly sharp-nosed were the hickory-nut dolls made in the American colonies; they had sticks for bodies, arms, and legs. American dollhouses of the nineteenth century often were inhabited by wooden clothespeg dolls with hair and features painted on their knobbed tops, and padded arms sewn into their sleeves. These dolls are called "peg-woodens."

Many makers of miniature rooms include costumed dolls whose clothing helps in establishing an exact period, or whose position indicates the usage of an unusual tool or accessory, and some miniaturists like to make the dolls themselves. Today's wooden clothespins that are smaller than the handmade clothespegs of the last century sometimes are used for little boy dolls, and character dolls—old sailors and ancient crones—occasionally are made of hickory nuts and sticks, with cotton or lamb's wool for hair.

A much more attractive and usable doll has a large round wooden bead for a head, and a wire-armature body. To make the armature, bend two lengths of thin flexible wire—one long and one short—together at the middle. Wrap the four wires tightly at this bend with hair-fine wire to create a pointed neck; spread the two short wires outward, for shoulders and arms, and wrap the upper portion of the two long wires together with plastic tape to form the doll's torso.

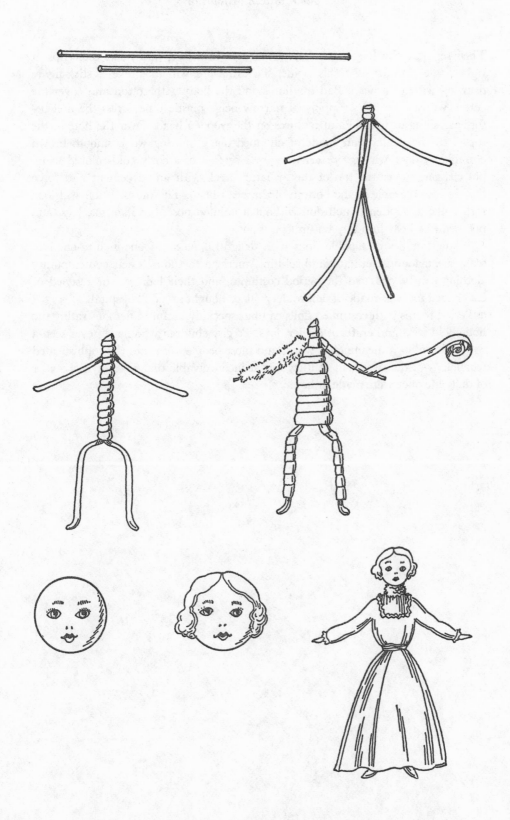

Then separate the long wires below the tape into legs, and bend their tips at right angles for feet. At this point, the armature will look like a stick-figure drawing without a head. Pad the limbs and the body with cotton and cover the cotton with a spiraled wrapping of narrow beige plastic tape; dress the doll before attaching its head. Paint features on the wooden bead. Over the hole in the top of the head glue hair made of chopped black knitting wool, smooth brown embroidery floss, wiry gray steel wool, or a section of a curly gold-colored metal pot cleaner. Cover the top of the armature neck with liquid cement and force this tip into the hole in the bottom of the bead head. The finished doll will look rather like a wooden Dutch doll without a pointed nose, but its arms, legs, and body can be bent into any natural position.

Whole families of flexible dolls with delightful faces, in one-inch-to-one-foot scale, are made in Germany and sold in American toyshops. Their contemporary clothing can be changed for period costumes, and their hair can be restyled or exchanged for wigs made of embroidery silk or bought at a doll hospital.

Period rooms with costumed dolls can be especially useful in demonstrating the household tasks and crafts of earlier days. To city children who have never seen a cow, "churn" is a meaningless word, and most people born into the sophisticated technology of the twentieth century find it inconceivable that so many necessities of daily life once were made at home.

VI

Flower Arrangements for Miniature Rooms

Making miniature flower arrangements is an exacting endeavor that demands saintly patience and a *very* steady hand, yet no room—be it full or mini-size—is at its best without the flowers that complement a color scheme or pinpoint a period.

A good miniature arrangement resembles a full-scale floral design that is seen from a great distance. Clarity of line is essential, and unless there are sharply defined voids, the tiny blossoms and leaves will run together in an indiscriminate mass. Like its large prototype, the miniature should be made with a specific location in mind; its height and width must be tailored to the spot, and its plant materials should be selected and sized accordingly.

A miniature arrangement made of real flowers no more than one-fourth inch in diameter may sound like an impossible dream, yet such an arrangement is not only plausible but practical. Gardeners have known for centuries that certain flowers can be preserved by air-drying, and that if these dehydrated blossoms are protected from dampness and the fading effect of strong sunlight, they will retain their shape and color almost indefinitely. A surprising number of the flowers that air-dry well are very small, but their thin petals are extremely fragile. Coating the dried blossoms, front and back, with hairspray (or with the colorless acrylic plastic sold in pressurized cans at paint stores) will give them strength to survive the handling necessary to arrangement.

Peruvian starflowers lead the list of suitable dried blossoms; these tiny many-petaled circles can be found in every mod boutique and come dyed in all the colors of the rainbow. Individual florets of the dried statice and yarrow used by florists in their winter bouquets furnish interesting contrasts in shape and size, while sprigs of dried baby's breath or acacia are excellent fillers. Fluffy tips of celosia, spiky bits of heath or heather, and curving sprigs of polygonum are all valuable background materials.

A second type of miniature blossom exists in seed pods, which are air-dried by nature and require only painting to be ready for arrangement. In mid-winter, tall dry ironweed stalks end in bouquets of perfect woody flowers a mere quarter-inch in diameter, with mounded centers and well-defined outer petals. Brush these with white enamel and center them with orange, for daisies; color them solid yellow and call them coreopsis; then add dark brown centers to turn them into black-eyed Susans; paint them red or purple, with black centers, and they become rudbeckia. Silvery santolina's insignificant flowers leave behind large-centered, curly-petaled little ghosts that can be painted yellow for marigolds, or brushed with all the colors of Joseph's coat to imitate zinnias and chrysanthemums. Rhododendron's clustered seed pods look like bunches of miniature Darwin tulips; each tulip on its own short stem can be quickly dipped in yellow, pink, or red enamel. Perennial salvia's seed pods encircle the dry stalk in rings of perfect little lilies. Cut the stem with scissors just above each circle of pods and paint the lilies white (for Madonna), pink (Lycoris), yellow (lemon), blue (Aga-panthus), or orange (for daylilies).

One final flower form can be found on the seed-packet rack in a grocery store or a garden center. Open a package of beet seed, and pour out a palmful of per-fect miniature rosebuds that can be enlivened with paint from tan to red, pink, yellow, or white.

Although these natural materials are both realistic and charming, man-made miniature flowers do possess a sturdiness for which an arranger will be grateful. Nor do wire stems crumble at a touch. Be on the lookout for arrangement raw materials at the costume-jewelry counter of a variety store, as well as at bazaars and flea markets—watch for necklaces and earrings made of tiny metal or plastic flowers. Pierced earrings frequently consist of single roses or flat daisylike blossoms mounted on metal posts that serve as ready-made short stems. In contrast, dangling earrings sometimes have one or more flowers held on by jump rings, while the metal or plastic blossoms in a necklace usually are pierced from side to side for stringing. Such blossoms must be removed from their settings and given stems before they can become part of a miniature arrangement. Cut the thin wire or plastic thread on which a necklace is strung and pull the flowers off. If a blos-som is attached to an earring by a metal jump ring, open this ring by forcing an awl or a nutpick through it to let the pendant fall free; a smaller ring will remain on one side of the flower itself, and this should be very carefully broken off with the tips of a pair of needle-nosed pliers. Metal flowers soldered on a costume brooch are more difficult to loosen. Push the point of a corsage pin or a darning needle under the back of the flower and pry it up—it may be necessary to repeat this process several times, working around the setting, to break the bond. If such a flower has a bead or rhinestone center, remove it in the same manner with pin or needle point.

The best material for stemming metal flowers is the lightest weight green florist's wire, which supports the blossoms yet bends easily; it can be cut with scissors. With the tips of needle-nose pliers, curl one end of a 2″ length of wire into a loop ⅛″ in diameter and bend this loop at right angles to the straight wire. Dip the

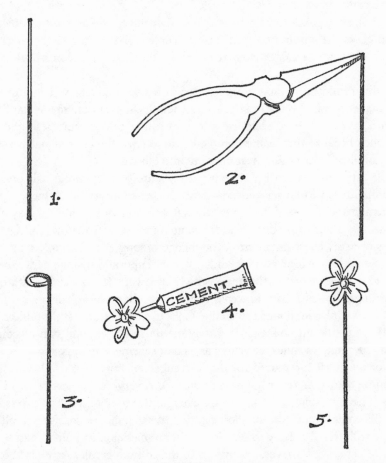

loop in clear liquid cement and center the back of a flower upon it; settle the flower with a fingertip and then prick the wire stem into a block of styrofoam to hold the bloom upright and steady until the cement is perfectly dry.

Costume-jewelry flowers that came enameled in natural colors will now be ready for use, but gold, silver, or neon-bright blossoms still will need to be tinted. Nail polish is a very useful coloring agent for red or pink roses, coating metal or plastic quickly and evenly and drying within seconds. The best all-purpose flower paint is, however, the enamel made for plastic airplane or automobile models and sold in half-ounce bottles where the model kits are displayed. Buy only one bottle each of white, red, blue, and yellow enamel since any desired shade may be obtained by mixing minute quantities of primary colors and lightening with white. Apply the paint with a number-two artist's brush.

There are potential miniature flowers in the packets of sequins intended as trimmings for styrofoam Christmas balls. Choose the very tiniest star-shaped and cup sequins that have center holes, and stem these round or five-petaled blossoms with straight pins—small yellow- or black-headed pins are better for this purpose than the common steel variety. Dip the head of a pin in clear household cement and push the pin point down through a sequin center, pulling the pin down until its head closes the sequin hole and forms a center for the flower; the shaft of the pin is now a sturdy straight stem ready to be touched with a brushful of green enamel.

The tiny round beads that are packaged in assorted colors, and sold in variety stores, make excellent buds in sequin- and jewelry-flower arrangements. Straight pins with very small heads also are sold in assorted colors, and these make even better buds because they come complete with stems. Small oval oat-pearls look like the swelling buds of lilies just bursting into bloom.

At the artificial flower display in a variety store or a boutique it is possible to find composite shrub-flower clusters—lantana, for example—that have especially good arrangement possibilities even though the individual florets may require judicious trimming with curve-bladed manicure scissors. An entire cluster, with a few tips of artificial cedar inserted for foliage among the blossoms, may be balanced in a wide bowl for a quick-and-easy contemporary arrangement; the same cluster also could serve as the supporting framework for an eighteenth-century mass arrangement of mixed flowers. The very smallest white bells removed from the top of a plastic lily-of-the-valley look like miniature white tulips when cemented cup side up on stems of fine green florist's wire, and can of course be painted red, pink, lavender, or yellow as a color scheme demands.

No foliage at all is required for mass arrangements of dried everlastings in the eighteenth-century manner, and very little greenery for other types of floral designs. This is fortunate, for leaves are even harder to obtain than flowers in tiny size. If foliage is a must, the smallest plastic leaves should be considered, although each one will probably have to be trimmed with manicure scissors to half its original size. There are, however, exceptions to the trimming rule. Artificial boxwood twigs, shorn of all but a few dark green shiny leaves, can provide a background of evergreen magnolia for a tall contemporary arrangement. Plastic ferns have center spines along which miniature strap leaves or feathery fronds are attached in matching pairs. These miniatures of the large fern leaf can be cut off with scissors and curved—after soaking in hot water for ten minutes—by rolling from the tip down. Miniature artificial pine is sold at Christmas time in florists' shops and at variety stores. Each tuft of needles is circled around a central hole, and pressed down over a knobbed protuberance on the plastic twig. Pull off the tuft and cut the circlet into segments for lily, tulip, or narcissus leaves; curve each plastic needle by pulling it across a thumbnail. Tips of plastic cedar or juniper are the most useful of all finds for background support or filler foliage in posy, line, or mass designs.

Whatever period it represents, and whatever design it embodies, a miniature arrangement demands a container of suitable styling and proportion. One looks first for containers among the vases, bowls, baskets, and pitchers that have accrued along with furniture in one's own miniature collection. Sometimes items that are slightly out of scale can be utilized for this purpose. An undersize brass goblet might double as a bud vase on a contemporary coffee table, or a sugar bowl from an overlarge china tea set could become a colonial boughpot.

Modern classic containers of proper scale are quite as rare as genuine antique miniatures, so it often becomes necessary to improvise, turning small everyday objects into the flower holders they so much resemble. Tiny suction cups are shaped like miniature footed compotes, and child-size plastic thimbles look like colorful cachepots, while the caps of felt-tipped pens and magic markers seem to be patterned after tall vases, columnar or flared. A small artificial grape dislodged from its bunch becomes a colored "glass" bubble bowl. A button box holds many a hidden treasure: flat buttons with raised rims that can serve as camellia bowls or holders for line arrangements; mound-shaped silvery buttons that turn into silver bowls when their shanks have been removed with pliers; wooden half-round hollow buttons that make fine seventeenth-century treen containers. To transform a button bowl into a compote, it is only necessary to cement it upon a stand, and

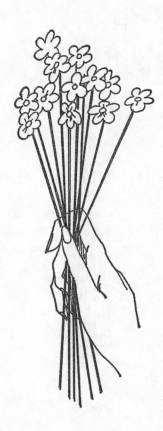

these stands can be of unlikely provenance: collar studs, metal grommets, short metal bolts, and clear plastic pushpins.

Hobby shops and mail-order catalogues offer findings for costume jewelry, and the filigree metal mountings for key rings and cuff links often are shaped like bowls or tulip vases. Christmas catalogues feature cone-shaped filigree bases for mounting decorated styrofoam balls, and these can be turned into cornucopias by curving their pointed tips with pliers. Little metal or plastic clapper bells, in assorted bright colors, are sold on cards as holiday package decorations. Remove the clappers, and cement the inverted bells on metal grommets to make flaring footed vases.

The costume-jewelry counter of a variety store will be a happy hunting ground for the large beads—round, square, oval, oblong, or faceted—that are the best of substitute miniature vases. Some beads made in Japan even boast tiny hand-painted oriental motifs that complete the illusion. To make a bead stand steady when it is placed on end in the upright vase position, mount it on an inverted thumbtack. The color of the thumbtack head will show as a thin rim around the base of the bead, which should be coated with liquid cement before being fitted over the shaft of the tack.

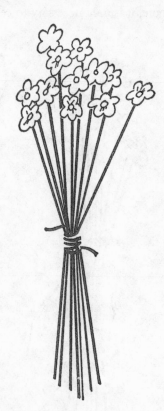

Combining infinitesimal flowers and foliage in such minuscule containers is exceedingly difficult—not because the materials are so small, but because fingers are so large and clumsy. For this reason, many miniaturists prefer to work with tweezers, but tweezers cannot be used for the tied arrangements that are easiest of all to make. Bunch a few flowers between thumb and forefinger of the left hand and wind hair-fine wire around their stems; then adjust the blossoms, turning them to face outward, pulling some up and pushing others down, until the bouquet is pleasing. Trim the stems off evenly just below the twist of wire, and the posy is ready to be popped into a jug, jar, pitcher, or tall vase. This easy method will even work for clear-glass vases if the stems are tied with colorless "in-

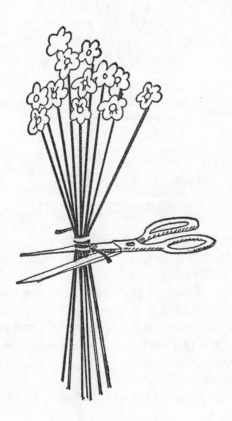

visible" thread instead of with wire: Make a loop in the thread and insert the bunched stems; pull the loop tight, and knot the thread to secure it; then trim off the ends of the thread. A few drops of clear liquid cement squeezed into the glass container before the flowers are added will look like water in the vase while it permanently steadies the arrangement.

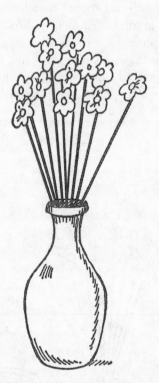

Wide-mouthed bowls require a different technique, and this is where tweezers may come in handy. Fill a bowl almost to the brim with wax dripped from a white candle and wait until the surface of the wax has barely solidified. Now work quickly to set the flowers in place before the wax hardens completely. First outline the design with tall background material; then place a center of interest; and finally add smaller flowers as fillers. To make a mound-shaped arrangement on a flat compote, tray, or basket, begin with a small piece of green floral clay. Roll the clay between the palms to form a ball the size of a large bead; put a drop of white glue in the center of the container and press the clay ball down upon it. After this glue has dried, dip the stems of the flowers in white glue before pricking them into the clay.

Adding another tiny air-dried blossom or just one more bead bud to an arrangement that hasn't quite "come off" is almost a reflex action, but in all probability this will only make matters worse. The advice so often given to novice flower arrangers should be taken to heart by the makers of miniature floral designs: "Do the arrangement and if it pleases you, let it alone. If something seems to be the matter with it, take out half the flowers and rearrange the remainder."

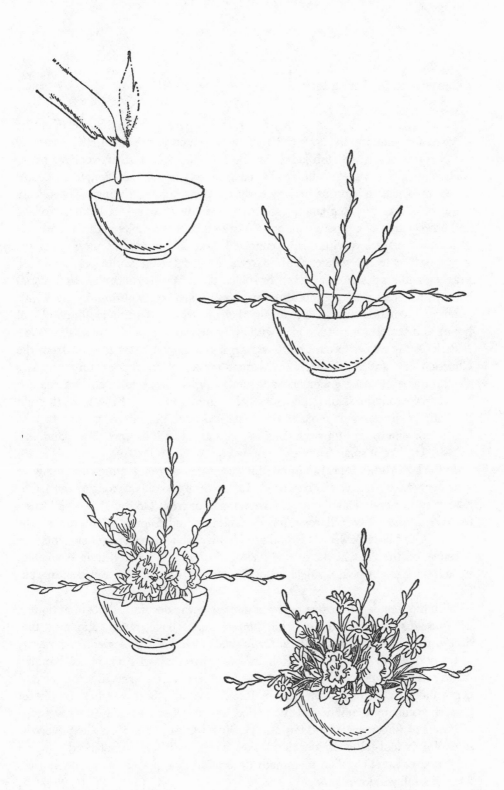

Arrangements for Period Rooms

Flower arranging is so much a part of contemporary living that we might be forgiven for assuming the craft to have been invented in the twentieth century by a committee of garden club ladies, but nothing could be farther from the truth. Elaborate foliage wreaths, floral chaplets, and stylized hand bouquets of lotus leaves and blossoms appear in very early Egyptian tomb paintings. The Greeks wore wreaths of ivy, stephanotis, and narcissus; they carried garlands of foliage and flowers in public processions, and decorated banquet tables with flat garlands of leaves interspersed with short-stemmed blossoms. Fruits were pleasing to the eye as well as to the palate, so the Greeks heaped their favorite pomegranates, peaches, and grapes on flat baskets or spilled them from cornucopias. In imperial Rome, walls were decorated in summer with swagged scarves brimming over with poppies, anemones, and roses; during the mid-winter Saturnalia, the walls of homes and temples were festooned with evergreen wreaths and garlands.

Perhaps the earliest record of flower arranging as we know it dates from the Christian Era, and is depicted in a Vatican mosaic of the first century A.D.; this airy grouping of roses, anemones, and pinks with delicate foliage has a shallow basket for a container. In richly colored Byzantine mosaics of the third through the sixth centuries, much more elaborate baskets or tall bronze urns are shown as holders for slim towering pyramids of foliage wound with narrow ribbon and dotted with clusters of small fruits and flowers.

In the late Middle Ages, an interesting reversal occurred. Gothic churches were ornamented with marvelous baskets of flowers and garlands of foliage and fruits, all carved in stone, while "rosaries" were made of fresh blossoms: ten pink roses for Ave Marias; five red roses for Paternosters and Glorias. Paintings of the Gothic Period used flowers as symbols to identify biblical personages or saints; for example, on the floor at the feet of the Virgin Mary, a vase with an elongated, slender neck might hold a single spray of white Madonna lilies, representing purity.

With the Renaissance came renewed interest in the decorative arts of antiquity. The wreaths and garlands of fresh flowers and foliage, cones, and nuts that decked the walls of Italian palazzi for festivals have been preserved for posterity in the carvings of Andrea della Robbia. Huge pyramids of fruit graced banquet tables to serve as decoration and dessert, and these were copied in stone for garden ornaments. Although the Italian Renaissance did borrow from the distant past, the exuberant freshness of the period was manifest in a new and novel type of flower arrangement: Blossoms and curving wands of foliage spilled over the sides of a six-foot-tall container that looked like a shallow bowl balanced upon an elongated candlestick. The mammoth decoration was placed in a corner or in front of a tall window.

This sort of container, perfect for a miniature cinquecento room or a modern art gallery, can be made by cementing a saucer from a small doll's tea set on a slender 4″ pedestal. Make the pedestal by alternating square, round, oblong, and faceted beads of any color on a core of wire as heavy as their holes will admit, and base the shaft on three stacked metal faucet washers of graduated size. Paint the entire container antique gold to disguise its diverse components, and secure a small ball of floral clay in the center of the bowl with a dot of white glue. Make several tied groupings of flowers and foliage, including one tapering curved cluster long enough to reach halfway down the pedestal. The flowers should be mixed in form and color; the arrangement could include deep reds and pale pinks, rich purples and bright golden yellows. Prick the tied bunches of flowers into the ball of clay to form a loose, spreading mass, and angle the long foliage spray into one side of the arrangement, letting it trail down and curve across the front of the pedestal.

The Renaissance reached its height in England during the reign of Elizabeth I, and flower arrangements for Tudor-style houses were "to the Queen's taste." Posies (tight bunches of a single variety of flower) in jugs were placed on side tables or on window sills, while perfumed flowers and aromatic herbs were combined in bowls to sweeten the air of poorly ventilated rooms. These herb-and-flower arrangements were called "tussie-mussies." In summer, gaping fireplaces were masked with cut foliage or with potted "chimney flowers." For a dark-paneled Elizabethan room, tie a few small, bright-colored blossoms in a tight clump, and place the posy in a brown glazed jug. Miniature wide-mouthed jugs are made in Mexico today, and one of these would be just right in style.

In the Low Countries and Germany, Renaissance arrangements were undistinguished masses of mixed flowers in tall plump jars. By the early seventeenth century, however, a new style called Baroque was flourishing here—to the opulence of Renaissance designs, an insistent asymmetry had been added. Wide pyramids of fruit still were used on banquet tables, but fruits also were combined with richly colored flowers in huge S-curve arrangements that were placed on massive side tables. Dutch traders had begun to bring back blue-and-white Nanking pottery from China, and Dutch potters at Delft were copying the oriental designs; flowers mixed and massed in wide blue-and-white delft bowls and tall delft jars became commonplace in castles and in more humble homes.

To imitate a tall delft jar of the Baroque Period, a smooth cylindrical lipstick case can be painted blue and decorated with small white flowers and curlicues. Begin a massive Baroque arrangement by bending a length of heavy green florist's wire into the shape of a capital letter S. Bind tiny fruits and dark-colored blossoms in tight clusters with hair-fine wire, and wire the clusters close together along the S-curve. A great many fruits and flowers will be required to make the arrangement as weighty and luxuriant as it should be; apples, peaches, plums, and pears would be the appropriate fruits to combine with wine-red, magenta, dull orange, and sulphur-yellow blooms. Place the center of the clustered S-curve across the container opening, and adjust the wire by bending until the arrangement is well balanced. Then slip a small wire hairpin over the center of the curve, burying its rounded top among the fruits and flowers, and spreading its points until they scrape the sides of the jar as they are pushed down into it. Tension will hold the heavy clustered wire steady on top of the lipstick-case container.

In the mid-seventeenth century, a more elegant asymmetrical style that originated in France was called Rococo, which meant "rock and shell." Scallop-shell motifs were popular in carvings and paintings, and vases for flowers often were shell-shaped. The heavy S-curve of Baroque arrangements was shortened and lightened to a scrolled C, and fruits returned to the dining table. Flowers were small, colors were pale, and blossoms sometimes were combined with curved plumes in fan-shaped arrangements.

A typical Rococo container can be made of two tiny scallop shells, found on the beach or purchased from a shell or hobby shop. Cement together the straight hinge sides of the two shells, separating the curved outer edges to leave a fan-shaped opening ⅛″ wide at the top; then cement the straight base of this fan to

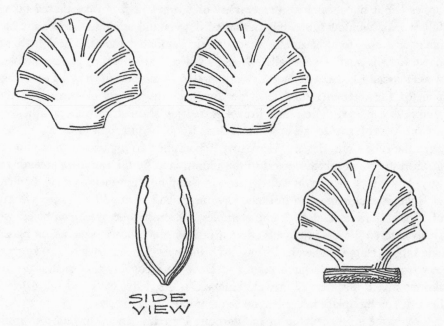

SIDE
VIEW

a thin white-painted oblong of wood, to hold the shell container upright and steady. Select very tiny pastel flowers and cut all their stems the same length; dip the stem of each blossom in white glue before angling it into the vase opening. The flowers will thus follow the contour of the shell vase and form a floral fan. As an optional addition to this design, borrow three fuzzy "plumes" from a pink or pale yellow feather duster bought at a boutique, and trim them down to appropriate length and width. To curl them, hold them over the spout of a steaming

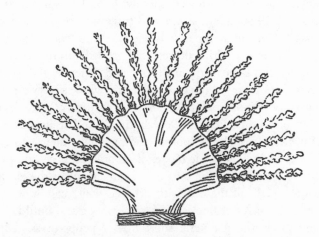

teakettle and then pull the spine of each feather across the dull edge of a knife blade. Add the curled plumes to the center of the fan vase, letting them nod forward over the tallest flowers.

Seventeenth-century English settlers brought only basic necessities to the American continent where wild flowers abounded in spring and summer, and where autumn leaves were miracles of brilliance. Early ships were so crowded with new colonists and their scanty belongings that it was a long time before there was room on board for such nonessentials as vases for flowers, but color-starved colonial housewives could not wait. They made do with baskets and treen (wooden) bowls as containers for flowers, fall foliage, and the "everlastings" that dried naturally in the fields in winter.

Half of a small black-walnut shell remarkably (and most appropriately) resembles a crude treen bowl of the type used in the early colonial period. As a cheerful accent for a starkly simple seventeenth-century interior, fill a wooden walnut-shell bowl with dripped white candle wax to support as many flower stems as can be crowded in. Red and pink, orange and purple, yellow, blue, and white blossoms should form a variegated mass above the rim of the shell, for flowers were not "arranged" by early-American housewives, but were merely massed for color.

In the eighteenth century, prosperous colonists along the American seaboard avidly followed the fashions of their English homeland. The furnishings and decorations of their large and comfortable homes reflected the elegance of the Georgian Period, and favorite flowers of the Old World grew alongside native plants in New World gardens. Trading ships at last had space for flower containers from Europe and the Orient, so fan-shaped and finger vases were popular mantel decorations while tall delft jars held peonies or flowering tree branches on wide window sills. China tureens were also used to hold flowers, and for very large arrangements there were monteith (silver) or Chinese export porcelain punch bowls.

Empty fireplaces were filled in summer with cool green leaves in low, wide, handled urns called boughpots. Bowls and tureens were packed with wet sand to support masses of mixed summer flowers; the same containers, with dry sand, held "buxom bouquets" of dried flowers and pressed autumn leaves in winter.

During the eighteenth century, in Europe and America, the most popular of all dried materials for winter bouquets was lunaria, whose silvery circles earned it the common names of "money plant" or "St. Peter's penny." Dried peppergrass is a miniature version of this favorite "everlasting," and if its tiny white disks are touched with clear frosted nail polish, they acquire lunaria's opalescent sheen. Since a sake cup looks like a scale model of an oriental porcelain punch bowl, it is precisely the right container for a winter arrangement in the elegant eighteenth-century manner. Half fill the cup with dripped white candle wax and cover the wax at once with a layer of fine sand. Let the wax stand until it is thickened but not hard and prick into it several short tips of peppergrass. Adjust the disked stems into a low, wide, airy mass, and add no foliage or other flowers. Such an arrangement would have served to decorate a side table in a hall or drawing room, or a serving table in a dining room, and would have remained on display from September until early spring.

Following the discovery of the ruins of Herculaneum and Pompeii in the mid-eighteenth century, the decorative arts of the ancient world were recalled during a Classic Revival Period that lasted from 1762 to 1830. No distinction was made between the legacies of eastern and western Europe, so the tall pyramids of Byzantium were as frequently used and as highly esteemed as the wreaths and garlands, cornucopias and swags, of Greece and Rome. Floral arrangements were self-consciously geometric as people professed an avid interest in Euclid; cones and crescents, half circles and ellipses of flowers were rigidly symmetrical. Timely copies of Grecian urns were made at the Wedgwood pottery to hold these designs, and the completed decorations were displayed on columnar or tripod pedestals. Slim wreaths and slender garlands spiraled with narrow ribbon were favorite motifs for carved wood and molded plaster in the Adam manner and were copied in fresh foliage and flowers for wall decoration. Once again, fruit was mounded on flat platters or spilled from cornucopias, and the cornucopia shape was adapted to wall pockets that contained fresh flowers.

During the brief Empire Period of the early nineteenth century, Napoleon's campaigns in Italy and Egypt raised fashion's preoccupation with the ancient world to the *n*th power. At this time, when popular decorating colors were deep green and antique gold, obelisk pedestals supported black or dark green tole urns holding stylized pyramids of flowers in which dull yellow was the predominant color.

A very practical basis for a Classic Revival pyramid arrangement—a shape that also can double as an Empire decoration—is a 1″-long pointed tip cut with a knife from a dime-store "velvetized" green styrofoam Christmas cone. Cover the entire surface of the styrofoam with flowers, beginning at the base of the pyramid: Remove the stems of the flowers and dip the back of each blossom in white glue before setting it in place; press down on the face of the flower with a fingertip to seat it securely. Encircle the cone base with blossoms and allow the glue to dry thoroughly; then add a second circle of flowers above the first and continue until the styrofoam cone has entirely disappeared beneath a pyramid of color. End with one flower glued face up on the very top. Cement the pyramid to the rim of an urn-shaped vase about 1″ in height, which could be a sugar bowl from an oversize metal or china tea set, and display the arrangement on a 5″ fluted corinthian column from a set of four cake separators which your bakery probably can supply. (Cake separators also can be ordered from catalogues; see Sources of Supply in the Appendix.)

Favorite flower hues of the Victorian Era were muddy magenta, dusty rose, mustard yellow, and faded mauve. Blossoms in these dismal colors often were combined with drooping ferns, trailing ivy, or weeping willow branches in so-called "sentimental" arrangements. The sentimental Victorians also were fond of waxed flower wreaths and tall shell-flower pyramids; they covered these "keepsake" designs with clear glass domes to protect them from dust and damage. Roses were preferred above all other flowers—as motifs for paintings and embroidery as well as in fragrant actuality. They were bunched with their own leaves in hand-painted vases: bulbous jars with stubby necks, or china cornucopias shortened and flattened almost to fan shape. As the era grew older along with the Queen, no marble parlor mantel was well-dressed without twin "dust-catcher" arrangements of peacock feathers or pampas grass.

A shell-flower pyramid (or a wreath of waxed flowers, *sous cloche*), is the ideal finishing touch for a Victorian room, but miniature glass domes are rather hard to come by. It is, therefore, wise to find the dome first, and then make an arrangement to fit it. Some miniature-manufacturers' catalogues offer gilded clocks under slender glass domes that make fine covers for slim pyramids of beads, sequins, and minuscule shells; after their domes have been removed, the clocks still are useful mantel decorations. Vending machines in variety stores sell cheap gewgaws sealed in clear plastic half-rounds that are good miniature "glass" shades for mound-shaped bead-and-shell designs. Best of all, there are clear plastic hen-size Easter eggs, meant to be filled with candies and used as party favors, that come apart at the equator. The pointed end of such an egg nicely follows the contours of a plump floral pyramid, while the blunt egg half is the perfect protective dome for a wreath of waxed flowers. Miniature waxed flower wreaths can be made of the tiniest of plastic blossoms and bits of artificial asparagus fern, dipped in melted paraffin and dried face up on waxed paper; the backs of the coated ferns and flowers may then be dipped in white glue and arranged in a wreath upon a circlet of lace paper cut from the center of a very small doily. Set the flowers so close together that they touch and overlap, and add bits of fern to the top of the wreath as well as to its outer edges.

All these historic types of flower arrangements have been adopted and adapted by twentieth-century enthusiasts. Egypt's chaplets and hand bouquets are recognizable in bridesmaids' floral headbands and brides' bouquets, while six-foot Renaissance-style containers have become traditional holders for church flowers. The evergreen wreaths and garlands of imperial Rome vie in popularity with tall Byzantine pyramids as Christmas decorations. Posies are perfect on ubiquitous modern coffee tables, and a renewed interest in herb gardening has revived the tussie-mussie. Every neophyte garden club member must learn the mechanics of the Hogarth curve that stems from the Baroque Period, and flower-show schedules keep alive the contrived symmetry of Classic Revival crescents and ellipses. As Empire and Victorian fashions in furnishings come round again, so do nineteenth-century decorative touches done this time with tongue in cheek.

Even though the past persists, line arrangements are especially suited to the simplicity of contemporary architecture and furniture. These designs are lineal descendants of long-established patterns in Japan and China, but they have gradually acquired a freedom of form that stamps them twentieth-century American. Unorthodox color combinations are quite acceptable, and containers can be flat or tremendously tall.

In an informal contemporary setting, a driftwood design would be an attractive focal point. A small gnarled twig, a corkscrew spiral of honeysuckle vine, or the twisted tip of a dried wisteria cane will double for driftwood in a shallow container made of a square button with a raised rim. Fill the button cavity with clear liquid (or epoxy) cement and allow the glue to become almost hard before setting the woody material in place; steady the driftwood branch with a fingertip until the cement grips it in firm balance. For maximum security, brace the branch with two or three small gravels and then add a cluster of short-stemmed flowers to hide the pebbles and tie the driftwood visually to the container.

A small compote-shaped suction cup makes a splendid container for a Japanese-style line arrangement using three branches of different lengths curved out and upward in the familiar heaven-man-earth design. Flowering shrub or fruit-tree blossoms can be simulated with white, pale pink, or yellow knitting wool. First cut the end of a strand with scissors into fine fuzz; make the branches of thin brown florist's wire, dipping each one lengthwise in white glue and rolling it in the chopped wool. Blow away the excess wool, leaving the brown branches lightly covered with "bloom." Sprays of "berries" can be used instead of spring-flowering branches in this design, and the *modus operandi* is much the same. The lengths of brown wire dipped in white glue can be rolled in blue poppy, black lettuce, or wine-red collard seeds, and shaken to remove any tiny balls that are not firmly seated. Fill the bowl of the suction-cup compote with epoxy cement and let it become almost hard before setting the branches upright in it. While waiting, curve the wires carefully and decide exactly how they should be placed, so that they need not be disturbed once they are in position. Accessories are an important part of contemporary arrangements, and for this oriental composition a tiny Japanese figurine would be the perfect accompaniment.

Period Centerpieces

Incredible though it seems, floral centerpieces were not used on dining tables until the middle of the nineteenth century! For this reason, every maker of miniature period centerpieces is perforce a collector of miniature fruits. Italian catalogues usually offer necklaces of Venetian glass apples and pears, strung in clusters along with flowers and tiny birds, but suitably small plastic apples, pears, and peaches are so seldom available that it is wise to lay in a goodly supply whenever they can be found. Look for them in florists' shops at Thanksgiving and at Christmas; search for them all year round in boutiques and party shops. Party-favor packages of mixed fruits will include bunches of grapes molded all in one piece, but these will be much less realistic than those you can make yourself by stringing the smallest of green or purple round beads on hair-fine wire.

Oranges and lemons, strangely enough, are much easier to find in properly small scale than apples and pears. Lemons traveled so well and were so highly prized in Europe and America that one or two of them may be included in period designs, but oranges were more rare and should be omitted except in Italian, Spanish, or West Indian settings. For some unknown reason, bananas are more common than any other miniature fruits, but they should be used only in twentieth-century centerpieces because they were generally unavailable before the days of rapid transportation.

Throughout the Middle Ages and the Renaissance, the place of honor in the center of the table was reserved for a standing saltcellar as large and as elaborate as the family's finances allowed. By 1700 small salt dishes placed at intervals along the table had replaced the single showpiece, and "dormants" were in vogue. These were platters of meat or poultry—a roast suckling pig with an apple in its mouth, for example, or a pheasant skinned, roasted, and returned to its plumage—that served as decoration at one meal and as the main course at dinner the following day. To make a roast pig dormant, cut off the legs of a piglet from a plastic farm set, and paint the pig's head and body with brown enamel. Slash the mouth crosswise so that it can be forced open, and press a small red apple into the opening; then place the roast pig on an oval pewter platter, and garnish the dish with a ring of apples.

By 1750 dormants had disappeared and epergnes were gracing dinner tables in pretentious homes. (In more modest houses, tables were simply centered with empty covered tureens.) Eighteenth-century epergnes were of silver: a shallow fruit bowl on a tall footed base was surrounded by three or four smaller dishes supported by branching arms that rayed out from the pedestal at a lower level. Fruit often was used in the small containers as well as in the large bowl, but sometimes the smaller dishes held almonds, raisins, or sweetmeats. A reasonable facsimile of an eighteenth-century epergne can be fashioned from a miniature pewter compote and cup-shaped silvery earring backs. Footed compotes often are included in German pewter tea sets and also are sold separately in toyshops and

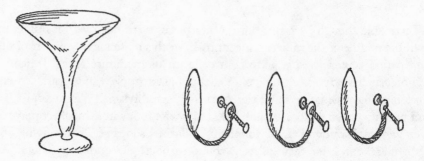

in the toy departments of major stores. Earring backs are among the jewelry findings in hobby shops, and for this purpose they must be of the screw type.

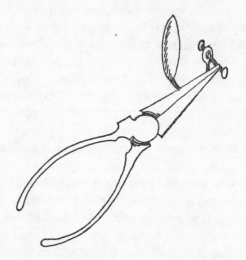

Remove a screw post by cutting through it with pliers or tin snips, leaving a curved metal arm ending in a tiny shallow bowl; the soft metal can be reshaped with the fingers to make its arch more graceful. Use liquid solder to attach three or four earring-back arms to the compote: Place a dot of solder on the end of an earring-back arm from which the post was removed, wait ten seconds, and press the coated area firmly against the compote pedestal. Hold the arm end under pressure for one minute, and then allow the solder joint of this first arm to set for half an hour before adding a second arm. Leave the finished epergne undisturbed overnight to be sure the solder has bonded, and then fill the bowls with minute apples and pears, adding bunches of tiny green or purple bead-grapes strung on hair-fine wire. Medium-size red or yellow beads nestling among the larger fruits will look like plums and help to fill the bowls.

The fruit arrangements of ancient Greece were copied and enlarged upon during the Renaissance, when lavish pyramids of apples, peaches, pears, and grapes ornamented banquet tables and formed the final course of the meal. During the Baroque Period, fruit pyramids for banquets frequently were made on tiered holders of metal or porcelain. A modest version of these banquet designs, the apple pyramid, was the most popular of all centerpieces in the American colonies during the seventeenth and eighteenth centuries. Although this became a traditional decoration for the Christmas dinner table, it was used on state occasions all year round. The basis of such a pyramid was a wooden cone studded with rows of headless nails on which the apples were impaled, and short sprigs of greenery tucked between and behind the fruits concealed the cone from view. Along the eastern seacoast, where pineapples imported from the West Indies could be obtained, the apple pyramid was proudly topped with a pineapple sprouting a tuft of green foliage.

To make a miniature apple pryamid, cut a section 1½" long from the tip of a green styrofoam Christmas cone. Use dull red beads, about ¼" in diameter, to represent the small apples of the colonial period. (If red beads are not available, pearl beads can be colored with mandarin-red model enamel.) Cut brown florist's wire in ½" pieces and thread these short wires through the beads; allow one end of each wire to protrude only a bit to look like the apple's stem. Begin with a row of apples around the base of the cone, dipping the longer end of each brown wire in white glue as it is pricked into the styrofoam, and build up the pyramid with successive rows placed so close together that the fruits touch. Top the cone with a tiny artificial pineapple—make it yourself, if necessary, of a casuarina cone with a trimmed tuft of plastic pine needles for foliage. (Little toppers for Christmas packages often include these smallest of all pine cones.) Tuck bits of glue-dipped plastic asparagus fern among the apples and place the finished pyramid upon a pewter plate.

During the Classic Revival Period, "plateaus" were the most coveted ornaments for dining-room tables. These were mirrors—usually long and narrow, with curved ends, to follow the shape of banquet tables. They were framed with wide bands of silver that raised the glass above the table surface, and on such a mirror an ormolu or silver candelabrum often was flanked by twin fruit arrangements in tall compotes. An acceptable miniature plateau may be made by bending a silvery bangle bracelet to the desired shape and topping this frame with a mirror cut to fit it at a glass company.

In the Victorian Era, something new in centerpieces made its appearance. Although it was called an epergne, this container bore no resemblance to its eighteenth-century namesake; on a footed pedestal sat a shallow fruit dish, and from the center of the dish rose a trumpet-shaped vase. In this two-part container that looked like a tiered fountain, flowers arrived on the dining table at long last.

A few Victorian epergnes were made of silver or of porcelain, but the vast majority were of clear glass. It is possible to construct a "glass" epergne in miniature by combining a watch crystal with a clear plastic pushpin and a party-favor wineglass. Procure from a jeweler a thin round replacement crystal 1" to 1¼" in diameter, and buy a package of pushpins at an office-supply company. Miniature wineglasses, footed and trumpet-shaped, are among the wedding favors at a party shop; the smallest of these come in cellophane packets and are about three-quarters of an inch tall. Remove the metal point from the pushpin with pliers, leaving a footed base. Cover the top of this base (the end from which the pin was pulled) with clear household cement and let it stand for fifteen seconds before centering the watch crystal on it to form a flaring shallow bowl. After the glue has dried hard, center a wineglass on the shallow bowl, and cement it there. Adorn the bowl with tiny fruits—preferably apples, peaches, grapes, and pears—and then fill the wineglass vase half full of colorless liquid cement. Wait one minute for the cement to thicken and add a tight bouquet of miniature roses or mixed flowers; tie the stems of the blossoms with invisible thread and place them as a unit in the vase.

VII

How Miniature Gardens Grow

No stately home of England is without its gardens on the grand scale, and Queen Mary's Dolls' House is no exception, although in this case the scale is one inch to the foot. Now that the royal residence has come to rest in a glass enclosure at Windsor Castle, with its outer shell permanently raised the better to display all its inner wonders, the casual viewer is struck by the perfect proportion of the garden on the east front but is blissfully unaware of the mechanical problems involved in its construction. It is hard to believe that the tall poplar trees, the stone balustrades, the standard roses, and the wrought-iron gates of its outer edge can disappear entirely underneath the house's foundations but, like the garage on the west front, the garden is actually a drawer that must be pushed back out of sight before the shell of the facade can be lowered into place.

In order to close its aperture as it slides back beneath the house, the entire front of the garden must bend upward at right angles to the bottom of the drawer. This fold has cleverly been placed just where the edge of a paved crosswalk meets velvety green grass, and is visible only as a hairline crack where the crosswalk intersects a pathway leading from the gate to the house; the hinges are hidden underneath the drawer. When the balustraded front is folded up, the gate, the rose trees, and the wall are in horizontal position above the crosswalk, while the Lombardy poplars extend back over the garden itself, barely clearing the tops of the flowers.

The ingenious plan was devised by Miss Gertrude Jekyll, one of the most imaginative gardeners in a nation noted for gardening, and a lady whose delightful sense of humor inspired the small touches that lift this *chef d'oeuvre* above the ordinary. On either side of the walkway leading from the gate to the ground-level entrance of the house are rectangular flower beds outlined with clipped boxwood hedges and planted with blue and purple perennial iris. A standard rose adds height at each corner, and the beds have a filling of bright summer flowers—Madonna and tiger lilies, poppies, marigolds, gentians, sweet peas, and fuchsias—all perfectly in scale and instantly recognizable! Behind these beds, the niched wall of the house is planted with climbing roses; the high windbreak walls to right and left support espaliered *Magnolia grandiflora*. As if all this were not enough, there are portable planters here and there: wooden tubs holding hydrangeas and hybrid rhododendrons; round terra-cotta pots of Agapanthus; and troughs of budding annuals. All these plant materials are made of various metals; every petal and leaf was curved and colored by hand before the flowers and foliage were painstakingly assembled.

Painted wooden garden seats are conveniently placed near the broad smooth paths, and there is a lawnmower waiting to shear the green velvet grass. Furthermore, birds are nesting in the trees; butterflies sip nectar from the roses; snails are visible (but just barely); and a fairy ring of toadstools has sprung up overnight.

The garden of Queen Mary's Dolls' House is perfection itself—in fact, it well may be the paragon for all time since its creation was a co-operative effort in which the most able technicians of an entire nation were available to carry out Miss Jekyll's delightful design. Seeing this masterpiece for the first time, a do-it-yourself miniaturist is bound to experience a sense of overwhelming inadequacy and is sure to give up gardening on the spot. Only a manufacturing jeweler could make such stamps and molds for metal leaves and petals, and only an artist could color and shape each one so perfectly. The patience and precision of a watch-maker would be required to assemble all the individual bits and pieces into trees, shrubs, and flowers. On second thought, however, one realizes that although it *would* be quite impossible to duplicate this particular garden, it is well within the realm of possibility to plan and construct other miniature garden scenes that are totally different but equally interesting. A special challenge lies in making these of materials that are everywhere available at reasonable cost.

It is encouraging, too, to remember that the size of Miss Jekyll's garden was established by the dimensions of a drawer that fitted underneath the Dolls' House, and that its design was dictated by the mechanics of the folding drawer front. Amateur gardeners-in-miniature work under no such restrictions. Their gardens' size is limited only by practicality, and their designs are circumscribed only by the limits of their ingenuity. For example, a walled eighteenth-century formal garden might be made in the tray of an old trunk found in the attic, or a country garden bounded by a picket fence could be constructed on a wood-framed cork bulletin board from a variety store.

A supremely practical container for a miniature outdoor scene is an aquarium, which comes with glass walls and requires only an additional top covering of glass or sheet plastic to be completely and transparently dustproof. Aquariums are sold at pet shops and variety stores, and the size selected should, of course, be suited to the type of garden planned. An almost square 2-gallon tank makes a charming container for a dooryard garden or a detail from a larger landscape, while a narrow city back yard can better be displayed in a 5-gallon oblong. A Victorian scene, complete with summerhouse, croquet lawn, and round flower beds, will fit into the 10-gallon size, and so will an informal outdoor living area featuring a terrace and greenhouse. For a large formal garden, or a sunken swimming pool with bath house and terraced plantings, only the gigantic 15-gallon tank will do.

Since these gardens are freestanding, they should be planned to be seen from all four sides. This requires extra effort in design and execution, but it also makes possible an element of surprise. A squirrel climbing up a tree trunk will no longer be visible when one walks to the opposite side of the container, but an acorn-cup bird's nest with tiny pearl eggs will be seen nestling among the leaves near the top of the tree.

Such freestanding scenes have the extra advantage of portability. A garden in a trunk tray or on a bulletin board is very light and easy to handle. Because they are made of plate glass and have steel frames, aquariums are heavy; the larger they are the more they weigh and the more awkward they are to carry—in fact, the 15-gallon size can be considered portable only in the sense that it can be lifted by two strong men.

A portable garden in a *small* aquarium would make a splendid gift for apartment dwellers in an urban area, or for former gardeners living in a retirement home, but this is not its only use. A small contemporary aquarium garden is an ideal door prize for a flower show or a plant sale; where lotteries are legal, extra money can be made by selling chances on it. A garden on a bulletin board or in a trunk tray would be a most attractive and appropriate decoration for the entrance to a flower show, or for the registration area of a garden club conference. A series of portable scenes, demonstrating various types of garden design, would constitute an excellent teaching device for horticulture seminars or for natural history museums.

If it does not have to be moved too often, a large aquarium can be a very special gift. Many a house museum is now hemmed in by streets and buildings, having lost its extensive grounds through the encroachment of a growing city. A large aquarium garden can give visitors some idea of the house's original setting and is in itself an attractive addition to the museum's displays. If photographs, drawings, or plans of the vanished garden are available, a scale model can be constructed; in the absence of documentation, an imaginary garden of the proper period will serve the purpose very well.

Portable miniature gardens are nothing new. In ancient Egypt, small models of useful objects were placed in the tombs of royal and wealthy personages, to serve the needs of the dead in the afterlife. Such models—houses, boats, shops, and gardens, all peopled with servants—were patterned after the actual possessions of the deceased. The Egyptian collection of New York's Metropolitan Museum of Art includes furnishings from the tomb of Meket-Rē, a court official who lived at Thebes about 2000 B.C. Among these treasures is Meket-Rē's walled garden, which looks like an oblong clay box raised and covered at one end; this roofed section represents a porch, with horizontally striped columns supporting its painted ceiling. The open garden area, surrounded on three sides by high walls, is centered with a shallow copper pool that could actually have held water. Between the pool and the walls stand seven recognizable sycamore trees; the sycamore was doubly valued, not only for its shade but for its aromatic gum that produced the precious perfume, frankincense. Four thousand years have passed since Meket-Rē's garden was entombed with him, yet it exemplifies certain elements of good design by modern standards. Having the garden adjacent to the porch of the house was a convenience, while high walls ensured privacy. Tall trees provided desirable shade, and the pool gave the garden a center of interest as it added the grateful coolness of water.

Although this ancient example of miniature gardens is portable and "in the open air," there is historical precedent for placing an outdoor scene on a cabinet shelf. Like other eighteenth-century Dutch curio cabinets, Sara Ploos van Amstel's "house" at The Hague's Gemeentemuseum includes a garden. This one is placed in the central space below the entrance hall, and its walls are covered with *vue d'optique* paintings. Looking across the inlaid terrazzo floor, past the fountain with its mosaic bowl and mermaid waterspout, one gazes beyond tall trellises and a painted balustrade to a distant *allée* of cypress trees. The perspective is perfect, but the garden is disappointing since its only flowers are in the mural paintings.

It certainly is possible to create a garden (or a whole series of gardens, for that matter) within the confines of a cabinet or a bookcase, and it is not necessary to forgo the flowers. For obvious reasons, the higher the ceiling of the shelf the greater the illusion of outdoor spaciousness. The sun always shines on miniature gardens, so a sky-blue painted ceiling is a must; the side and back walls of the shelf also should be blue for an effect of background distance that will lend enchantment to foreground plantings. The illumination should be brighter than that used in an indoor scene, and it is interesting to experiment with colored bulbs—yellow for the look of midday sunshine, blue for twilight, or pink for early morning. The wiring can of course be placed at the front of the shelf and hidden behind a wide strip of molding attached to the shelf above, but it also would be practical to bring the wires in from one side of the shelf and conceal the bulb with plantings or architectural detail. In such an arrangement, the light source represents the position of the sun, highlighting plantings placed directly in front of it and casting realistic shadows.

Once the background painting is done and the lighting is installed, a garden-on-a-shelf is easier to complete than one that is freestanding. Because it will be seen from one direction only, each tree, shrub, flower, and ornament can be so placed that it presents its best side to the viewer. In this type of scene, a large and spreading tree is a good focal point since its overhanging branches can be supported by attaching them to the ceiling of the shelf. Place the tree in a corner or against one side wall and fit double-pointed tacks around the long upper branches. Hammer the tacks into the ceiling, and hide them by rearranging the foliage.

The symmetry of a formal planting is most apparent when the design is viewed from above, and the same is true of a knot garden's interesting pattern of narrow beds laid out in loops and swirls. To obtain a bird's-eye view automatically, a garden could be housed in a glass-topped curio table or hidden in a deep drawer. A glass-topped coffee table, with a well deep enough for shrubs and flowers though not for trees, can be made of a piano bench. Remove the solid wooden bench top by unscrewing it from the hinges and replace the top with heavy plate glass edged with wooden picture frame strips. The glass can be cut to size at a company listed under "Glass: Retail" in the Yellow Pages of the telephone directory, and frame strips with mitered corners are sold in several lengths at variety stores. An old wooden filing cabinet or a new "field" chest with deep drawers can conceal a secret garden complete with tall miniature trees, and the sides of the drawer will be ready-made windbreak walls.

Originally the word "garden" meant an enclosed space, and it still is customary to define the boundaries of a planted area with walls, fences, hedges, or paths. If a diminutive rock wall is wanted, there are two ways to obtain one. A thin cork wall tile can be cut into strips and rubbed lightly on both sides with white paint; this will give its cracked brown surfaces the look of gray fieldstone, and the easy-method wall can be cemented on edge to serve as a background for shrubs or flowers. Purists probably will prefer to construct a rock wall of actual gravel on a cardboard core. Cut a strip of cardboard the desired length and height and lay it flat on a pad of newspaper. Pour a small amount of white glue into a saucer and dip the pebbles into the glue before fitting them closely together on the cardboard. Let the glue dry overnight before turning the cardboard over to cover the other side with stones.

For mosaic work, hobby shops sell tiny oblong tiles that look exactly like miniature bricks. These come in sheets, attached to a coarse cloth mesh; they usually are available in yellow-brown, gray, and beige, but only rarely are they white or red. However, gray or beige tiles can be metamorphosed into mellow red bricks with one quick coat of translucent nail polish, which colors well, dries almost instantly, and does not obscure the realistic roughness of the tiles' surface. A miniature brick wall requires no cardboard core, and the tiny tiles need not be removed from their cloth backing and glued individually. Cut between the rows of bricks with scissors to form two strips of the right length and height. Then, with a paintbrush apply a thin coat of white glue to the cloth back of each brick strip and press the two glued surfaces firmly together. Lay the double-faced strip flat and weight it overnight with books to prevent buckling. Finally, give the wall a neat finish by adding a single row of bricks glued face up on its top edge.

For some types of gardens, fences are more appropriate than walls, and fencing can be found ready-made in hobby shops and toy stores. White plastic picket fencing is sold in snap-together sections as an accessory for model railroads, and plastic farm sets always include board or rail fences. Furthermore, thin wooden tongue depressors are ideal building materials for a high board fence—a druggist will sell these by the dozen or by the box. Stake fences can be made of precut wooden skewers, floral picks and lollipop sticks, or of bamboo plant stakes and thin dowel sticks cut to the desired height. Dowel sticks also make good posts for wire-mesh fences—strips cut (with scissors) from aluminum or plastic window screening, or cut (with tin snips) from ¼″ mesh hardware cloth. Square balsa dowels can be sized and roughened with a serrated knife to furnish fence rails for a rustic scene, and large black metal hairpins will simulate the scallops of a wrought-iron fence. A contemporary enclosure, tall and opaque for privacy, can be found in corrugated aluminum flower-bed edging which is sold at garden centers. It will stand on edge unsupported; it can be bent or curved to any shape; and it can be painted in a solid color or with a mod design.

When architects and city planners add greenery to their scale models, they indicate hedges with strips of sponge. Man-made sponge—not the smooth plastic, but the cellulose variety that is full of holes—is a practical though recognizable material for miniature garden hedges. Cut thin green sponge with scissors to the desired shape; the holes will give it natural-looking irregularity. To deepen its color, soak it for twenty minutes in dark green liquid dye diluted with boiling water. Remove the sponge bits from the dye bath with tongs and rinse them under cold running water; then place them on several thicknesses of paper toweling to shrink back into shape as they air-dry. Very realistic hedges can be made of steel wool, which is sold in sheets at paint stores and can be shaped with shears. Pour a small amount of dark green enamel into an aluminum pie tin and dredge a section of steel wool in the paint to coat its outer edges; transfer the hedge to a thick pad of newspaper to dry. If the steely gray of the wool still shows through, dab on more green paint with a brush. For the easiest and most effective hedge of all, use a number of sprigs of artificial cedar or juniper, placing them so close together that their stubby needle foliage is intermingled; level their tops with scissors, and shear away all straggling needles to obtain the effect of a well-pruned row of evergreens.

Paths can outline an entire garden or define the various areas within it. A most effective miniature walkway can be made by removing brick tiles from their cloth backing and laying them in a herringbone pattern, using white glue for cement. The same hobby shops that sell brick tiles for mosaic work also stock sheets of small flat polished stone tiles that are pleasingly varied in size and shape. In white, dull brown, or streaked gray, these make good flagstones for garden paths. Fine sandpaper, pale beige in color, is sold in large sheets at paint stores; for miniature purposes it has the texture of rough concrete. Instead of cutting it in strips for straight paths, cut it in 3″ or 4″ squares. When the squares are laid end to end, the cracks between them will look like joints of cement. A curved concrete path is most easily made by outlining it in chalk, and filling in the outline with antique-white latex paint into which a small amount of sand has been stirred. Fill in the outline of a gravel path with a thick coat of white glue, and add a liberal layer of white sand. Allow the glue to dry overnight and then lightly flick the surface of the path with a soft dry paintbrush to remove unattached grains of sand. Grass paths are appropriate for a formal garden or for one composed entirely of flower beds. Velveteen and plush have traditionally been used for miniature grass, but terry toweling is more realistic. It should of course be solid green—dull rather than bright, and light rather than dark—in color. Cut the toweling with shears and do not hem the edges. Brush the path outlined on the garden floor with white glue; lay a strip of toweling carefully and smooth it immediately, then weight it overnight with books to prevent wrinkling as the glue dries. In the same way, larger pieces of green terry cloth may be laid down for lawns.

A quick-and-easy tree to shade a terry-cloth lawn can be made of a large, green-dyed sponge. For many years, natural sponges were almost impossible to obtain, but they have reappeared in housewares departments and at auto-supply stores. They differ enormously in shape as well as in size. Some are irregularly scalloped, flattened orbs while others are symmetrical mounds, and their small branching growths vary in form and texture from sponge to sponge. Their natural straw color can be changed to green by soaking for thirty minutes in liquid dye diluted with water as hot as it comes from the kitchen faucet. Wear rubber gloves when lifting a sponge from the liquid, and squeeze the sodden mass over the bowl to remove all excess dye. Then rinse the sponge under cold running water, squeeze it again, and let it dry on a pad of newspaper. Give this green tree crown a sturdy bark-covered twig for a trunk by dipping the smaller end of the twig in white glue before forcing it far enough into the bottom of the sponge so that the tree crown is well balanced and securely supported.

Lacier trees can be made of artificial greenery, and a prospective gardener should constantly be on the lookout for suitably small plastic foliage. Before Christmas, boutiques and florist shops display "picks" of evergreen twigs almost delicate enough to be termed miniature; sprays of pale, feathery spring greenery appear at Easter time. Available all year round are ferns of several sorts that can double for poplar, cedar, walnut, or heaven trees. In autumn there are clusters of yellow, red, and brown maple or oak leaves that are only slightly oversize; it is tedious and time consuming to trim each leaf with curve-bladed manicure scissors, but it is perfectly possible to do so. If all else fails, choose plastic foliage with a great many close-spaced leaves of whatever size and turn each leaf into a tiny ginkgo fan by cutting it straight across, with scissors, $1/4''$ above its stem.

If you should come upon a bushy bit of artificial foliage with many branching twigs, very tiny leaves, and a thick brown stem—rejoice, for you have found an instant tree. Most plastic stems and some plastic twigs are stiffened with cores of

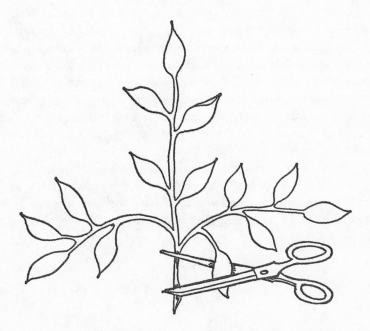

heavy wire. This means that a foliage cluster can be reshaped by separating and bending its small sprays, but unwanted "limbs" cannot be cut off with scissors. Prune your instant tree with tin snips or wire-cutter pliers.

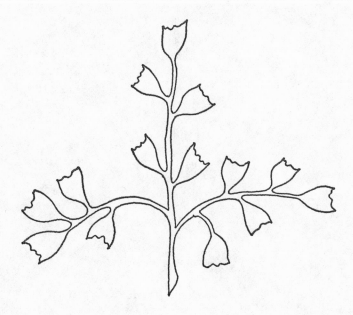

Lacking a ready-made tree, you can construct one on any thick brown plastic stem. The better-quality artificial flowers and leaves are molded separately and attached by hand to their stems. Flowers have center holes, and leaves usually are borne on short stalks that end in hollow cups; stems are studded with knobbed protuberances, over which the flower holes or foliage cups are pressed. The original leaves and blossoms can easily be removed by tugging them up and over the knobs so that this miniature tree trunk can sprout new branches of your choosing. Dip the cupped end of each leafy branch in white glue (or plastic cement) before pressing it firmly down over a knob.

Whether their foliage is sponge or plastic, miniature trees are top-heavy. Their slender, rootless trunks offer inadequate support to spreading crowns, and before the advent of epoxy cement it was necessary to nail the base of a tree trunk to the garden floor. This hold-everything glue comes in two tubes—one of epoxy and

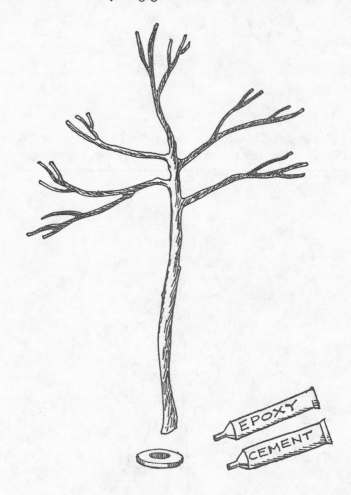

one of hardener—which must be mixed and used immediately thereafter. For optimum balance, force the tip of the trunk into the tight-fitting hole of a flat faucet washer, and then spread cement on the bottom of the washer as well as on the garden floor. Wait at least ten seconds before setting the tree in place; then brace the trunk with stacks of books for twenty-four hours and hope for the best when

the books are finally removed. If the tree still stands perfectly steady, you have only to disguise the washer beneath bits of terry-cloth grass. If, on the other hand, the tree top slowly begins to lean, it may be necessary to brace the tree permanently—with one or more stones cemented at its base, with a "pruning" ladder propped against its weak side, or with a garden bench artlessly placed in its shade. Another bracing idea is to use two trees instead of one, placing their trunks so close together that their branches touch, to give each other mutual support.

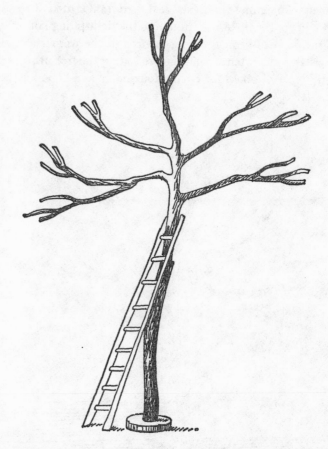

Evergreens are essential to good garden design, and Christmas is the time to buy the miniature pine and cedar trees of various sizes that are intended for mantel and coffee-table decorations or for place favors. These usually have flat circular bases of wood or cardboard on which they balance well. By coating its base thickly with white glue, such an evergreen can be instantly transplanted in the garden. Disguise its circular base by brushing it with white glue and sprinkling on a layer of cigarette tobacco, which will look like a peat-moss mulch. Among the holiday package toppers and party decorations may be found mound-shaped picks of pine and cedar which miniaturists recognize at once as evergreen shrubs. Remove a pick stem and settle the shrub on a circle of white glue for permanent planting.

In hobby shops and toy stores, the accessories for model railroads include evergreen trees that stand quite steady on spreading networks of brown plastic roots. The roots show up well against green terry-cloth grass, and white glue will quickly attach them to it. Green-dyed lichen, which often is packaged with evergreen trees in a "landscaping" set, perfectly imitates low-growing juniper.

Model-train accessories also run to autumn- and spring-flowering trees; the smallest of these, minus their spindly trunks, make excellent mound-shaped shrubs that can be secured to wood, wallpaper cleaner, or terry cloth with white glue. These trees are made of stiff wire clusters dipped first in glue and then in colored fibers, and by the same method such flowering shrubs as spirea and for-

sythia can be simulated with thin brown or green florist's wire and chopped knitting wool. Cut across the end of a twisted white or yellow skein, as close to the tip as possible; the wool will fall from the scissors blades in the form of fine fuzz.

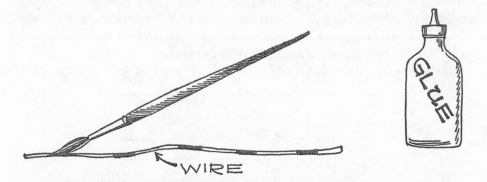

Spread the fuzz out in a thin layer on a sheet of waxed paper. Touch a wire at intervals with a paintbrush dipped in white glue, and then roll the wire in the chopped wool—the fibers will cling to and cover the glue spots with a mist of color. Use matching plastic tape to bind several of the green or brown wires together at the base, and curve the canes into a spreading bush; prune with tin snips, if necessary, to achieve a look of natural growth.

Vines that climb up walls and clamber over fences should have canes of the very lightest weight green or brown florist's wire. Here foliage will be a special

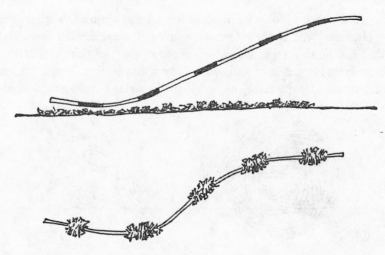

problem because, with the exception of grapevines, most climbing plants have tiny leaves. Use miniature artificial ivy for grape foliage, trimming and blunting the leaves with scissors, and make bunches of grapes from the smallest of round green beads strung in clusters on hair-fine wire. Foliage for other vines can be cut with a paper hand punch from green-on-both-sides florist's foil. Punches may be bought from an office- or school-supply company; most of them make round holes no larger than a match head, but some cut diamonds or crescents that are fine-pointed vine leaves. Attach punched dots or diamonds to the vine after its canes have been secured to a wall or fence by squeezing a tube of clear liquid cement until a bubble of glue appears; lift a leaf with tweezers and dip it in the glue bubble; then touch the leaf to the cane. The tiny circle or rectangle will be so nearly weightless that the cement will adhere instantly.

Heavy brown wire should be used for espaliers trained on walls or fences. The

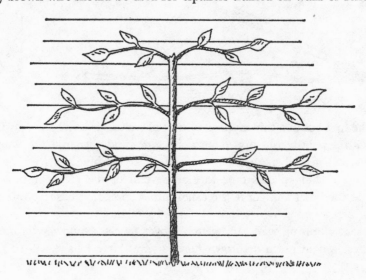

easiest espalier is *Magnolia grandiflora*. It can be made by gluing tufts or single leaves cut from artificial boxwood twigs to the brown wire. Espaliered fruit trees call for small pointed leaves—trimmed miniature foliage or punched out foil diamonds with side points removed. Bunches of tiny fruits on wire stems—oranges, lemons, apples, peaches, and pears—can sometimes be obtained from florists at Thanksgiving time; boutiques and variety stores usually have miniature fruit toppers for Christmas packages. Other sources are dollhouse accessories and party-favor packets from toy and party shops.

Now for the flowers that are the glory of any garden. It is satisfying, as well as

esoteric, to fill the miniature flower beds with real dried flowers. For centuries, gardeners have known that certain blossoms kept all their shape and most of their color if they were hung head down in a dark room to air-dry. Among these are

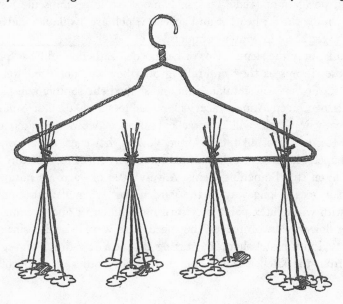

yarrow, statice, celosia, baby's-breath, and Queen Anne's lace. Gather the flowers in the late afternoon of a hot sunny day and do not put their stems in water. Wire them in small bunches, hook several bunches to the crossbar of a coat hanger, and hang them in a dark closet for about three weeks. By this time, the dehydrated

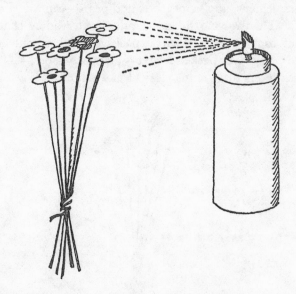

stems and petals will be rather brittle to the touch, but they will regain strength and acquire durability if they are coated with hairspray or with colorless acrylic plastic (which is sold in pressurized spray cans at artists' supply shops).

Other dried flowers are suitable in size for miniature gardens: tiny bright-colored Peruvian starflowers which are sold by florists and found in "mod" boutiques; polygonum (red Mexican bamboo) whose minuscule rosy disks dry naturally on the shrub; heather and acacia, which are available ready-dried from florists who use them in winter bouquets.

Obviously, only the slender tips of celosia or heather should be "planted"; set out in loose clumps as they naturally grow, they will not need foliage. A tied cluster of starflowers will simulate a mound-shaped chrysanthemum plant, while a few florets of Queen Anne's lace will resemble shasta daisies. Small sprays of baby's-breath or acacia will be excellent fillers between and among the other blooms. Most useful of all the air-dried flowers, however, is yarrow, whose flat parasol-shaped blooms can be separated into many small tufts of tiny round blossoms borne on stiff branching stems. A very little of yarrow's natural mustard-yellow color goes a long way in the garden, but when its clustered florets are brushed with white latex paint they turn into candytuft and become the perfect edging for flower beds. Moreover, they need not always be white, since latex paint can be tinted any pastel shade by stirring into it a few drops of vegetable food coloring from the kitchen shelf. Four half-ounce bottles of food coloring—red, yellow, blue, and green—come packaged together, and by mixing one or more of these with a small quantity of white latex, a veritable rainbow of flowers can be culled from a few heads of yarrow.

One final and very welcome addition to the list of natural plant materials is not a blossom but a seed. Small tan beet seeds may be purchased in paper packets at grocery stores and garden centers. Each one is covered with swirled corrugations like half-open petals and looks like a perfect miniature wooden rose. Paint these red, pink, yellow, or white and glue them in clusters to climbing rose vines on the garden wall.

Instead of (or in addition to) these natural dried materials, artificial flowers can, of course, be used. Look for long wands of blossoming shrub with composite clusters of very tiny florets; good possibilities are white spirea and orange lantana. Just as they are, the clusters can go into the garden as mound-shaped plants; they also can be cut apart with scissors to enable the florets to be set out individually.

Low-growing bedding or edging plants can most easily be imitated with the bushy tips of artificial cedar or juniper, and they can be made to bloom with sequins. For the crumpled look of petunias, crush the smallest size white sequins between thumb and finger and press the center hole of each one over the glue-brushed tip of a plastic cedar-sprig needle. The tiniest of red star sequins, mounted on cedar or juniper needles, will simulate sultana admirably.

Tall hollyhocks are an integral part of every English dooryard or American country garden. Using a dime for a pattern, cut seven circles from red, pink, or white crepe paper for each hollyhock stalk desired. Grasp the center of a circle between thumb- and fingernail, and pinch it to form a flat triangle about ⅛″ long—as you do this, the paper circle will ruffle itself into a blossom ¼″ in di-

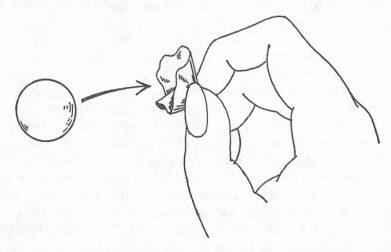

ameter. Cut a 5″ stem of lightweight green wire, and attach the blooms with green plastic tape narrowed with scissors to a strip ¼″ wide. Begin with a flat blossom near the tip of the stem, wrapping its flattened "tail" to the wire with a twist of the tape. Then spiral-wrap the tape down the wire, adding the remaining six blossoms at intervals, on opposite sides of the stalk, by overwrapping their flat pointed ends. Use a flat circle of the smallest green plastic geranium leaves for

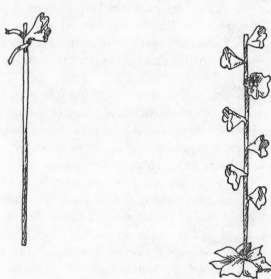

hollyhock foliage, splitting each leaf in two lengthwise and shortening it if necessary for scale. Cement the flowering stalk in the center of the foliage circle.

As in a full-size garden, the ground must be prepared before plants can be set out, and the best basis for a miniature flower bed is (of all things!) the type of non-crumbly wallpaper cleaner that is sold at paint stores. As it comes from the package, wallpaper cleaner is a moist pink mastic mass that is quite stiff but very pliable. For this purpose, it has one distinct advantage over modeling or floral clay: It retains its own shape, and permanently grips anything imbedded in it as it gradually dries rock-hard when exposed to air. Paint the outline of a flower bed liberally with white glue. Knead the wallpaper cleaner until it is perfectly smooth and press it down firmly upon the glue; then flatten and spread the cleaner into a ½" layer with the fingers, leaving its surface slightly uneven. Now give the cleaner the color of rich earth with a coat of dark brown flat paint or brown scuff-coat shoe polish, and planting time is at hand as soon as the paint (or polish) is dry. Dip the stems of flowers in white glue before pressing them down into the cleaner; for very fragile stems, make holes with a toothpick or a darning needle.

A bed of seedlings is fun to do and amusing to see: groove the wallpaper cleaner, before painting, with the tines of a fork. Cut ¼" and/or ½" tips from plastic pine or cedar and dip the cut end of each green bit in white glue before pricking it down in a brown furrow.

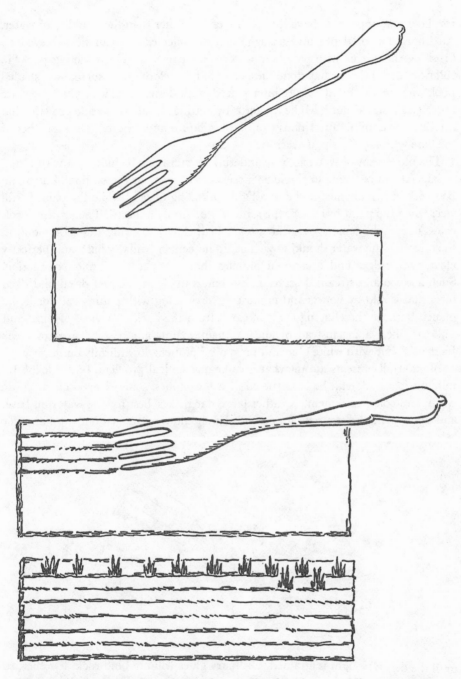

Water—in the form of a quiet pool, a purling brook, a tumbling waterfall, or a sparkling fountain—is a special delight in any garden. Because still water reflects light and images, a mirror can best represent a garden pool; an untreated mirror, however, appears to have the solidity of ice rather than the liquidity of water. An impression of depth and a suggestion of reflected sky can be achieved by brushing the mirror with pale blue water-color paint. Edge a reflecting pool "in full sun" with brick or flat-stone tiles, or with terry-cloth grass; surround a shaded pool with small round stones interspersed with ferns so placed that they are reflected in the "water." Make the ferns by cutting the alternate side growths that are themselves miniature fronds from a plastic fern and binding them together at the base with a ¼″ strip of green plastic tape.

The movement of water in a meandering stream must be indicated with a material that can be made to ripple as it seems to flow. Coat the outline of a stream bed with brown enamel, and add a light sprinkling of sand while the paint is still wet; when the paint has dried, the sand will be firmly adhered. Then squeeze colorless household cement over the stream bed, slowly drawing the tube along in the direction the water should flow. The liquid cement will dry hard and perfectly clear, with ridges and occasional bubbles that enhance the illusion of motion. Such a woodland stream deserves mossy banks made of the real dried and dyed moss that is sold by florists and in variety stores along with potting soil for house plants. Remove the clinging clods of earth from the back of a sheet of moss and pull the fibers apart instead of cutting them; paint only a small area of creek bank at a time with white glue and press a bit of moss down firmly on it.

A waterfall presents a somewhat greater mechanical problem, but a delightful miniature cascade can be constructed of a few stones, some clear kitchen plastic wrap, and colorless cement. A rather large flat rock is best for the waterfall base, and upon it smaller stones of graduated size should be arranged one atop another

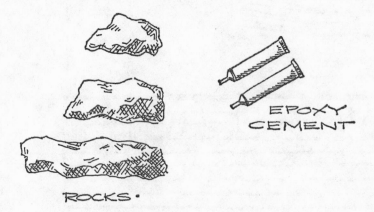

ROCKS·

EPOXY CEMENT

until the desired height is attained. Ordinary glues will not bind rocks together, so epoxy cement should be used. Spread the cement over the entire undersurface of the smaller of two stones, and press this rock down firmly on the top of the stone below; the weight of the rock itself will hold it in place as the glue dries to an unbreakable bond. When the terraced pyramid of stones is complete, cement it to

Madurodam is a bustling Dutch city — just 1/24 actual size! Every building here has a famous counterpart somewhere in the Netherlands: the "oldest" structure is this medieval castle complete with moat and portcullis, a reconstruction of one built on the island of Voorne about 1000 A.D. Madurodam, Holland. PHOTOGRAPH BY BETSEY CREEKMORE

Mrs. Thorne's eighteenth-century dining room of Gunston Hall shows the influence of the Orient on the American colonies. Hand-painted Chinese wallpaper, "temple doors," and a needlepoint oriental rug provide a proper background for museum-reproduction Chinese Chippendale furniture. PHOTOGRAPH COURTESY OF THE ART INSTITUTE OF CHICAGO.

The first Thorne Rooms were built to house their owner's collection of antique miniatures, and the furniture for this Victorian parlor came from a nineteenth-century dollhouse. Wall-to-wall carpeting and a large gas chandelier are added comforts; for the lived-in look, there are newspapers and a potted aspidistra. Dulin Gallery of Art, Knoxville, Tennessee. PHOTOGRAPH BY BETSEY CREEKMORE

Like all rooms designed by Robert Adam, this classic Revival dining room is formal — a balanced entity, with furniture that borrows its motifs from the architectural embellishments. To keep the scene from being too precise, Mrs. Thorne added a view outside the windows: a winding river and irregular clumps of trees. PHOTOGRAPH COURTESY OF THE ART INSTITUTE OF CHICAGO.

But you *can* do it yourself! This scenic wallpaper was a free sample from a decorator's pattern book. Window panes are mirror squares; floor boards were cut with a razor blade from a pressed-wood panel; and the oriental rug is a washcloth, wrong side up. Only the dried flowers are real. The authors' collection. PHOTOGRAPH BY BETSEY CREEKMORE

MIRROR

the garden floor and place a small mirror at its base. Hide the edges of the mirror with a ring of flat pebbles to form a catch basin. Now cut a strip of clear kitchen plastic wrap, about 1″ wide and long enough to reach from the top rock to the one below it. Attach one end of the strip to the edge of the top rock with a dot of

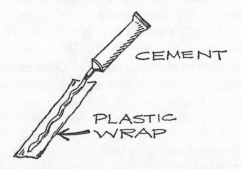

CEMENT

PLASTIC WRAP

liquid household cement and allow this glue to dry thoroughly. In the same way, bridge each level of the cascade to the one below, making each strip of plastic wrap slightly wider than the one above and ending with a 2″-wide strip from the flat base rock to the mirror surface. Now slowly squeeze a very little colorless liquid cement from the tube onto the edge of the top plastic strip, letting it trickle down the strip to the rock below; squeeze more cement over the next strip and

CEMENT

continue until the pool is reached. The cement dries so quickly that it coats the plastic, sometimes stringing off in droplets on each side, and hardens as it touches the mirror into a miniature whirlpool.

By the same method, a lion-head wall fountain can be given "flowing water." Cut off the head of a plastic lion (from a dime-store set of zoo animals) just behind the mane and cement the flat cut surface to a rock or brick wall. Below the lion head, use a scallop shell of appropriate size for a drip-basin, or make a semi-circular pool from the shallow lid of a half-round plastic or thin wood container that held imported soft cheese. The lion head and the basin can be made to look like concrete by brushing them with white latex paint; they also can be antiqued with a coat of flat black paint rubbed sparingly with light green enamel. Cut a ¼″ wide strip of kitchen plastic wrap; attach one end with household cement to the lion's mouth and the other end to the basin bottom. Then squeeze a drop or two of clear cement onto the top of the strip, adding more cement very slowly until it trickles down into the bowl. Wait six hours for this vertical strip to become completely dry and rigid and then cover the entire bottom of the basin with ¼″ of household cement, which will dry clear and transparent as water.

A classic tiered fountain, the ideal center ornament for a formal garden, can be constructed of a small footed alabaster bowl and one matching low candleholder. Mount the candleholder on a wooden block in the center of the compote to raise its base to the level of the rim of the larger bowl. Once again, household cement can serve as water, filling the candle cup and trickling down prepared jagged

strips of plastic wrap into the compote bowl. For an unusual simulation of a jet of water, use an "optic reflector" from a string of Christmas tree lights. Each optic reflector is a circle of clear curved plastic filaments that are transparent yet reflect light. Cement the base of a reflector in the cup of the fountain's candleholder and water will appear to spray outward and downward into the compote bowl.

In a less formal setting, a birdbath may be a more appropriate center of interest than a fountain. Metal bowl-on-pedestal stands are sold as display bases for alabaster eggs, and require only painting to become tall birdbaths. The same effect can be obtained by cementing a saucer from a doll's plastic tea set on a fluted metal lipstick case and mounting the case on a small square block of wood. Antique-white latex paint will blend these unrelated materials into a harmonious whole. A tiny scallop shell, brushed with white latex for the look of cement, makes a fine ground-level birdbath underneath a spreading tree.

For architectural interest, a formal garden might be centered with a circular Greek temple instead of with a fountain. A "temple of love" decoration for the top of a wedding cake would be perfect for this purpose, but is expensive. The same round structure with white fluted columns can be achieved by inverting a small shiny-white plastic mixing bowl over a cake separator with four 8″ columns—the cake separator can be bought at a bakery or purchased from a mail-order catalogue. In a Victorian garden, no building would seem so much at home as a gazebo. Plastic holders for potted plants are modeled after these nineteenth-century garden rooms with peaked roofs and balustraded sides; they are sold in variety stores and garden shops. A greenhouse would be a marvelous addition to a contemporary scene, and miniature greenhouses—for starting seeds indoors or growing herbs on a kitchen window sill—are available at garden centers. Even smaller greenhouses are offered as toys by mail-order houses.

A hanging basket, filled with spreading ferns or pendant flowers, is a good ornament for the greenhouse, but it could equally well be hung from a tree limb or a summerhouse ceiling. A large gold-colored metal sunburst of the type sold for trimming Christmas ornaments makes a fine frame for a "brass" basket: With pointed pliers, gently bend each spoke upward so that the flat wheel becomes a deep cup. To form a hanger, attach three or four lengths of very thin gold-filled chain to the spoke ends with dots of liquid solder and gather the end links of the chains onto a metal jump ring.

Potted plants for the greenhouse are easy to make and are attractive accents for gardens, steps, terraces, and miniature rooms. The screw-on caps of toothpaste, ointment, and glue tubes are absolutely perfect flowerpots! Fill a cap cavity with wallpaper cleaner and brush the surface of the cleaner with brown shoe polish before setting the flowers in place.

Larger caps from perfume or shaving-lotion bottles make fine planters for ferns or single tips of plastic cedar shaped like arbor vitae. Other planter possibilities are: low candleholders, shaving-brush handles, the smallest square plastic pots for

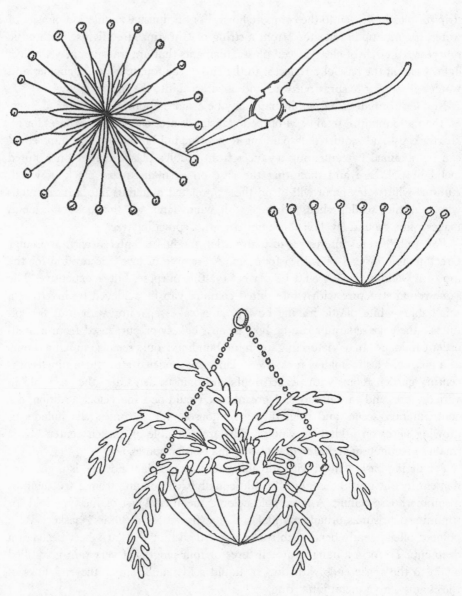

house-plant seedlings, and little square or oblong plastic boxes. A small hand bell, with its handle and clapper removed, can be inverted and mounted on a square of wood to become a tulip-shaped planter with a flaring rim. Coat any of these planters thickly with antique-white latex paint for the look of concrete, or "bronze" them with equal parts of brown and black enamel and highlight them with the rub-on patina finish that is sold in tubes at artists' supply centers. A "redwood" planter can be made to size, from thin balsa strips put together with liquid cement, and stained red-brown with oxblood liquid wax shoe polish.

Tiny tools—spades, rakes, trowels, wheelbarrows, and watering cans—often are found among plastic party favors, and a coil of shiny green ground-wire will look like a garden hose. (Obtain a snippet of this wire at an electronics shop or from a television repairman.) Fan-shaped plastic trellises, for training house plants, are sold at variety stores and garden centers; they end in stakes that are pushed down into the potting soil to hold them upright. The stakes can be shortened (and the outer ribs of the trellis removed if necessary for scale) with tin snips, and the trimmed trellis can support a climbing rose or a clematis vine in the miniature garden.

Gardens are made to be enjoyed, so there must be some evidence that they are visited by people. "Cast-iron" furniture from Germany is fashioned of silvery pot metal in lacy patterns popular in the Victorian Era. Painted white (or black antiqued with green), these little loveseats, chairs, and tables make marvelous garden furnishings. From Germany, too, come contemporary metal chairs and chaises upholstered in bright printed cloth, with tables holding beach umbrellas that actually can be raised and lowered. Such a set is the perfect furniture for a terrace paved with tiny glazed tiles or made of a cork mat rubbed with white paint to simulate stone. "Ice cream parlor" chairs and tables are offered in mail-order catalogues, as well as "redwood" chairs and picnic tables. Slatted wooden benches of wood or plastic may be bought at toyshops, while "concrete" benches can be made of balsa wood thickly coated with antique-white latex paint. An outdoor barbecue fireplace can be built of brick tiles or of gravel glued to the outer and inner sides of a cardboard box, and a grill can be added with strips of black wire. If crumbled bits of real charcoal in the firepit are touched with red nail polish, they will look like glowing coals.

For a final fillip, one can add a sense of life and movement to an otherwise static scene by careful placement of a few wild creatures. A tiny brown bunny could be almost hidden in a flower bed; a gray squirrel could scamper toward a tree; a tan tortoise could amble across a path; and a minuscule green bullfrog could poise on the bank of a stream. Birds (from a child's charm bracelet or a Venetian-glass necklace) might perch on the rim of a birdbath or a fountain, and a remarkably real acorn-cup nest holding tiny pearl eggs can be balanced in the crotch of a tree. Butterflies alighting on the blossoms can be made of the smallest size star sequins. With sharp-pointed scissors, excise the top point of a star and bend the sequin between thumb and finger to slant the pair of pointed wings.

Centerpiece Gardens

Centuries ago, some artisan turned his fine Italian hand to the making of miniature formal gardens. Traditionally, these sets of glazed white porcelain included four straight and four curved shallow containers like narrow planters, plus four taller urns or four statuettes of proper scale; as a variation on the norm, some or all of the sections were sometimes balustraded. Japan's clever copyists now reproduce these classic designs, and inexpensive sets are sold in boutiques and offered in mail-order catalogues.

A miniature garden of fresh flowers for the dining-room table will be a conversation piece as well as a centerpiece. Treat both the curved and the straight sections of a porcelain set as flower-box planters, filling them with short-stemmed composite blossoms such as ageratum, candytuft, spirea, or lantana. Large composite shrub or tree flowers with small florets can be divided into segments for this purpose; good possibilities are hawthorne, lilac, snowball, and pyracantha. Arrange the planters in accordance with the shape of the table, alternating them with miniature statuary. To keep the design completely floral, remember that the same footed alabaster compote and matching candleholder that formed a fountain can become a tall tiered planter for the center of a garden if compote bowl and candle cup are filled with flowers.

As an alternative to fresh flowers, the curved and straight sections of the centerpiece set can be treated as hedge planters to create a formal evergreen parterre. Fill the planters with sprigs of small-leafed foliage—boxwood, azalea, cotoneaster, or *Ilex microphylla*—or with tips of spruce, hemlock, or juniper; cut all the bits of foliage the same length, and crowd them into the containers to form a dense mass. Center the green garden with a single statuette or with a tall urn holding a feathery air-fern.

The best support for fresh foliage and flowers in such a garden is green Oasis; this solid substance that soaks up water like a sponge can be bought in large blocks from a florist and cut to size with a sharp knife while dry. It should be soaked in cool water for forty-five minutes before being pressed down into the shallow containers. The most fragile of flower stems can be pricked into its moist soft surface, yet it will support the blossoms firmly. In shallow Oasis-filled containers, fresh flowers will last several days while foliage sprigs can be kept for two or three weeks.

A miniature centerpiece garden can be a lasting rather than an ephemeral decoration if permanent flowers and foliage are used instead of fresh plant materials. Artificial boxwood twigs, trimmed all the same length, are the first thought for an evergreen parterre. For bright beds or urns filled with mixed blossoms, there are miniature air-dried flowers—baby's-breath, statice, Peruvian starflowers, feverfew, heather, and yarrow—and painted pods of ironweed, pearly everlasting, crape-myrtle, and salvia. Plastic posies can of course be used, alone or in combination with delicate artificial foliage. Fill the porcelain planters with green floral clay or with strips of green styrofoam to hold natural or artificial permanent plant material; make holes for flower stems with toothpicks and dip each stem in white glue before setting it in place for unshakable arrangement.

Topiary forms and "standard" trees will add interest to a permanent garden. Simple "poodle trees" can be made by wiring together several sprigs of artificial cedar, spruce, or juniper and pruning the mass with scissors into three vertical balls graduated in size. For the basis of a standard, cover a very small (1¼" diameter) styrofoam ball with green florist's foil, and mount it on a 4" twig or dowel stick. Fill a party-favor flowerpot with wallpaper cleaner, and press mustard seed "pebbles" or coarse sand down upon it. Dip the end of the twig trunk in white glue, and push it down through the cleaner to touch the bottom of the planter. Then cover the ball with plastic or dried flowers. Cut the stems off ¼" below the flower heads; make holes in the styrofoam with the point of a toothpick and dip each stem in white glue before pricking it into a prepared hole.

The stylized conical and animal shapes of eighteenth-century topiary can most

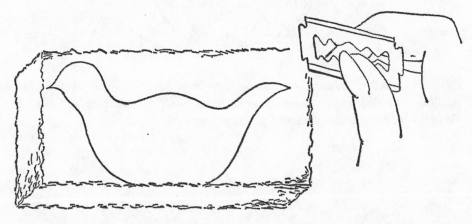

easily be made of a thick sheet of smooth green plastic sponge. Rough out the design on the plastic with a ball-point pen, and cut it out of the sponge block with a razor blade. Then shape the topiary carefully with the sharp points and curved

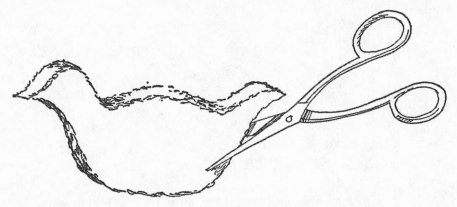

blades of embroidery and manicure scissors. Soak the finished shape for thirty minutes in dark green liquid dye diluted with boiling water. Lift the sponge with tongs, rinse it under cold running water and place it on a thick pad of newspaper

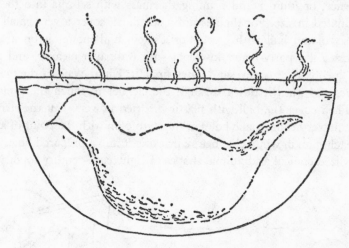

to drain and dry. Then plant the topiary in a square, white-painted plastic seedling pot. Weight the pot with a filling of wallpaper cleaner and hide the cleaner with a top coating of small pebbles or coarse sand.

Any centerpiece garden can be arranged on a bare table top, but a better background for it is a dark green tablecloth—linen, burlap, or felt—which adds

the look of grass around and between the planters, turning the whole table into a garden.

A porcelain centerpiece, Italian or Japanese, is not an indispensable part of a table garden, nor is its formality always desirable. Flower-bed planters of various shapes and sizes can be made of shallow tin cans: oval shad roe, oblong sardine, and round potted ham. Remove the can tops smoothly with an electric or wall-type can opener, wash the insides of the cans with hot soapy water, and coat the outsides with white or green latex paint. Another garden set might combine oblong photographic slide files made of shiny black plastic with round shallow boxes of clear plastic that held cheese wedges. Paint the clear boxes with glossy black enamel and then antique the round and rectangular containers by rubbing their sides sparingly with light green enamel.

Other flower-bed container ideas include brown-glazed ramekins or fluted white individual soufflé cups, aluminum tart shells, clay flowerpot saucers 2″ or 3″ in diameter, and ivy rings of glass or pottery. Carrying this last idea one step further, make a mini-miniature garden for an invalid's tray or a coffee table by painting the outside of an individual aluminum salad ring mold white and filling its cavity with colorful florets. Center the ring with a very tiny figurine or with a small porcelain bird.

Because they are made in sectional flat-bottomed containers that can be fitted onto a tray for carrying, centerpiece gardens can be classed as portable. A porcelain planter set stretched to its full length by placing straight and curved segments, urns, and/or statuary along the outer edge of the speaker's table is a marvelous decoration for a garden club luncheon. The garden is visible from both sides, and is low enough to permit those seated at the head table to see and speak across it. Small round guest tables can be centered with ivy rings and statuettes; long guest tables lend themselves to elongated arrangements of rectangular plastic planters interspersed with urns or statuary.

VIII

Portable Scenes and Shops

In 1928, when the motion picture industry was in its glittering heyday, America's most elaborate "dollhouse" began to take shape in Hollywood, California. It belonged to Colleen Moore, a silent screen star of the first magnitude, who rejoiced in an abiding Irish love for fairy stories. Having owned a succession of seven dollhouses during her childhood, she envisioned yet one more—a miniature fairy-tale castle that would become an eighth wonder of the Little World.

In Hollywood, the capital of the Land of Make Believe, Miss Moore's ambitious scheme found ready acceptance. Since she intended to take the finished palace on a tour of major American cities for the benefit of children's charities, she asked architect and set-designer Horace Jackson to create a lightweight structure, in a scale of one inch to the foot, that would instantly be recognized by everyone as an enchanted castle. The base of the completed building was nine feet square, and its tallest tower rose to a height of seven feet; although it was made of cast aluminum, it weighed approximately one ton. Nevertheless, it could and did travel, for it was cast in two hundred separate, interlocking pieces that came apart for shipping, and were fitted together again upon arrival. Each room was an entity, and all the lighting and plumbing were interconnected. Many of the craftsmen who worked on this modular marvel already were expert in producing scaled-down scenes for First National Studios, where hurricanes and holocausts, sea battles, and the ruins of antiquity were filmed in miniature.

The castle's interior decoration, in Early Faerie Period, was planned by Harold Grieve, A.I.D.; and the theatrically beautiful lighting effects were achieved by Henry Freulich, Miss Moore's personal cameraman. The rooms and the courtyard were filled with more than two thousand miniature treasures—among them King Arthur's Table Round, Sleeping Beauty's bed, Aladdin's lamp, and Cinderella's coach—for the comfort and convenience of resident fairies. Determined that the castle should transcend the realm of possibility, and become the fulfillment of childhood's fondest dreams, its owner parted with a pair of diamond and emerald clips that were turned into shield-shaped chair backs for the bedroom of the Fairy Princess, and ordered for the drawing room a floor tiled with rose quartz and bordered with green jade. In her recent book, *Colleen Moore's Doll House,* Miss Moore vividly describes the creation of another extravagant accessory:

> When I decided that the drawing room chandelier had to be made of diamonds and emeralds recruited from several pieces of personal jewelry, I took my problem to a prominent Beverly Hills jeweler. He looked a little dubious at first, fingering the diamond necklace and brooch, the emerald bracelet, and the diamond pendant I held out to him in my handkerchief. "It could be very interesting," he said at last, "but it would be sacrilege to use this." He handed back the six-carat pear-shaped diamond pendant on its chain. "Take this home. You have to have something to wear." Two weeks later he telephoned me. "Bring back that pear-shaped diamond," he demanded in a refined shout. "I have to have it for a drop at the bottom of the chandelier!"

By the time its solid-gold cornerstone was laid in 1935 by Mrs. James Roosevelt (the mother of the President of the United States), the castle and its furnishings had cost half a million depression dollars. Wherever it was displayed, huge crowds flocked to see it; Colleen Moore's fairy-tale castle seemed to typify America's ebullient ingenuity as Queen Mary's Dolls' House had exemplified England's dignity and tradition. The Queen's dollhouse had been completed only a decade earlier, and inevitably the two miniature mansions were compared by newspaper reporters in the cities where the castle was on view. Many feature writers implied that the American production was a brash attempt to go the British one better, pointing out that Miss Moore had borrowed several ideas from Queen Mary's Dolls' House and enlarged upon them. Indeed, the castle's verdigris-copper library shelves are filled with inch-square holographic books by American authors and, in addition, there is a guest book containing the autographs of great and royal personages from around the world. Distilled water not only flows from bathroom taps, but also drips from a weeping willow tree into a garden pool. Both houses are electrically lighted, and in the dolls' house electricity also runs an elevator and powers household appliances; in the castle, it simulates dancing flames in a fireplace, and sways the treetop cradle of the Rockabye Baby.

Miss Moore's Hollywood extravaganza is now on permanent display at the Museum of Science and Industry in Chicago. Each day, visitors by the hundreds circle the shining little building in its glass enclosure as they listen to the recorded music of the gold pipe organ in its chapel. While children joyfully point out the "jewels" in the Cave of Ali Baba, adults linger outside the chapel, with its jewel-toned stained glass windows, and its ceiling motifs borrowed from Ireland's eighth-century Book of Kells. Here are the true treasures of the castle. The stained glass screen behind the gold baptismal font is a fragment of a Lambeth Palace window blown out during a London air raid in World War II; the portrait bust of Pope Pius IX is the Prelate's own seal that disappeared during an insurrection at the Papal Palace and was eventually sold at auction in Boston. In the gold monstrance on the altar is a sliver of wood believed to be from the True Cross. The relic was presented by the Pope to Clare Booth Luce at the time of her conversion to the Roman Catholic faith and was given by her to the castle as a memorial to her young daughter, Anne Brokaw, who was killed in an automobile accident.

Children who visit the castle are invariably enchanted by it, and even the most pragmatic adult comes away with a feeling of having seen something out of the ordinary, something unique. And yet, "Is there any thing whereof it can be said, See, this is new?" (Ecclesiastes 1:10).

Despite its size and flamboyance, Colleen Moore's itinerant castle belongs to a large order of portable scenes that had its origin in Germany during the seventeenth century. At the same time that curio cabinets were being filled with costly miniatures and mechanical toys, Philip Hainhofer of Augsburg was designing castle courtyards walled with turreted and towered buildings, peopled with soldiers and servants, and crowded with animals, vehicles, and household equipment. These seven-foot-long courtyards were acclaimed as art objects, and were highly esteemed by noble ladies to whom they were presented by Duke William of Bavaria. In later times, the tradition of large but transportable displays was continued in fortified castles besieged by armored knights, in battlefields with opposing armies of lead soldiers, in working models of mining apparatus, and in model railways with tunnels and towns.

Many of the large mechanical displays were designed to be informative. For example, in 1911, a new railroad was about to be built across the Zara and Katsina districts of Nigeria, but the native rulers of those provinces had never seen a train. The British entrepreneurs wisely presented each emir with a model railway, made to a scale of three-fourths inch to one foot, with clockwork locomotives pulling long strings of cars through a miniature Nigerian landscape.

During the seventeenth and eighteenth centuries, humbler portable rooms and scenes were made by the thousands for educational purposes. Nuremberg kitchens and miniature shops were teaching toys, and with them children learned by participation. Miniature portrayals of biblical scenes and historic events were welcomed by stay-at-home tutors and traveling evangelists, who used them in teaching by the show-and-tell method.

The concept of reinforcing a textbook knowledge of history with visual displays is still a valid one, and obviously it is easier to take one miniature museum-quality exhibit to students in their schoolroom than to transport an entire class to the museum. A civic-minded miniaturist can make a much appreciated contribution to a city's public schools by constructing for them a portable, historically accurate scene—provided the subject of the display has been approved in advance by school authorities. Relevance is an intangible requirement that may have been overstressed of late, but a miniature exhibit would be welcomed by history teachers only if it were pertinent to some phase of the curriculum.

Local history touches students more nearly than events that were far away in place as well as in time, and the offer of a diorama showing the founding of your city would surely be accepted with surprise and pleasure. A more general scene, showing what daily life was like in the newly settled town, would be more interesting to develop and would have broader application as a teaching aid.

In a city where textile mills are an important part of today's economy, a two-story weaver's house of the late colonial period would serve the dual purpose of demonstrating how eighteenth-century artisans lived and how cloth was made before the Industrial Revolution. The unheated, windowless loft of a weaver's house often served as his workshop, and to reach it, he climbed a steep flight of stairs from the family's one-room living quarters on the lower floor. Such a house can be constructed from a rectangular wooden packing box by taking off one side. The top that was prised up to remove the contents of the crate can be utilized as a slanting roof. Support the roof with graduated blocks of wood glued to the upper rims of the box ends so that it slopes away from the open front of the house.

Measure the interior dimensions of the box, and have a rectangle of heavy plywood cut at a builder's supply company to fit across the box and form a second floor; have a 3"×4" piece cut out of one corner of the plywood, for a stairwell. Nail ½" square strips of wood around the inner walls of the house, 10" above the bottom of the box, to support the floor of the second story. Cement square wooden strips across one side of the plywood, to look like exposed rafters; then cement the plywood floor to its nailed strip-supports, with its crossbeams down and the cutout stair opening at the back of the box.

A simple boxed staircase leading to the upstairs loft can be made of a strip of balsa wood 1" wide and ½" thick. Cut the strip into sections 2½" long. Cement

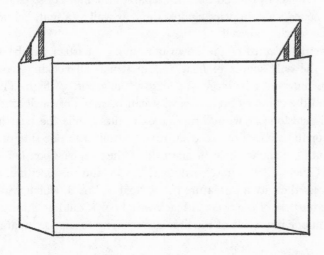

the bottom edge of one section over the top edge of another, to make a tread ¾″ deep and a riser ½″ high. When this cement is dry, add another step, and continue until the flight of stairs is long enough to reach from the floor of the house to

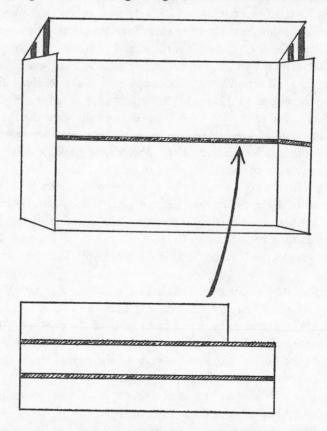

the opening in the ceiling. Then cement one long edge of the joined wood strips to a thin rectangle of plywood that will separate the flight of steps from the room, and set the boxed stairs in place against the rear wall as a unit, below the hole cut in the ceiling for the stairwell.

The principal feature of the downstairs living quarters will be the fireplace, which was the only source of heat and in which all cooking took place. The fireplace opening must be large—at least 6″ long and 5″ high. The protruding fireplace and the chimney breast above it can be made of cardboard boxes faced with gravel-fieldstone or with "brick" mosaic tiles, while the hearth can be laid with brick or flat stone tiles. An oven may be built into one side of the chimney piece by cutting a square hole in one side of the fireplace box before it is faced with brick. Glue a small square cardboard box behind this opening, and place inside this recessed cavity a miniature brown loaf of bread, which will immediately identify the purpose of the oven. A black wire hook should be imbedded, with liquid solder, in one inner side of the fireplace opening to support a large open kettle

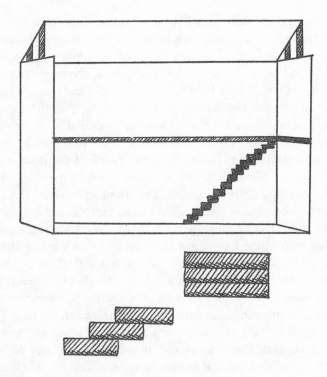

above the fire. Use rather thick bark-covered twigs for logs and simulate flames by gluing jagged bits of red and yellow cellophane between them. Around and below these logs, there should be ashes. Cover the floor of the fireplace thickly with white glue and immediately add a layer of cigarette ash; then place a long-handled skillet-spider or a covered Dutch oven among the ashes, in front of the logs. Other cooking utensils may be hung on the sides of the chimney breast, and a long rifle should be supported on pegs above the wooden mantel shelf.

The other furnishings of this single ground-floor room would have been extremely simple and functional: a trestle table, flanked by backless benches, before the fire; a dresser on whose open shelves a few pewter or delft plates were displayed; an armoire for clothing and a chest for storing linens; a low-post bed with a trundle bed beneath it; one or two joint stools, and a Windsor chair for the master of the house. The inevitable cradle on one side of the fireplace would have been balanced on the other side by a flax wheel, on which any member of the family not otherwise engaged was expected to spin linen thread. (All these early-American pieces are currently being reproduced in miniature, and are pictured in various catalogues.) A pierced tin candle lantern and wooden candlesticks would have served as lighting fixtures, and there should be a braided rag rug on the floor.

Cement two rectangular purse mirrors, horizontally, to the back wall of the room for windows, gluing on small square-patterned sash strips cut from a plastic berry box to imitate the little leaded windowpanes of the colonial period. One handwoven placemat, of the sort that repeats a traditional weaving pattern in reduced scale, will supply short curtains for these windows plus a spread for the low-post bed. Upstairs, no windows will be required; the eave ends beneath the sharply slanted roof would have been left open for light and ventilation.

The chief feature of the weaving loft must be a large cloth loom, but looms scaled one inch to one foot are not commercially available. After examining a full-size antique loom, it is possible to copy it in miniature with balsa wood, but one must have photographs to follow. The framework of the loom is not hard to imitate, but it is exceedingly difficult to make a working model that actually weaves. The warp threads must stretch from front to back of the frame, with their ends tightly wound on wooden rollers; these taut threads must pass through cord loops suspended from a high, movable bar stretched across the middle of the loom from side to side; the loops must be attached in such a way that when the bar is turned, alternate loops are raised and pull up with them alternating warp threads. The weft thread must be wound on a shuttle that is passed from one side to the other, between the row of raised threads and the level warp. For a traveling display, such a stupendous undertaking is unnecessary. So long as the loom *looks* as if its heddle lifted alternate warp threads to admit the passage of the shuttle, all will be well. Place before the inoperable loom a model of the high backless bench on which a colonial weaver perched, making it of balsa.

The tall "walking wheel," which was used for spinning carded wool into thread, can be simulated with a base and wheel hub of balsa and round wooden toothpicks for wheel spokes. For the rim of the wheel, soak a ¼" strip of thin balsa in warm water for five minutes, and bend it into a circle; butt the ends of the strip together, and hold them in position with a block of balsa cemented across this join on the inner surface of the rim. A spoked reel, which was used to measure spun thread, is among the early-American miniatures often found in museum shops and offered in better catalogues; from the same sources, an adjustable weaver's double candlestand may be obtained. Dye pots should be grouped in a corner of the loft, and masses of dyed wool (actually tufts of absorbent cotton tinted with vegetable food coloring) should hang from open balsa rafters. Shelves along one wall should hold tiny bolts of cloth—indisputable proof of the weaver's skill.

All the furnishings of this movable house must be firmly attached with generous dots of white glue, to prevent damage in transit. When the display is complete, a sheet of lightweight, transparent Plexiglas can be permanently installed with narrow molding strips, to cover the open front side, and the Weaver's House will be ready to begin its travels.

As an interesting contrast to colonial textile manufacture, one might make a simpler display of Indian weaving. Small-scale upright looms that hold half-finished Navaho blankets, and have squaw weavers seated before them, are sold in souvenir shops throughout the Southwest. Such a miniature is attractive in its own right, but it will be even more interesting and instructive in a proper setting. First, cement the loom and weaver in the center of a rectangle of plywood that has been covered with pale beige sandpaper, and then build over the loom a "ramada" made of slender bark-covered sticks. This primitive shelter should consist of a pole roof supported at the corners on long posts. As though you were making a miniature raft, put an uneven number of sticks together, side by side, with brown twine looped over and under each pole near its ends. Use epoxy cement to attach the upright corner posts to the sandpaper-covered base, and to secure the roof to the tops of the posts. Suspend a clay water olla from the roof; wrap an Indian papoose to a narrow back board with strips of cloth, and prop the board against a ramada post; add a clay bowl of cardboard tortillas, and a basket holding balls of colored wool thread. Finally, cement two or three miniature artificial cacti near the edge of the sandy base, to identify this as a southwestern desert scene.

In Colleen Moore's enchanted palace, the world's best-loved fairy tales are illustrated in various ways. Murals tell the stories of Cinderella, Rip van Winkle, the Pied Piper, Puss in Boots, and the Three Little Pigs; bas-reliefs depict characters from *Gulliver's Travels* and the *Wizard of Oz;* etched glass windows show Jack and the Beanstalk and Prince Charming; medallions portray *Aesop's Fables;* and tapestries commemorate the *Idylls of the King.*

These and other children's favorites are retold year after year at library "Story Hours," and a miniaturist might render a real service to the public library system by constructing a portable scene that would serve as a three-dimensional illustration for a children's classic. At the risk of seeming to disparage Miss Moore's glistening nine-foot-square aluminum castle, it must be frankly said that the best possible showcase for an illustrative scene is an ordinary oblong metal breadbox. The brightly colored box is lightweight, and of manageable size; its magnetized door completely hides the scene inside until the exciting climax of the story has arrived.

With a diminutive plastic castle for its center of interest, the portable diorama could illustrate more than one fairy tale, plus many historic incidents. As a challenge to its designer and a delight to its beholders, the scene might be extended outward from the hollow box onto the lid of the fold-down door. This can be done by attaching tiny buildings, trees, equipages, and persons (with epoxy cement) to the green-painted inside of the door in such a way that they do not touch the walls of the enclosed castle when the box is shut. Let a drawbridge span the gap that appears between the inner floor and the edge of the door when the box is opened, and hide the magnet near the door's outer edge with a knoll made of cork or styrofoam. If a tiny magnet is cemented inside a hollow in its base, the knoll will remain in place even though the door is sharply slanted.

Sometimes it is possible to combine community service with social comment, in portable scenes that capture the flavor of present times. (1) For the waiting room outside the admitting office of a children's hospital, one might make a miniature kindergarten playground, with which an apprehensive mother could distract and amuse a frightened child. (2) For the conference room of the local planning commission, or the office of a neighborhood improvement association, prepare a model of a mid-city pocket-park. (3) For the reception room of a college art department, or the studio-classroom of a museum, construct a miniature sidewalk art show. (4) For the entrance lobby of a large flower show, or the headquarters of an environmental protection agency, nothing could be more appropriate than a card-table-size conservation exhibit.

(1) A rectangular wood-framed bulletin board, from a variety store, will be a lightweight yet sturdy base for the children's playground. Fence the bulletin board, just inside its frame, with 5″ wide strips of plastic window screening stapled to dowel posts, or build a high board fence of vertically cemented wooden tongue depressors. For access to the play yard, cut a bright red or green gate from the bottom of a plastic tomato carton.

In one corner of the fenced area, use epoxy cement to plant a shade tree with a thick brown artificial geranium stem for a trunk, and the smallest of green plastic foliage. Cover most of the yard with green terry-cloth grass by spreading white glue evenly on the bulletin board and pressing the cloth down firmly on it, but leave a narrow walkway from the gate to a slatted garden bench sheltered by a large beach umbrella. The light tan color and semi-smooth texture of the bulletin board's surface will perfectly resemble a playground path.

Large toy stores usually stock small-scale playground equipment imported from Germany. The well-made wooden miniatures include A-frame swings, seesaws, slides, and carousels as well as coaster wagons and tricycles. Any or all of these would be splendid additions to the bulletin-board scene, but the larger pieces are quite expensive. In the light of the new emphasis on imaginative play, you might prefer to design your own free-form equipment—crawl-through tunnels, curving slides, styrofoam blocks of all shapes and sizes for building forts and mountains—and make it yourself. Whatever else it contains, the yard should have a sandbox for the romper set. Any square shallow box made of wood, metal or plastic can be turned into a sandbox with a camouflaging coat of paint, but real sand is so coarse that it would be out of scale. Substitute baking soda or powdered borax as a filling for the sandbox.

This playground scene will come to life the moment doll children are added to it. Choose little boy and girl dolls with flexible arms and legs, and arrange them in natural positions on the slide, the swing, the seesaw. Place a seated romper-clad baby in the sandbox, along with a miniature shovel and pail. Since so many of today's young mothers work outside the home, the care of small children often devolves upon middle-aged mother substitutes. For this reason, the play supervisor seated on the slatted bench might be a "grandmotherly" doll with gray hair and glasses.

(2) In many cities, once prosperous neighborhood business districts have sunk into untidy poverty as rent receipts and property values have declined. If one small building burns, or is condemned as unsafe and torn down, it usually is not replaced, and so a block of shops is left with a gap like a missing tooth. This is the very sort of inner-city area in which elderly residents outnumber the young, and public parks are nonexistent. Urban planners have found that a rubble-covered vacant lot can be transformed into a much needed mini-park for senior citizens, at minimal expense, and any miniaturist interested in garden design will be intrigued by the idea of making a model pocket-park.

Begin with a piece of plywood that follows the dimensions of an actual lot in a scale of one-half inch to one foot. This means that a lot with a 30' frontage and a depth of 50' would be represented by a model 15" wide and 25" deep. Cardboard boxes, painted brick-red, can be used to indicate the buildings that flank the vacant lot, but for ease of carrying, these should not be attached to the plywood.

First screen the back of the lot from the alley behind it, with a high fence made of wooden tongue depressors or of corrugated aluminum lawn edging; soften the bare look of the fence with a network of green-wire vines. Lay walkways with squares of coarse sandpaper, and use epoxy cement to plant two or three spindly trees and a few evergreen shrubs. Maintenance is always a problem in public parks, so instead of masking the remaining area with terry-cloth grass, mulch it with pebbles and confine the flowers in raised planters. Mustard seed from the spice shelf or bird gravel from a pet shop, pressed evenly over a coating of white glue, will be in interesting textural contrast to the sandpaper paths, and unpainted clay flowerpot saucers will make fine planters. Choose shallow saucers no more than 3" in diameter, and fill them with wallpaper cleaner to support tight masses of very tiny varicolored flowers. Give the area a center of interest in the form of a diminutive piece of sculpture, or a birdbath complete with cake-charm doves standing in for a park's ever-present pigeons. Add a street light for safety and a bench or two for comfort—look for the lamp and the benches among the model-railroad accessories in a hobby shop—and then people the park with small stooped, elderly dolls.

(3) Today, Americans of all ages are engrossed in art. Inspired by the example of such admirable amateurs as Dwight D. Eisenhower and Winston Churchill, world-worried mature citizens have taken up painting as a distraction and a hobby; in reaction against all forms of materialism, the younger generation has turned to op art as to an anodyne. All over the country painting classes abound, and art shows are the order of the day.

Fashions in art are constantly changing, almost as rapidly as clothing styles and slang phrases come and go. In a miniature sidewalk art show, it is possible to capture an evanescent art fad and preserve it—like a fly in amber—for posterity. As a side effect, the costumes worn by miniature artists and prospective purchasers will provide an interesting fashion commentary, and tongue-in-cheek touches can recall to mind the catchwords that were all too often heard.

As a setting for such a show, use a long and rather narrow strip of plywood for the sidewalk, and nail at right angles to it a slightly wider plywood piece of equal length to represent the wall of a building on which pictures will be hung. Cover the sidewalk with squares of sandpaper, for the look of cement, and paint the side of the building to resemble brick or stucco.

On this wall, art works might be grouped by categories: copies of famous paintings; original oils, water colors, and drawings; framed prints; and posters. An artist would undoubtedly enjoy making some or all of these drawings and paintings, but an untalented miniaturist will have no difficulty in obtaining them. Miniature oil paintings are sold in most art shops and department stores; many of the world's masterpieces are reproduced in color on the backs of playing cards, or on postcards sold in museum shops; museum booklets are illustrated with small-scale color photographs of abstract oils and water colors; publishers' catalogues are filled with tiny drawings, prints, and posters—some in color, but more in black and white. Gilded metal snapshot frames, from a variety store, will serve for the traditional works of art, while plain frames of balsa rubbed with white or gray paint will better suit the abstract pieces. A drawing or print attached with library paste to a cardboard backing can be matted with colored craft paper from the stationery counter of the dime store.

On the sidewalk, a prize-winning original painting might be shown with its blue ribbon, on an easel. Statuary in the prevailing artistic mood should be prominently displayed, and there should be felt-covered tables crowded with small art objects and "miniature" paintings. (Mini-miniature color prints, cut from catalogues, can be sized and shaped to fit frames made of gold buttons with raised rims.) A show official should be seated, with the cashbox, at a table near one end of the walkway. Painters and sculptors should stand ready to explain their works to the art lovers who are inspecting the exhibits.

If the present moment seems artistically uninteresting, look to the past and select a vintage year like 1969, which was hailed in song as "the beginning of the Age of Aquarius." Men were wearing saucer-sized pendants on long chains with their Nehru jackets; afro hairdos were "very big," and bushy beards were vying for attention with drooping Fu Manchu mustaches. Girls in micro-miniskirts and knee-high boots had waist-length, ruler-straight hair. Population control was the burning issue of the day, and Ivy League colleges were offering courses in black studies. By popular demand, newspapers were printing daily astrological forecasts. Andrew Wyeth's name was at the top of the list of contemporary painters, but Andy Warhol's preposterous posters were selling like mad in mod boutiques. The "beautiful people" had discovered pre-Columbian Art.

(4) Conservation is a word often used but seldom defined by the organizations that are sworn to preserve, protect, and defend the nation's natural resources. As

acrimonious verbal battles rage over fossil versus atomic fuels, scenic rivers versus flood control, or destructive pests versus dangerous pesticides, it is important to understand just what it is that we are all so determined not to lose. As an affirmation of involvement, a miniaturist might devise a visible definition of conservation—an idyllic scene that shows how land and water, animals and plants, should be harmlessly enjoyed in recreation areas.

To provide for water in such a scene, one could use as the foundation for the whole display a mirror cut to fit the top of a card table. This large mirror would be heavy and awkward to carry in horizontal position, so the land masses of the miniature scene should be made separately on shaped pieces of very stiff cor-

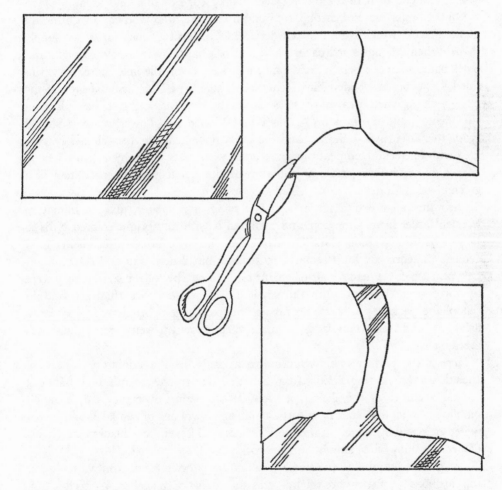

rugated cardboard. In showing a wooded area where a small creek flows into a large lake, begin with a square of cardboard 4" smaller than the mirror. Draw the indented outline of a lake shore on one side of the cardboard, and cut along this outline with tin snips. Decide at what point on the shoreline the stream should enter, and mark the place. Then cut the cardboard, beginning at the marked spot, into two pieces, and separate the pieces so that their straight outer edges and sharp upper corners are fitted over the edges and corners of the mirror. A strip of mirror, representing the creek, will now be exposed between the divided sections of the cardboard.

For level land, cover the smaller piece of cardboard with terry-cloth grass, and place a weeping willow tree with pendant, pale green branches where it will be reflected in the water. Add low flowering shrubs and short-stemmed flowers growing between outcropping rocks. Build a small balsa bridge to span the brook and attach one end of it to the inner (creek bank) edge of this land area.

On the larger piece of cardboard, build up a contoured landscape with instant papier-mâché, which is sold in powder form (with directions) at artists' supply shops. When the moistened paper has dried rock-hard, cover the sloping lake and creek banks with terry-cloth grass, and moor a canoe on the lake shore. An open-sided, slant-roofed wooden bird feeder will make a perfect picnic shelter at the edge of the wooded area that should crown the rise. Inside the shelter, place on the picnic table a miniature camera and binoculars. Towering trees should shade this little rustic building, and the forest floor beneath them should be covered with fine-crumbled peat moss instead of with grass. Evergreen shrubs belong here, along with ferns made of miniature fronds cut from the center stem of a green plastic fern leaf.

Near the full-size bird feeder that is serving as a shelter, place a miniature wooden feeder from a toyshop, and surround it with tiny bright colored birds to be viewed through binoculars. On a tree branch that overhangs the shelter roof, cement an acorn cup for a remarkably realistic birds' nest, and add three minuscule pearl eggs. Cement a pair of parent birds to nearby foliage so that they seem to hover over the nest. Buy the smallest size white doves that are sold in cellophane packages as wedding favors and paint them bright red (for cardinals), or bright blue (for jays), to make them show up well against their leaf-green background.

Here is the perfect habitat for native animals from a miniature collection. Include a fawn peering timidly from behind a tree trunk, a skunk high-tailing it around a corner of the shelter, a squirrel scampering over the roof, a rabbit nibbling at a tender blossom, a turtle climbing slowly out of the lake, and a frog poised on a water-lily pad in the creek. There could even be a blacksnake (made of a coil of shiny wire) sunning upon a rock.

For perfect portability, the small flora and fauna must be as firmly attached to the cardboard "land" as are the tall trees and the wooden shelter. When it is time to exhibit the conservation scene, the folded card table, the shining mirror, and the two landscapes will travel safely in the back of a station wagon.

Any permanent portable scene should have a protective covering that is light in weight and, of course, transparent. Cutting and cementing Plexiglas is hardly a project for the home hobbyist, so select a company listed under "Plastics: Retail" in the Yellow Pages, and order a bottomless, frameless case that will fit comfortably over the scene and be supported by the model's own base. The clear, rigid top and sides of the case will be cemented to each other with plastic in liquid form, which will harden to seal the joints in an invisible bond.

Using miniatures as attention getters is an accepted gimmick of commercial advertising. A model of a cruise ship in the window could almost be called the trademark of travel agencies, and the tourists expect to see scale models of the company's latest jets in every airline ticket office. Model houses are sure to be present in the reception rooms of real estate developers, and no one is surprised to find a model of a new suburban branch on view in the lobby of a downtown bank.

Following the precedent thus set by advertising professionals, a miniaturist may assist a civic organization in its fund-raising campaign, help to publicize a coming event, or keep before the public a continuing civic project. A miniature scene made for publicity purposes has various useful possibilities. Its photograph could illustrate a newspaper feature story. It might be a conversation piece on a local television station's talk show, with the camera moving in to show each detail as it is described. Alternatively, a "close-up still" of the model could be used in spot announcements donated by the TV station as a public service. A large bank or a major office building might permit the model to be exhibited in its lobby, but the best possible location for it would be the window of a department store. Displaying a miniature scene in a large store window has the effect of a whisper in a crowded room. People come close to find out what is going on.

For this sort of short-term advertising, miniatures borrowed from their permanent settings can be given temporary mobile homes, and protective plastic cases usually will not be required. Collapsible cardboard theaters, already fitted with footlights, can be found in (or ordered through) department stores whose toy departments feature marionettes and puppets. The smallest size marionette theater would be the best of backgrounds for a scene from a forthcoming community theater production. For an indoor set, decorate the stage as though it were a miniature room. For an outdoor setting, follow the same techniques used in making a garden on a bookcase shelf.

To publicize the membership drive of a local museum, a rectangular cardboard apple box (begged from the manager of a supermarket) might be metamorphosed into a miniature art gallery. Paint the outside of the box and its inside ceiling white; then tape a night light on a long extension cord above the slit in the box top, and hide the light beneath a small box disguised as a chimney. Floor the gallery with sheets of adhesive-backed wall tiles, and cover the walls with marbleized black self-stick plastic. Title this marbled hall "The Culture of the Yellow Race," and fill it with a collection of miniatures from the Far East: blue-

and-white porcelain beads doubling as tall Ming vases; a small costumed Japanese doll in its original glass box; embroidered wall hangings cut from an eyeglasses case; tiny brush paintings culled from place cards or bridge tallies; ivory or porcelain statuettes displayed on black-painted box bases. Museum-type showcases can be made for the gallery from the sort of transparent plastic boxes in which men's black bow ties are sold. Invert the shallow lid of such a narrow oblong box, and mount it on four black-painted golf tees, which will look like tapered legs. Line this lid with black felt or velveteen, and arrange thereon a few "priceless" treasures: hand-painted oriental bowls and vases, a jade Buddha from a charm bracelet, a graduated group of ivory elephants, several miniature Japanese fans opened to show their microscopic designs. Touch the rim of the box with plastic cement, turn it upside down, and fit it into its top to form a "glass case" over the valuables.

A longer, shallower cardboard carton can be turned into a tile-floored, marble-walled hall of statuary for displaying small-scale models of such masterpieces as the "Pieta," the "Discus Thrower," and the "Venus de Milo." Very tall cake-separator columns spaced at intervals along the rear wall will add architectural interest to this long, narrow hall, and large masterpiece paintings could be hung between the columns. As a final touch of elegance, add a colorful flower arrangement in a towering Renaissance-style container.

The best advertisement for a garden club's outdoor plant sale would be a model of the sale itself, made on a bulletin board or in a large trunk tray. It is great fun to reproduce in miniature all the horticultural delights—the potted house plants and perennials, flats of annual seedlings, balled and burlapped evergreens, hanging baskets, cut flowers, and dried-flower arrangements—of the show. Birdbaths, fountains, and garden ornaments of all sizes probably would be on sale, and there might be a display of framed bird and flower prints. Inevitably, there must be a white elephant table!

Often, at a plant sale, the wares of each committee are temptingly arranged beneath a brightly colored tent, a gaily striped awning, or a huge, flowered beach umbrella. Such a compartmentalized sale bears a strong resemblance to the street fairs that were prevalent in Europe during the eighteenth and nineteenth centuries. A hundred years ago, miniature fairs were very popular. A typical street scene consisted of a row of colorful booths built along one side of a wooden plank that had been grooved and painted to resemble paving stones. Each booth offered a different attraction: cakes and confections; ribbons and notions; baskets; pots and pans; or toys. A balloon man often had taken his stand at one end of the row, and a scissors grinder might have set up his whetstone wheel at the other. A muffin man, carrying sweetcakes and buns on a tray, could usually be seen among the strolling customers.

Essentially, a model street fair was a series of shops made individually and put together to create a more impressive display. The juxtaposition was something new, but single shops had been around for a long time. A good many eighteenth-century commercial establishments have survived in miniature to become museum pieces and to provide an insight into the business practices of their day.

At the Metropolitan Museum of Art in New York City, it is possible to purchase a model of a colonial silversmith's shop, complete in a lighted wooden case. Samples of the smith's artistry are displayed on shelves, and are seen through the many-paned glass show window. The same silver miniatures are sold separately, so that a customer need buy only the inkstand, the gravy boat, or the Chippendale tray required to complete a collection. This lighted shop shell would be a splendid showcase for any specialized collection of antique miniatures. Instead of with silver, its shelves might be stocked with a variety of pewter plates and serving dishes, with early-American articles of brass, copper, and tin, or with oriental porcelain tea sets, figurines, and vases.

As the antithesis of this elegantly simple colonial shop, it would be amusing to construct a cluttered country store of the late nineteenth century in a shallow wooden packing box with a framed and hinged glass front. Open shelves should cover the rear wall, behind a long boxed counter made of balsa. Here all the little unrelated antique oddments from a miniature collection could be displayed to advantage. If they fail to fill the shelves, the store's stock can be augmented with "antique reproductions" now being made in Hong Kong and Japan for sale in American toyshops. These inexpensive scale copies of old-fashioned household effects run to kerosene lamps, bowl and pitcher sets, coffee grinders, washboards, churns, and sadirons. The copies of antique store fixtures that are available in a few specialized catalogues include pot-bellied stoves; barrels, kegs, and crates; droll posters advertising long-vanished nostrums; and for the counter top, wrapping-paper dispensers and balance scales. It is even possible to order a country postoffice—with a letter slot, and numbered mailboxes surrounding a grilled window—to be placed at one end of the long counter.

Another reminder of bygone days is the miniature roll-top desk now being made, surprisingly enough, in Spain. This desk might serve as the focal point for a turn-of-the-century doctor's or lawyer's office. An attorney's office can appropriately be contained in the sort of old-fashioned metal breadbox that has a slanting top, and looks like a little house. (You probably will find this outmoded kitchen convenience among the junk in a dark corner of a secondhand store.) A law office often occupied all of a small building at the corner of a residential lot or on a village street, so paint the outside of the breadbox to resemble a yellow-frame or red-brick cottage with a green roof.

Even in those days, a lawyer's library would have been rather extensive; his office also would have boasted wooden filing cabinets and a large iron safe for storing deeds, wills, and documents. Miniature reproductions of old-fashioned office safes, complete with combination locks, are now sold as coin banks, but filing cases must be contrived by stacking little wooden matchboxes; pulls for the file drawers can be made of double-pointed tacks. Provided he was sufficiently busy and prosperous to require the services of a clerk, a tall writing desk and a high stool would have stood opposite the attorney's own roll top. There would have been one or two straight-backed wooden chairs for clients, an octagonal eight-day clock, a large wall calendar, and a spittoon beside the shaker stove. A high silk hat on the wooden hat rack would have been the badge of his learned profession.

An oblong wooden box will provide better housing for the doctor's office, which would have consisted of a waiting room and an examining room. Divide the box with a plywood partition. Paper the waiting room in a nondescript brown, and furnish it with a hat rack, an umbrella stand, a parlor stove, and several rocking chairs grouped around a center table holding a stereopticon and a pile of slides. Over the table, suspend a kerosene hanging lamp. In addition to the roll-top desk at which he wrote his prescriptions, the physician probably would have furnished his gray-painted inner office with a glass instrument cabinet, a leather couch, a straight chair for the patient with a revolving stool for the doctor beside it, a medicine cabinet, and an examining table concealed behind a screen in one corner. A row of heavy textbooks on top of the desk would have constituted his entire medical library, and his "little black bag" would have held his traveling pharmacy.

The Swiss toy firm of Franz Carl Weber still makes and sells a type of folding shop that has been in constant demand since its introduction during the late eighteenth century. When closed and latched, the shop looks like a square block of wood with convenient handles for carrying; when the cube is opened, it reveals two walls of compartmented shelves, a generous amount of floor space, and a large counter. Its remarkable adaptability has justified the continuing production of this toy. In its earliest days, it often was a milliner's establishment or an apothecary's shop. During the long Biedermeier period, its shelves seemed equally right for bolts of cloth and ribbon, hand-painted china plates and vases, or the brown loaves and iced cakes of a bakery. Today, in the Zurich toy store, this same shop is called a mini-market. Canned goods and packaged soap flakes, fresh vegetables and fruits, milk, meat, poultry, and eggs are sold separately to stock its shelves.

As a gently ironic commentary on its history, it would be amusing to turn this folding case into a toyshop filled with playthings old and new. One tier of shelves could be devoted to the things that interest little boys: balls, blocks, boats, cars, planes, soldiers, horns, drums, a bicycle, and a rocking horse with flowing mane and tail. On the opposite side of the shop, the toys for girls would certainly include dolls of all sizes, in old-fashioned and contemporary dress, dollhouses and furniture, a toy stove, a tiny piano, and a phonograph with records. On the large counter top, a model railroad might be assembled, with tracks running through tunnels and alongside stations, and some of the floor space could be given over to pedal cars and coaster wagons. It may be necessary to add a third set of shelves—a wooden drawer divider intended for silverware—to hold stuffed animals and sports equipment.

Footballs, bowling pins, baseball bats and gloves, tennis or badminton rackets, golf clubs, ice skates, and boxing gloves all are sold in cellophane packets as children's party favors, and many other tiny toys can be culled from a large package of mixed favors bought at a party shop. Actually, since children's playthings come in all sizes, any miniature too small for use in a scene scaled one inch to one foot could be considered a candidate for the toyshop.

The dime-bank cash register should be presided over by a sales clerk, and there must of course be customers: a mother making a purchase; a small boy trying out the rocking horse; a little girl standing entranced before a dollhouse.

An identifying characteristic of miniaturists is their unwillingness to throw *any* little thing away. Therefore, if you already have made several miniature rooms and scenes, you undoubtedly are harboring a shoe box crammed with leftover miniature accessories. In order to obtain the statuette of Bob Cratchett holding Tiny Tim that was absolutely irresistible for a Victorian library, you had to buy a set of six brass pipe tampers shaped like Dickens characters. Five pipe tampers were packed away for future reference. Needing a pair of armored knights on horseback for lamp bases or bookends, you decimated an army of tiny plastic crusaders; the remaining medieval figurines joined the pipe tampers in storage. In a corner of the same box, opened packets of party-favor miniatures contain more plastic fruits, wineglasses, birds, and trophy cups than they have contributed to prior undertakings. A paper bag labeled with the name of a hobby shop holds a handful of wooden beads, a few shells, and some bits of dyed coral; a larger bag contains the remnants of a bunch of Peruvian starflowers. Here is the nucleus of a delightfully different contemporary shop called, "The Unique Boutique."

In the garden center at a discount store, seek out the largest size bird feeding stations. One of these is sure to look like a little wooden house, with glass walls and a slanted roof crowned by a weather vane; the feeder will be centered on a sturdy tray with a raised rim. You will immediately recognize this as a prefabricated portable shop. A small light bulb anchored to the underneath side of its removable roof will illuminate the interior of the glass-sided building, but the source of light will be concealed by the down-slanting roof.

Showcases for its tempting miniature merchandise will be found in a hardware department: shallow, see-through plastic boxes, divided into graduated compartments to hold nails and screws of various sizes. A smaller version of this clear plastic box, with oblong or square divisions for thread spools or bobbins, is sold at sewing centers. Remove the lid of a nail box, and then paint the bottom of the box black. After cementing an item of appropriate size inside each compartment, glue the set of shelves behind the glass at one end of the feeder, facing outward, so that the merchandise is seen from the outside as through a show window. Paint the bottom of a second lidless box, fill its shelves, and cement it behind the first shelf section, back-to-back, so that its tiny treasures face the inside of the feeder. Repeat this process, using two more divided boxes, at the other end of the feeder. Cover the wooden floor between these double-sided sets of shelves with red shag carpeting made of a terry-cloth hand towel, and stand a bobbin box on end in the middle of the rug to hold the tiniest bijoux. Pave the feeding tray outside the shop with little oblong tiles, coating them with dark red nail polish for the appearance of glazed bricks. Decorate each side of the bricked terrace with a piece of modern metal sculpture, and suspend a hanging basket filled with ferns from a cuphook on the front of the shop.

As an exercise in ingenuity, try to stock the shelves with as many different boutique items as possible: découpaged wastebaskets made of plastic pill vials; lipstick-case umbrella stands; cuff-link bookends; pill boxes masquerading as make-up boxes; Danish modern candleholders made of wooden beads; bracelet charms and party favors converted into desk or book-shelf ornaments; bead vases; pictures framed in buttons with raised rims; arrangements of artificial fruits; artificial flowers by the bunch, wrapped in green waxed paper. As you work, ideas will come so thick and fast that there may not be room for all your clever inspirations.

While full-size boutiques have been luring customers with luxury items, the purveyors of beauty products have certainly not been idle. Even in a business accustomed to instant fads, the sudden, overwhelming popularity of wigs could be accounted a phenomenon.

Meanwhile, the rewriters of history were presenting American Indians as a much-abused, heroic minority. Indian headbands, beadwork, fringed leather, and brightly colored designs were adopted as high fashion by the counterculture. To any punster, here is an obvious connotation that could be turned to good account as a droll footnote to social history.

The Wigwam. What other name would suit a miniature wig shop half so well? The scene could be made in a heavy cardboard box about 16″ square. Gift-wrap paper in Indian design, coated with hairspray after it is pasted in place, will simulate an inlaid vinyl floor. Bright yellow walls, contrasting with bright blue draperies, can be ornamented with Indian beadwork appliques bought at a hobby shop. A set of beauty-parlor fixtures, from the toy counter of a variety store, can be enlivened with imaginative touches. An Indian scout (part of a dime-store cowboy-and-Indian set) might support the hood of the hair dryer on his grounded rifle; a smaller plastic Indian brave, with knife in hand, could hold a long blond "fall" as though it were a scalp; an Indian canoe could be filled with sale-priced braids and buns. Wigs for display on shelves at the back of the shop can be purchased from a doll hospital and fitted over glass wig stands made by inverting small round grape molds, with slender flaring necks, that are sold at hobby shops for casting fruits in plastic. There is, however, a better and cheaper way of obtaining wigs complete with stands. Unlike the perfectly proportioned residents of German dollhouses, most little American-made dolls look deformed because their heads are too big. Usually their hollow heads are molded separately, and fitted over the knobby necks of solid-plastic bodies. When, as in the case of the "Sidewalk Art Fair," a miniature scene calls for lifelike dolls attired in the fashion of the moment, it sometimes is necessary to remove the overlarge heads from well-dressed dolls and replace them with proportionately correct heads taken from dolls with smaller bodies. The disembodied oversize heads left over after this exchange are ideal mannikin heads with pert noses and long eyelashes, wearing high-style wigs.

An aquarium and a bird cage will provide peculiarly appropriate housing for the type of pet shop that maintains a petting zoo for children as an added attraction. Now is the time to bring forth all your animal miniatures, of whatever species, because to be effective, the pet shop-plus-zoo must have a large number of inhabitants.

If one long side of a two-gallon aquarium is given a coat of paint or a coating of self-stick plastic, the glass tank at once becomes a shop with three glass walls. Cover the open top of the tank with the colorful plastic roof of a rectangular bird cage, first taping a small bulb on a long cord beneath the rooftree to light the shop interior. When little cardboard trinket boxes with clear-plastic tops are stacked against the painted rear wall of the pet shop, they will look like cages with glass doors. Cover the floor of each box cage with kitty litter, and fill the cages with pedigreed dogs of several breeds, each in a separate compartment; an assortment of mongrel puppies; a mother cat with kittens; and a family of white rabbits. Bird cages on stands and glass aquariums complete with goldfish are among the imported miniatures found in toyshops, and a shallow clear-plastic box can be covered with wire screening to make a cage for white mice. At a pet store, one can buy a plastic parakeet toy that is shaped like a tiny Ferris wheel; encased in a screen-wire enclosure, this makes a spendid squirrel gym.

The shallow tray of a large footlocker will be a ready-walled enclosure for the petting zoo; face both sides of the wall with rock-patterned adhesive plastic. Then unscrew the bottom of the bird cage, reverse it, and replace it to form a flat-topped roof for the inverted wire cage. Set this barred enclosure crosswise at one end of the tray and cover the tray floor beneath it with brown sandpaper. The bird cage could be treated as a tremendous aviary, with a branched stick cemented upright within it to represent a dead tree. Surround the cage with plastic screen wire, and let miniature birds of every size and kind perch on the tree limbs, cling to the inside of the screening, or preen themselves on the ground. Alternatively, the cage could be partitioned into two or three sections to hold a rocky bear den with a mother grizzly and her cubs, a shallow pool with alligators and large turtles for its denizens, or a tree full of monkeys.

Cover the remainder of the tray's floor with green terry-cloth grass. Place a mirror "pool" with a coping of large pebbles in the center of the zoo's grass plot, and plant a large shade tree in one corner. Add all sorts of harmless baby animals—a fawn, calf, colt, lamb, some piglets, a hen and chicks, a duck with her ducklings swimming in the mirror pond—and little boys and girls to play with them.

When the converted aquarium is placed end to end with the tray zoo, there will be room in front of the pet shop for a separate cardboard strip covered with sandpaper paving. This third segment of the total scene needs only one embellishment: a spotted pony tethered to a hitching post.

In Holland's miniature city of Madurodam, slow-moving motorboats trouble the placid canals. Like fast-flying shuttles on a giant loom, trains streak back and forth along the railroad tracks. Brightly colored buses, trucks, and cars turn the superhighway into a kaleidoscope of ever-changing patterns. On the tall Binnenhof tower, clockwork figures move to strike the hours, and (whenever a coin is inserted in the proper slot) uniformed musicians on the bandstand in the park strike up a tune. Stripped of all its wondrous mechanization, Madurodam would be only an enlarged version of the sort of scale models used by urban planners to study the problems of existing cities or to design the layout of proposed new towns.

Strolling through the streets of the model Dutch city, one sees only the exterior of the waist-high buildings on either side. The architecture of some of these shell structures—the Binnenhof, the university, the cathedral, the airport, or the railroad station—makes them readily recognizable, while the modern office buildings and factories have identifying signs. The ground-floor shops in tall canal-side houses are distinguished one from another by characteristic merchandise in their windows; the bakery, with its coffeecakes and round rye loaves displayed on glass shelves, could never be mistaken for the butcher's shop with sausages festooned across its window.

Unquestionably it is easier to decorate one window of a small-scale shop than to reproduce its entire interior, and one look at Madurodam's typically Dutch shop facades is apt to inspire a traveling miniaturist to attempt a row of modern American store fronts. Following the format of a nineteenth-century street fair, make the fore part of each store in a separate shallow box, standing on edge. (Ask at the supermarket or at a wholesale grocery, for the thin oblong wooden boxes in which grapes are shipped.)

Plan and construct the show-window display for each store before closing the box front with a pane of thin glass or rigid plastic; then cement balsa doors and a siding of stone, brick, or shingles to the outside of this glass. "Redwood" shingles can be made of very thin 1"-wide strips of balsa by cutting ¾" slashes along one edge of each strip with scissors, and then staining the pale wood with oxblood

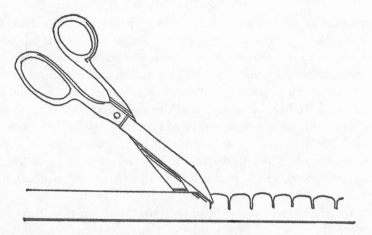

liquid shoe polish. When applying these shingles, begin at the bottom of the wall and overlap each row with the slashed strip cemented above it.

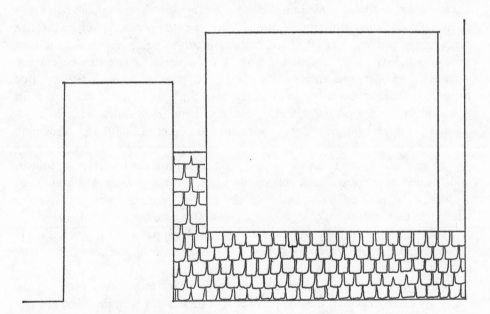

Every self-respecting suburban shopping center has its supermarket and its drugstore and may also possess a dress shop, a bookstore, and a bakery. The inside of each shallow box can be painted or covered with solid-color contact plastic to provide a bright background for the merchandise in its window. The sidewalk-to-roofline plate-glass windows of the grocery store should be plastered with signs advertising the specials of the week, cut from small newspaper ads. Behind the glass, there could be slanted bins holding fresh fruits and vegetables, plus balanced pyramids of canned goods and stacks of packaged soap flakes. All these items are sold in large toyshops, as dollhouse accessories. Fill one window of the drugstore with a melange of any little articles you have on hand—toys, jewelry, candles, perfume bottles made of glass beads, and so on. Immediately behind the glass on the other side of the door, place an ice-cream-parlor table and two wire chairs. The table-and-chairs set is one of the old-fashioned miniature reproductions now being offered in catalogues. In addition to bright-jacketed sets of books, toyshops sell tiny magazines, newspapers, airmail envelopes, and playing cards as dollhouse miniatures. These belong in the bookstore window, along with bookends, cameras, posters, and framed prints. In the dress shop's window, a drapery of dark velveteen will form a most effective backdrop for the smallest size fashion dolls that make such perfect mannequins. Other costumes from their wardrobes may be draped over chairs at the sides of the display space, while the purses, shoes, and stockings that came packaged with these extra outfits might be tastefully disposed in the center of the floor, around a large flower arrangement in a tall vase.

Grandmother Stover's miniature baked goods are sold in cellophane packets at party and toyshops, and these delicately browned dinner rolls, sugared coffee rings, and glazed loaves of bread will make a mouth-watering display for the window of a bakery. Round, diamond-shaped, or crescent cookies can be cut out with punch-presses from sheets of fine beige sandpaper, and arranged on large rectangular baking sheets cut from heavy-duty aluminum foil. Metal caps from soft drink bottles are perfect miniature pie pans. Brush their fluted sides with aluminum paint, and fill their cavities with instant papier-mâché pastry, browning the top of each pie delicately with enamel. Cakes are even easier to make. Simply paint the screw-on metal caps of aspirin and soft drink bottles white or brown, and you will have created layer cakes with vanilla or chocolate icing! For a tiered wedding cake, stack snap-on plastic pill vial caps of graduated sizes, and ice the whole pyramid with swirls of white latex paint. Decorate the top of the cake with a few tiny white flowers, or with a "wedding bell" snipped from a plastic lily-of-the-valley, and display this *chef d'oeuvre* in the center of the window, on a lacy mat cut from the center of a small paper doily.

There is a type of plastic ice tray that produces ice fingers instead of square cubes. By cutting between the compartments of such a tray with tin snips, one obtains a number of oblong containers shaped exactly like miniature window boxes. Paint the outside of these window boxes green or white and fit into them blocks of green styrofoam to support masses of white sequin petunias or red star-sequin sultana. Then cement one or more boxes below each show window to add continuity to the row of shops.

When all the stores are finished, set them up in a row with their sides touching and measure the distance from one end of the block to the other. Then make a 3″-wide roof that is long enough to cover the top edges of all the boxes. This could be a strip of cardboard covered with balsa shingles, or a strip of asphalt roofing with shingles painted on its gray-black surface. For a gutter to finish the lower edge of this overhanging roof, split ¼″ plastic tubing in half, lengthwise, and

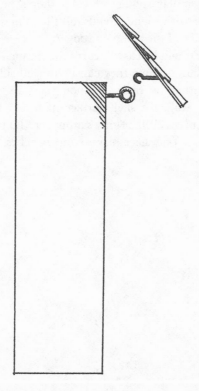

coat the outside of the little gutters with aluminum or copper paint. For ease of transportation, the strip of roof should be removable. Screw a small eyebolt into the upper edge of each box front, and screw a matching number of hooks along the back of the roof. It then becomes a simple matter to fit the hooks into the eyes and angle the roofline downward over the store fronts.

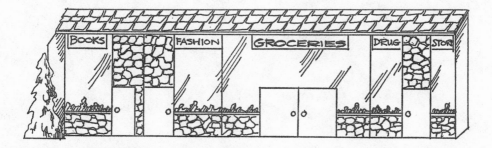

Large store-front signs could be spelled out with the gummed gold or silver letters that are sold in sheets at variety stores and party shops. Smaller signs, with white lettering on bright backgrounds, can quickly and easily be printed with a label maker, using tapes of various colors. Either type of self-stick lettering could be applied directly to the store fronts, but many shopping centers require all their stores to have signs of similar styling. If each shop's name is mounted on a wooden tongue depressor with rounded ends, all the miniature signboards can be cemented to the lower edge of the common roof.

The finished store fronts will be easy to carry to a branch library or a children's museum, where in less than no time they can be ranged side by side on an available shelf and tied together by their common roof. If the shallow shops are pushed back against the wall, the shelf surface in front of them can become a sidewalk covered with squares of light gray sandpaper. To turn the block of stores into a pedestrian mall, it is only necessary to add benches, planters, and a fountain to the sidewalk area.

IX

To Build a Mountain

For twentieth-century Americans who are harried by computers and hurried through life at an ever-accelerating pace, mountains have a powerful appeal. They represent solitude, untrammeled natural beauty, pure clear water, and clean invigorating air. We see eye to eye with the Renaissance artists who looked at small pyramids of precious stone and called them miniature mountains. Along with heightened concern for the future of our threatened planet has come a deepening awareness of its past. Ecology and archeology have ceased to be mere course titles in a college catalogue, and modern man's greatest technological achievement—the first exploration of the moon—turned out to be the greatest geology field trip of all time!

The mountain ranges of the United States are rich in industrial ores: coal and iron, copper and zinc, sulphur and lead, as well as silver and gold. These same mountains have also yielded a geological treasure trove of quartz, and minerals in colorful crystalline formations—golden yellow, pale green, amethyst, orange, rose-pink, sky-blue, and diamond-clear.

During the administration of President John F. Kennedy, a unique official gift for visiting heads of state was designed by Tiffany jewelers of New York: a perfect specimen of translucent, jewel-toned mineral crystal tied with a rope woven of gold wires, to represent a small symbolic part of America the Beautiful. In the late nineteen-sixties, fine stores began to display miniature silver statuettes mounted on mineral-crystal bases that were an integral part of each composition. This new art form was perhaps inspired in part by the President's gifts, but it is strongly reminiscent of Vienna's historic collection of jewel mountains enhanced with gold or silver miniatures.

More recently, brightly enameled blossoms with golden leaves and stems have been given crystalline or lava bases to become expensive and *recherché* ornaments for desks or coffee tables, and these miniature flowers definitely have their roots in history. Hundreds of years before the birth of Christ, Egyptian artists were making tiny flowers of gold or enameled metal and using them in miniature architectural or landscape scenes—garden pavillions surrounded by blossoms and tiny birds, or fields of flowers and grasses with grazing animals.

For amateurs, this old/new idea of combining geological specimens with miniatures can be not only a craft but a creative endeavor, and one need not be a professional geologist (or even a weekend rock-hound) to acquire the needed materials. Rock shops in large cities and resort areas offer a fascinating array of surprisingly inexpensive novelties. For example, fluorite, which is common in southern Illinois, is usually murky violet in color; occasionally, however, it is clear hyacinth blue, pale green, or canary yellow. Illinois' sphalerite (zinc sulphide) is black and shiny as jet, and sometimes is encrusted with small white barite crystals that sparkle like snow. The Rocky Mountains harbor clear quartz that bristles with prism-shaped crystals, and sulphur in crystalline form that is clear golden yellow. Shiny, scaly mica also is found there, as are glittering "fool's gold" (iron pyrite) and black "peacock" copper ore that shimmers with red, blue, and purple flecks. Quite often these types of mineral crystals are unearthed in cone-shaped chunks that look like jagged mountain peaks, or in flat masses whose angular top surfaces resemble the waves of the ocean.

To ornament these basic shapes, silver bracelet charms have obvious advantages: They are available everywhere in a wide variety of styles and, being mass produced, they are not costly. The secret of success in combining them with geological specimens lies in choosing the right charm for the selected substance. For instance, a charm in the shape of a steepled church might be placed near the apex of a clear quartz spire to symbolize mankind's search for immortality through religion. A more worldly representation of man's aspiring would be a knight-on-horseback charm so positioned upon a pyramid of amethyst-colored fluorite that the horse's forefeet are reaching for the topmost crag. The title of this composition might be "Excelsior!" Quartz or crystal ornaments should be displayed where light will enhance their color and clarity—in a sunny window, beneath a table lamp, or in a lighted breakfront—and they make treasured gifts.

The best gifts always are those that reflect the tastes of their recipients. Place a skier charm on the steep slope of a paperweight-size chunk of snowy barite, and present the unusual desk accessory to the winter sports enthusiast on your Christmas list. On a flat specimen of blue or purple fluorite with upstanding sharp-edged crystals like the waves of the sea, use one or more of the many types of ship charms: rowboat, canoe, sailboat, motorboat, steamship, or galleon. Add a large lighthouse charm to complete a seascape for a weekend sailor's office.

Useful though they are, charms are not the only possible decorations for mineral crystals. Tiny travel souvenirs of gold plate, silver, crystal, or porcelain can be displayed effectively on geological specimens of appropriate texture and color. No matter what the miniature is made of, it can be attached to the mineral with epoxy cement, of the type sold in drugstores and variety stores; there are two tubes in the package, one of epoxy and one of hardener. Squeeze out a few drops of the epoxy in a paper cup, add an equal quantity of hardener, and mix the two gluelike substances quickly but thoroughly with a wooden matchstick. Use a flat wooden toothpick to apply the cement to the miniature, covering its base completely with a thin coat. Wait ten seconds, and set the miniature in place. If necessary, steady it with a fingertip for a minute or two until the cement begins to grip, and then leave the decorated specimen undisturbed for twenty-four hours to allow plenty of time for the epoxy to harden.

Most of the semi-precious stone mountains in European museums are mounted upon baroque stands made of gold, silver, or bronze, and in many cases these holders have raised ornamental designs. To twentieth-century eyes, such stands seem overly ornate and actually distract attention from the displays they support. Before selecting a base for a crystalline specimen be sure the specimen really needs to be mounted. If its bottom is smooth and flat, it will stand perfectly steady on a shelf or table top and will probably be better balanced and more impressive freestanding. Covering the bottom with self-stick felt will insure against scratches. If, on the other hand, the bottom of the piece is slanting, rough, or uneven, mount the crystalline mass upon a simple stand of appropriate material and design. One good possibility is a low plain silver compote, and a lone plated compote often can be found in secondhand stores or at garage sales. For a small but very rough specimen, a silver napkin ring from an antique shop may prove a better solution. Lay the ring flat and cover its upper edge with chalk; then settle the base of the specimen on the ring, moving it gently until it balances unsupported on the thin silver rim. Chalk marks on the bottom of the crystal will then show where epoxy cement should be applied. In the same manner, a wide metal bracelet can become a base. A glass ash tray of a color that matches or blends with the glassy crystal is another suggestion; use the ash tray right side up or upside down, whichever way the specimen best balances upon it. A clear glass slab paperweight (from an office-supply company) might be right for a mass of clear quartz, while a rectangular black marble paperweight would better suit jetlike sphalerite. The most important thing to remember is that a base must be heavy enough to support the weight—actually and visually—of the specimen.

Once again, epoxy cement is the adhesive to use for attaching the mineral crystals to bases of whatever material. Be sure to use enough cement to obtain a strong bond since the completed ornament probably will be lifted by the base. Apply a coat of epoxy to the base *and* to the specimen, and wait thirty seconds before joining the two. The weight of the crystal will hold it in place without bracing, but it is wise to leave the mounted specimen undisturbed for forty-eight hours before lifting it.

Mineral crystals are by no means the only geological specimens that can be combined with miniatures to make conversation pieces or gifts. It is interesting and challenging to create a display that represents a region or a particular city, and for this purpose ores and stones are splendid raw materials. To symbolize the Rocky Mountains, one might choose a chunk of iron pyrite filled with the glittering flecks that earned it the common name "fool's gold," topping a piece of the ore with gold-plated pick-and-shovel charms arranged as though they had been carelessly thrown down. To portray the southwestern desert, a piece of bright blue-green copper ore could be enhanced with a silver thunderbird charm or with an Indian-crafted turquoise bear.

In general, industrial areas can be characterized with rust-colored iron ore or with shiny steel-gray marcasite, but it is more difficult to pinpoint a specific city. For Pittsburgh, for example, one would need to top steely marcasite with a gold-plated metal triangle—part of a dangling earring from the dime store—and center the golden triangle with a silver skyscraper charm.

As a volcanic island famous for flowers, Hawaii would be very easy to typify. One might begin by cementing a rough piece of lava rock in the center of an unframed round mirror. From the costume-jewelry counter of a department or variety store, choose the smallest metal or enameled flowers. Remove them

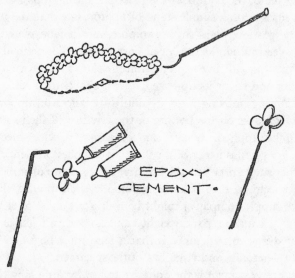

carefully from their setting, levering them up with a nutpick or a corsage pin; then use epoxy cement to attach each blossom to a short length of stiff brass wire (from a hardware store). The wire stems should vary in length, and some should be gently curved. Again with epoxy cement, attach the wire stem ends to the lava rock in a naturalistic clump. Take advantage of cracks or pockets in the lava's surface to provide sufficient depth of the cement to hold the bloom-tipped wires upright; if necessary, cement one wire at a time, bracing it overnight with small stones before adding another flower.

Coal—beautifully black and opalescent with surface oil—is the very essence of

Appalachia. With modern mining machinery it usually is cut in blocks too smooth and too precise to suggest the ruggedness of the area. It is, however, far more fragile than it looks. Drop a cube of coal on a paved driveway, and it will crack into two or more irregular chunks, many small slivers, and a circle of black dust. Choose the piece most interesting in shape, rinse off the dust, and rub the surface lightly with mineral oil to bring out its subtle colors. Then add the symbolism of the Great Smoky Mountains by cementing a tiny black bear to the mountain peak of coal.

The rough icicle-shaped stalactites and stalagmites that grow beneath the earth in limestone caverns make unusual and interesting displays. As a reminder of the cave from which it came, top a stalagmite with a tiny black bat from a set of Halloween cake charms, or cement to it miniature spelunker's equipment: a silver candle-lantern charm and a coil of lightweight twisted picture wire for rope.

The most common, as well as the most adaptable, materials for mini-mountains are ordinary fieldstones—rough marble, gray granite, white limestone, or soft red sandstone. Silver charms are perhaps too elegant for these mundane materials, but stones make perfect mounts for travel souvenirs or for oddments from the miniature collection.

In some sections of the country, rock is so common that it is free for the asking—from farmers, home builders, or road construction companies. Elsewhere it is a rarity, but stone can be bought in any city. Nurserymen stock natural and "cast" stones for rock gardens and ornamental boulders. Builders' suppliers rarely have stone on the premises but know where it can be obtained. The Yellow Pages of the telephone directory list the purveyors of rock, sand, and gravel under "Stone, Crushed." If all else fails, visit a monument maker and beg a few scraps of granite or unpolished marble. Sometimes it is well-nigh impossible to find a stone of exactly the right shape and size, but two or more small rocks can be put together with epoxy cement, side by side or one atop another, to build a mountain.

A tiny roadside shrine, of the type sold as a OO-model railroad accessory in German or Swiss toyshops, is a meaningful souvenir of a visit to the Bavarian

Alps, but its significance is lost if it is set upon a shelf among other, showier miniatures. As a background for displaying it, one might select a stone—the more eroded and earth-stained, the better—with steeply sloping sides like small-scale palisades. Cement the shrine on a promontory halfway up the cliff, as a reminder that its prototypes do cling to rocky crags, and add no further decoration to distract attention from it. For versatility, the other side of the stone could show an alpine waterfall. Cut a strip of clear kitchen plastic wrap about ½" wide and long enough to reach from the lip of an overhanging ledge to the base of the rock. Attach the ends of the strip at top and bottom with clear household cement and let the glue dry for an hour. Then squeeze liquid cement directly from the tube over the edge of the ledge, allowing it to dribble down the length of the plastic wrap. Do this slowly and carefully, for an excess of cement will run off too rapidly. A thin trickle of the clear glue dries so quickly that it forms a clear sheet over the plastic strip, with extra droplets stringing down on either side precisely like a miniature waterfall.

A miniature chalet, the almost inevitable souvenir of Switzerland, can be the inspiration for a typical Tyrolean scene. Balance the chalet on a narrow shelf near the top of a large rock, surround it with the Tyrol's ubiquitous red flowers, and place beside it a single fruit tree. Obtain the flowers and the tree where model-railroad accessories are sold. Buy a OO-size apple tree and a red "spring flowering" tree. Cut off the branches of the flowering tree with scissors, and lay them flat around the base of the chalet like a foundation planting. If the building has a balcony, lay a flowering limb along its railing, too. Trim the apple tree severely, for a gnarled and twisted look, and "plant" it close against one side of the house. As a crowning touch, turn the pointed tip of the mountain into a snow capped peak with a coating of materials from the kitchen cabinet. Measure two tablespoonsful of baking soda, one tablespoon of cornstarch, and one tablespoon of salt into a custard cup and mix them well. Add two tablespoons of cold water, and stir until a thin paste is formed. Drip the paste from a spoon onto the top of the mountain peak, letting it trickle down the rock and settle like glaciers in vertical crevices. The salt, which will have dissolved completely in the watery paste, will reappear as the "snow" dries to glisten on its surface.

The Western world has no monopoly on miniature mountain scenes. For centuries, the Japanese have enjoyed a unique type of decoration called *bon-seki*, which means "stones on a tray." *Bon-seki* may represent mountain peaks with waterfalls, or segments of rocky seacoasts, but water and rock are the two indispensable parts of such a design and no other materials are used. Real stones of appropriate size are combined on a lacquered tray with "water" made of marble dust which is brushed with the tip of a feather into a semblance of waves, cascades, whirlpools, and spray. The first impression made by the stark simplicity of these rugged rocks and moving water is one of solitude that verges on loneliness, but the longer one looks the more peaceful and soothing the scene appears.

This idea can be applied as well to seascapes and mountain rivulets of the American continent as to those of the Island Kingdom. For the basis of the composition, an inexpensive metal tray from a variety store can be "lacquered" with a half pint of flat black enamel into which one tablespoonful of clear varnish has been stirred. Chunks of gray granite, held together and to the tray with epoxy cement, will best simulate mountain peaks or rock-bound coasts. For the mountain cascade, build up a flat-topped, broad-based pyramid of stones to cover half the surface of the tray; place two flat stones side by side on the top of the pyramid, leaving a narrow space between them for the source of the waterfall. A seascape could be an island entirely surrounded by waves, a rocky promontory extending from one side of the tray into an expanse of water, or a semi-circular shoreline against which breakers hurl.

In New England or the southern Appalachian region, fine white or gray dust may be obtained at the marble mills that polish rough stones into smooth slabs. Outside these marble-producing areas, genuine marble dust is very difficult to procure, but an acceptable substitute for it can be found in baking soda or powdered borax. Unless the dust is attached in some way to the stones and the tray it will not stay in place. Paint the path of a mountain waterfall thickly with white glue, and cover the wet glue with a generous layer of marble dust or soda. Groove the pattern of the cascade with a toothpick and swirl a whirlpool in the white dust that has been allowed to form a pool on the surface of the tray at the base of the pyramidal mountain. The waves of a seascape can best be made of wallpaper cleaner pressed down on the glue-coated tray and shaped with the fingers into

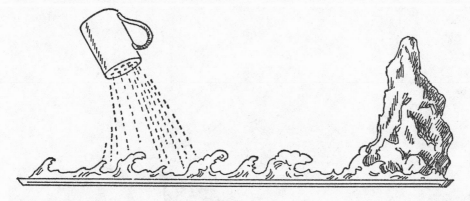

swells and troughs. Then paint the surface of the cleaner with white glue and coat it well with marble dust or borax—an easy way to do this evenly is to sprinkle the dust from a kitchen salt shaker.

Japanese *bon-seki* is a composition in grisaille, but one need not slavishly adhere to black, white, and gray. The wallpaper-cleaner waves of a seascape could be painted sapphire blue or emerald green and then white-capped with soda; a light dusting of white dust should be added to the base of the shore-line rocks for spray.

For a totally American version of stones-on-a-tray, one can build a miniature rock garden on a plastic turntable bought at a variety store. These small inexpensive lazy-Susans, intended to keep bottles and jars within reach in a refrigerator, come in several colors; the avocado green which will suggest grass would be a good choice for this endeavor. With epoxy cement and irregularly shaped stones, build a low pyramid that covers most of the rimmed platter. A tree—perhaps a "weeping cherry" made of brown wires dipped in white glue and rolled in chopped pink wool—cemented beside the mound would add asymmetry and attractiveness to the composition. Fill the crevices between the stones with tiny short-stemmed flowers for the look of low-growing rock-garden plants, and complete the design with a border of dried, dyed moss fitted around the jutting rocks at the base of the garden pyramid.

X

Under the Christmas Tree

America's Christmas traditions are a bright collage of customs brought to these shores by early European settlers. The Dutch were accompanied to Nieuw Amsterdam by their thin, red-robed and mitered St. Nikolaas, who underwent a gradual metamorphosis to become our chubby, jolly Santa Claus. German religious refugees introduced the lighted Christmas tree that had originated with Martin Luther. The evergreen wreaths and garlands that came to this continent with English colonists had long since migrated to the British Isles with Caesar's legions. Originally, these were pagan decorations, used to adorn the homes and temples of imperial Rome during the mid-winter Saturnalia. Since the Feast of Saturn coincided with the Christmas season, the early Christians defied their Roman persecutors by adopting the heathen ornaments and giving them secret symbolism. Evergreen foliage represented life after death, while the wreath, with no beginning and no end, signified eternal salvation. Indigenous to Britain were the Yule log and the mistletoe bough. Christian missionaries merely tolerated these ritual symbols of the tree-worshiping Druids, but they assigned a special meaning to wreaths made of English holly: the circlet of prickly leaves represented Christ's crown of thorns, and the red holly berries, drops of His blood.

Christmas is a time to keep alive the traditions of the past and to establish new family customs that will become traditional. Since the twelfth century, the manger scene made popular by St. Francis of Assisi has commemorated the Saviour's birth in homes throughout Christendom. In Italy and France, where the first miniature crèches were commissioned by pious princes, the human and animal figures were carved of wood and realistically hand-painted, molded of tinted wax, or modeled of delicately colored porcelain. In addition to the Three Kings from the Orient who came bearing gifts of real gold, frankincense, and myrrh, such a Nativity Scene often included the richly dressed royal family for whom it had been made. In the intervening years, the Holy Family, the shepherds, the patient beasts, the angels, and the Wise Men have been cast in gold or silver, carved from ivory, marble, or semi-precious stone, molded of glass or plaster—even fashioned of clay or plastic. Their size has varied, from early equestrian kings three feet in height to present-day standing shepherds less than one inch tall. Actual garments often have been added: fine white linen swaddling clothes for the Holy Infant; a sheer blue veil for the Madonna; tow-cloth tunics for the shepherds; rich velvet robes for the Magi, and jewel-studded golden crowns.

Many American families follow a venerable European timetable in putting up the crèche on a living-room mantel, a dining-room sideboard, or a hall console. First, against a backdrop of evergreen branches or small potted palms and ferns, the stable is set up and the straw-filled manger, the ox, and the ass are arranged inside. On Christmas Eve, the Virgin Mary and St. Joseph take their places beside the manger. A large star hangs among the green branches above the stable roof, and nearby, shepherds listen to the Herald Angel's tidings of great joy. At the farthest edge of the mantel or table, the Wise Men begin their journey. When the children awake on Christmas morning, the newborn Baby Jesus is asleep in the manger. The Wise Men have advanced a few inches toward the scene, and each day they move a little closer until, on January 6, they arrive at the stable and present their gifts.

Nativity scenes may differ in size and composition, but all portray the self-same event, with an unalterably fixed complement of human, angelic, and animal figures. In contrast, the secular Christmas scenes that developed in northern Europe had only one thing in common: They were invariably made of wood. Often a *putz* represented a simple wintry landscape—an isolated farmhouse, and a woodcutter trudging toward a clump of bare-branched trees. Sometimes, however, an entire village would be shown with narrow houses clustered about a steepled church, and a castle crowning a nearby hill.

When German immigrants introduced the Christmas tree to Pennsylvania in the early eighteenth century, they placed beneath its branches the sort of miniature scene that had been traditional in northern Europe since the Reformation. In Pennsylvania's Lutheran settlements, making a *putz* was a project for the entire family. Father taught his sons the elements of wood carving and carpentry as they whittled animals and people or built barns and houses for what their English neighbors called "the Christmas yard." Mother helped the little girls to paint the buildings and the animals and to dress the human figures in scraps of cloth. On Christmas Eve the whole family joined in setting up the *putz*, under the decorated tree, on a snowy landscape made of a linen sheet strewn with wisps of white wool.

Most American house museums are decorated for the Christmas season, in proper period style. For an early house whose history permits the use of a tall evergreen trimmed in German-colonial fashion with candles, red apples, thin spicy cookies, and popcorn chains, a *putz* beneath the tree will be a happy addition. Spread a length of white linen on the floor, covering the tree stand, and on it arrange the red-roofed houses of a miniature village.

Little wooden villages made in Germany today are sold in America as children's toys, but they are mass-produced copies of a type of early *putz*. Each one includes a church (usually with an onion-shaped dome), and several square wood-block houses with steeply pitched roofs. Larger sets also have stylized wooden trees, and tiny men, women, and farm animals.

The enormous *putz* in the basement of the Single Brothers' house at Winston-Salem, North Carolina, seems to bear little resemblance to a home-made Christmas yard of colonial days. It is so large (twenty-two feet long and eight feet wide) that it would fit only under the limbs of a giant of the forest; instead of an imaginary one-street village, it faithfully portrays the entire nineteenth-century town of Salem in a scale of one inch to eight feet. Still, the similarity is there. This is a secular Christmas display, entirely separate from the Nativity Scene shown in an adjacent cellar. Careful research and skillful construction have made this *putz* one of the wonders of the "Little World," but like its predecessors, it has been a composite achievement. An eighteenth-century yard was a family project, and this is the joint work of a church committee. Although drifts of white marble dust have replaced the quondam linen sheet, this is a traditional winter scene.

The differences actually are matters of mechanics. Early Christmas yards often boasted miniatures in motion, such as windlasses or gristmills that were activated by tightly wound springs. Old Salem's *putz* includes a mill at the edge of town, but its tall, constantly revolving water wheel is powered by an electric motor concealed under the platform that supports the entire display. A hidden loudspeaker fills the chill air with the recorded music of the Home Church organ. Twentieth-century technology also has made it possible to light the church, the college buildings, and the houses of the *putz* from within, using tiny model-railroad bulbs wired into a transformer under the platform.

This last idea is one that can easily be adapted for home use. Cover the tree stand and surround the tree with flame-proofed cotton batting to form a snowy background for a lighted village. As the focal point of the scene, use a little lighted church, of the sort that is sold complete with replaceable light bulb and long extension cord in Christmas shops. Little cardboard houses with cellophane-covered windows come in sets and are intended to be slipped over the Christmas-tree light blubs. Arrange these along streets made of wide black plastic tape and light them with a string of white grain-of-wheat-size bulbs. Add evergreens of various sizes and leafless trees made of well-branched twigs; flock these plantings with spray snow or encrust them with ice by painting each branch with clear household cement. Frost the black pavement very lightly with flocking, for the look of wind-blown dry snow on icy streets.

Instead of placing the lighted village beneath the Christmas tree, you might prefer to arrange it on a sideboard or a console table, where it would be raised to better viewing level. To protect the furniture, build the display on a large piece of heavy cardboard. This time, make the snow of materials from the kitchen shelf—by the same recipe used in schools for the construction of relief maps. In a large saucepan, blend 4 cups of baking soda, 2 cups of cornstarch, and 1 cup of table salt with 3 cups of cold water. Place the pan over medium heat and stir until the mixture boils; continue stirring briskly for about one minute, until the thickening mass has the consistency of creamy mashed potatoes. Spoon the paste onto a platter and cover it with a damp cloth until it is cool enough to handle. Then knead it smooth and press it over the cardboard in a thin layer. Set the houses in place at once, burying the wires that light them under drifts of snow, and use the last remaining bit of soda paste to make a snowman for one front lawn. As the snow dries, the salt crystals that appear on its surface will sparkle in the light streaming from the tiny windows. Use clumps of graduated evergreen trees for lawn plantings, along with leafless trees made of the dried woody stems of grape clusters. Spray the trees with white flocking and flock the top of 1"-long cars and trucks to be cemented along the streets.

In England and English-speaking countries, the Christmas tree did not gain general acceptance until it was sanctioned by Queen Victoria in the mid-nineteenth century. Remembering the joys of his own German childhood, Prince Albert ordered a tree at Windsor Castle, in 1841, for the infant Prince of Wales. The December 1850 issue of an influential American magazine, *Godey's Lady's Book,* carried a drawing of the British royal family that showed the Queen, the Prince Consort, and their children grouped around a large table tree. Its branches were decorated with blown-glass ornaments from Germany, and a waxen angel with outspread wings perched on the topmost twig. Queen Victoria's influence was strong in the erstwhile colonies, and Americans hastened to adopt the "pretty custom" that had received her stamp of approval.

During the nineteenth century brightly painted pewter *putz* figures were being made in Germany and sold in sets. The most popular scene was a skating party, meant to be arranged on a mirror pond edged with cotton snow. These two-dimensional skaters, sleighs, cottages, and trees are once again being cast from the original molds and are available in import shops. Such a skating scene would be an ideal Christmas decoration for an American house museum of the mid-Victorian Period, placed at the base of a table tree whose candle-tipped branches were laden with blown-glass balls, candies in paper cornucopias, and tiny toys.

The skating party would be equally at home beneath the branches of an electrically lighted space-saving table tree in an efficiency apartment. It also makes a splendid centerpiece for Christmas dinner or for a children's holiday party. On a snowy tablecloth, place an unframed full-length mirror to represent a long, narrow lake; disguise the straight edges of the mirror with irregularly cut cotton batting and clumps of artificial evergreen trees.

In some families, the best-loved toys are not banished forever when they are outgrown but are carefully packed away with the Christmas ornaments. Each year thereafter they reappear under the tree in a twentieth-century American version of Germany's traditional *putz*. A parade of antique model cars, outdated buses, bright red fire engines, and bright yellow delivery vans may encircle the tree stand; a rail fence might surround a little red barn, restraining a barnyard full of cows and horses, pigs and poultry; a collection of doll-size tools, now in the hands of bendable felt elves, could simulate Santa's workshop. Best of all, on tracks laid around the tree, the puffing freight engines and shiny passenger coaches of an electric train can rattle over bridges and rumble through tunnels on Christmas morning. In the Victorian manner, little "frozen Charlottes," kewpie dolls, and gilded filigree-metal dollhouse furnishings can be suspended on narrow velvet ribbons from the branches of the tree itself.

Collectors of Victoriana are constantly on the lookout for small Christmas decorations—china snow babies, wooden sleighs, wax angels, crocheted hat-shaped pincushions—to be combined with the tiniest of blown-glass fish, horns, and birds for decking centerpiece or coffee-table trees. To embellish an inherited marble-topped table, one might decorate a small artificial evergreen with silver bracelet charms, tying them on with crimson cord, and place the tree beneath a tall glass dome.

An easy but effective contemporary coffee-table ornament is a little gilded tree garlanded with prestrung seed pearls (from a sewing center) and trimmed with the tiniest white wedding-favor doves (sold in packets at party shops). An even smaller gilded tree—a place-favor-size evergreen lightly sprayed with gold paint—makes a marvelous Christmas decoration for a miniature contemporary room. Swag the tree with shiny silver cord and decorate it with beads and silver snowflake sequins. Attach the ornaments with sequin pins: push a pin through the hole in a bead; then dip the pin point in white glue and press it deep into the tree's foliage. Under the tree arrange a pile of presents. Wrap sugar cubes, sugar tablets, and the smallest of empty matchboxes in brightly colored flexible foil and tie them with gold cord.

It is especially interesting and challenging to make historically correct Christmas decorations for miniature period rooms. For a colonial interior in Pennsylvania Dutch styling, tip the branches of a little evergreen tree with liquid cement and carefully balance on these glue dots short sections of white wax matches for candles. Use scarlet thread to tie on tiny red plastic apples and ginger cookies cut from brown craft paper with a punch press. Turn a length of heavy-duty white thread into a string of popcorn by tying knots along it as close together as possible. Drape the popcorn chain over the branches as a spiral. Then place beneath the tree a village *putz*, making the houses of ¼″-square wood blocks and giving them steep-slanted roofs of red craft paper.

A stiff little place-favor tree of the type that looks like a cone-shaped green bottle brush will be a fine table tree for a Victorian parlor. Make candles for this tree by bending straight pins into an L shape, with pliers, and painting their pointed tips white. Then dip the head of a pin in white glue and press it deep into the stubby foliage; hold the white candle tip in upright position until the glue has set. Use sequin pins dipped in glue to attach beads of several sizes and many colors, which will look like blown-glass balls, and top the tree with a large sequin shaped like an angel or a star. Surround the tree base with charm-size toys and sugar cubes or tablets wrapped in white tissue paper and tied with red embroidery floss.

In most period rooms, a Christmas tree would be highly inappropriate, but this does not mean that miniature antique interiors must be deprived of seasonal decorations. Tips of artificial juniper will be a small-scale version of long-leaf pine when banked along the mantel shelf of an early-American keeping room. In colonial days a string of home-grown hot red peppers was used as a decoration as well as a means of seasoning. Bits of red needle-coral (from a broken necklace) strung on white thread and swagged above a fieldstone kitchen fireplace will remarkably resemble shiny, spiky peppers.

For the windows and the mantel of a formal eighteenth-century drawing room, wreaths and garlands can be simulated in miniature with artificial cedar cut into tiny sprays. As the basis of a wreath, twist a short length of green florist's

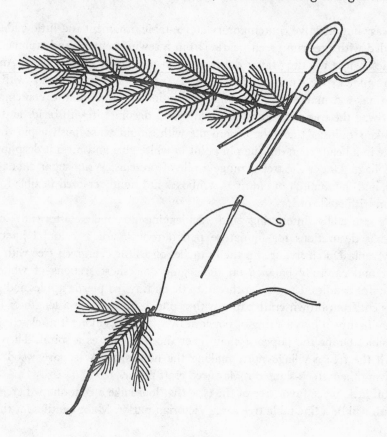

wire into a circle. Then use hair-fine wire to cover this frame with cedar tips. Wrap the stem of a sprig flat upon the frame; add a second sprig, letting its tuft of foliage overlap the stem of the first to hide the wire wrapping. Continue until the circlet is completely covered, tucking the stem of the last twig under the foliage of the first. Garlands can best be made on a core of green twine by sewing on overlapping cedar tips with dark green thread. Tie up the garlands and garnish the wreaths with bows of red satin baby ribbon cut in half, lengthwise.

In a room of the American Federal Period, sprays of evergreen might peep out from behind the gold frames of mirrors and portraits, while the mantel and the doorway could be outlined with cedar-sprig garlands. After Clement Clarke Moore's *A Visit from St. Nicholas* was published in 1823, "stockings were hung by the chimney with care" in homes throughout the United States. Tack Barbie-doll stockings (filled with beads for a properly lumpy look) to the mantel of a Victorian bedroom. Let a tiny doll or a toy animal protrude from the open end of each stocking, hiding the tack, and add a red-and-white-striped candy cane. Make the canes by twisting together two thin pipe cleaners, one red and one white. Cut the spiraled strip into 1″ lengths, with pliers, and curve the top of each cane.

In a dining area of whatever era, fruit is the most felicitous holiday decoration. For the trestle table in a colonial kitchen, heap bright red apples in a wooden bowl. An epergne filled with apples, pears, and grapes should center the banquet table in an elegant eighteenth-century dining room. Around the wassail bowl on the sideboard lay flat sprigs of greenery to form a wreath and top the green ring with fruits in the della Robbia manner. In a less ceremonious setting, an apple pyramid crowned with a pineapple (which was and is the symbol of hospitality) would be the perfect centerpiece. On a Victorian table covered to the floor with a white damask cloth, an arrangement of apples, oranges, and pears in a glass basket or a silver compote might be flanked by layer cakes on footed stands.

Last-minute preparations for Christmas could be amusingly detailed in an American farm kitchen of the turn of the twentieth century. Lean an evergreen tree against the wall and place beside it the crossed strips of wood that are to support it in upright position and the hammer that will nail the tree to its stand. Hang a stalk of bananas from a hook in the ceiling and set a crate of oranges on the floor; make the crate of narrow balsa strips braced with matchsticks. Open the oven door to reveal a roasting turkey and center a table with a bright red bowl of tempting doughnuts. (Oat-cereal Cheerios are perfect doughnut miniatures; glazed with a protective coat of hairspray, they will keep for years.)

Christmas is a time for giving, and James Russell Lowell has aptly defined the essence of generosity as:

> Not what we give, but what we share—The gift without the giver is bare . . .

Everyone has heard, and miniaturists are convinced, that "the best things come in small packages," but it goes without saying that the most appreciated presents are those that are tailored to the tastes of their recipients.

Unusual and very acceptable Christmas gifts may be made of small pieces of rock, ore, mineral crystal, or quartz by adding a miniature appropriate to the season. Perch a gold cherub on a small segment of rose quartz to make a perfect dressing-table ornament for a young daughter, or mount a miniature Madonna on sky-blue fluorite for a new mother's gift. Small angel musicians are sold in sets at boutiques, and each has a robe of a different color. For a music lover, mount a blue-robed chorister on a mound of copper ore, or a golden-brown clad harpist on an eroded clay-stained rock. Should you be fortunate enough to have a piece of soft sandstone, use it to make the cave-stable background for a tiny crèche. If the sandstone has no natural hollow, you can create one by outlining it with an electric drill and gouging out the necessary amount of crumbly stone with a thin chisel. Arrange the nativity scene within the cave and cement a shining star to the top of the sandstone. Mirror-backed glass stars are sold by mail and in hobby shops as trimmings for styrofoam Christmas ornaments.

In an import shop it usually is possible to find a wooden statuette of St. Francis, with tiny birds alighting on his outstretched hands, that is no more than eight inches tall. This could become the focal point of a miniature woodland scene that will delight a gardener or an environmentalist. In the center of a round wood trivet or a bark-edged slice of a tree limb, cement the brown-toned saint and add a background of shapely evergreens for height and color contrast. Then, in the foreground place one or more hand-carved animals of proper scale; a squirrel, a rabbit, a turtle, and perhaps a pair of fawns.

A vignette in a small wooden shadow box could echo a businessman's interests. Buy the box unfinished at a hobby shop and wax or stain the exterior, including the frame that holds the protective glass. As an example, to represent the mining industry of the Southwest, paint the inside of the shadow box sky-blue and floor it with sandpaper. Then paste a magazine photograph of the rugged Rocky Mountains on the rear wall. In the center foreground, cement a miniature miner leading his heavily laden donkey, and add a pebble boulder or a tiny artificial cactus at one side of the floor space.

Please a talented flower arranger with a miniature florist's shop in a shadow box fitted with narrow balsa shelves. Use the caps of marking pens for tall containers and mass in each one a different variety or color of real miniature dried flowers: Peruvian starflowers, baby's-breath, statice, mimosa, tips of celosia or heather. Fill flowerpots made of inverted toothpaste-tube caps with tufts of artificial pine and let the plants come into bloom by adding painted pod flowers: ironweed shasta daisies; salvia lilies; and rhododendron tulips. Arrange the flower containers and the potted plants on the shelves, securing them with liquid cement. A slender brass doorstop, of the type that has a short screw at one end and a half-round of rubber at the other, will be a splendid pedestal to hold a spreading floral bouquet in front of the shelves. Buy the door bumper at the hardware counter of a variety store and twist off its rubber tip with pliers. Screw the tapered shaft upright in the center of the shadow-box floor. Make a wide, shallow arrangement of mixed blossoms in a squat brass vase, and use liquid solder to attach the bottom of the container to the top of the pedestal. Finally, spell out FLOWER SHOP in gilt-paper letters cemented facing outward on the inside of the protective glass.

In a large oblong shadow box, make a miniature rendition of "This Is Your Life" as a unique Christmas (or birthday) gift for a brother or a son. Plan to hang the box vertically, and divide its interior into three equal parts by cementing in two balsa shelves. The lowest section should represent childhood. Paste a montage of little boy snapshots on the rear wall, and let memory guide you in choosing the favorite pets and toys that should be featured in the foreground: a tiny kitten, a lop-eared mutt, a Shetland pony; a bicycle, a sled, ice skates, a football, a baseball bat and glove. Reserve the center section for school days, using postcards of high school and college buildings as a backdrop and centering them around a graduation photograph in cap and gown. At one side of the shelf, cement tiny books in stacks, and top the tallest pile with a typewriter. Devote the rest of the shelf space to extra-curricular activities adding, perhaps, a pair of skis, swim fins, a guitar, and a model sports car. In the career section at the top of the box paste a postcard of the city's sky line between snapshots of the man's office building and his present home. Add the tools of his trade—an executive's flat-topped desk and swivel chair, an author's typewriter and filing cabinet, a lawyer's briefcase, or a doctor's medicine bag. Fill the remaining shelf space with miniatures indicative of his leisure-time activities: golf clubs, a musical instrument, a tennis racket, a boat, a tiny camper-trailer. Come to think of it, a doctor's life story in miniature could most fittingly be contained in an antique wooden medicine cabinet with a mirrored door.

There is a dedicated group of miniaturists who find articles of dollhouse size too large and too coarse for the type of portable outdoor scene that they delight in designing. They work primarily with those smallest of miniatures that are called "tinies" by toy manufacturers. "Panorama figures" is another, more euphonious, name for animals and persons one inch or less in height, which first were used in the foreground of perspective scenes inside peep-show eggs. The best of these are currently made in Germany, as accessories for HO-, N-, and OO-scale model railroads, and are sold in this country at hobby shops that specialize in electric trains. Animals or people are packaged in sets, on cards or in clear-plastic boxes. All the tiny persons are beautifully detailed. Under a magnifying glass, each one is seen to possess well-delineated features and a distinct personality. Some sets are contemporary in styling, containing workmen in coveralls, families in street clothes, or men and women in evening dress. Others are manifestly nineteenth century—men wearing swallowtail coats with top hats, and women in hoop skirts and bonnets. Occasionally a complete little vignette is offered: a housewife hanging out the laundry on a clothesline, or a barn with horses peeping out its windows and a farmer mending harness just outside the door. Other accessories in HO-, N-, OO-scale include: churches, town and country houses, trees, fences, mills, shops and factories, street lamps, and (of course) railroad stations.

Anyone accustomed to dealing with objects sized one inch to one foot will find it hard at first to adjust to this much smaller scale. Aside from the difficulty of adapting the eye and steadying the fingers, the problem is that the selection of minute model-railroad accessories is so limited. The solution lies in using these mini-miniatures in imaginative ways, combining them in some cases with panorama figures of molded plastic. These tiny articles are offered in wholesale confectioner's catalogues, as foreground figures for panorama Easter eggs. Often they can be bought at a bakery, where they are used in decorating cakes.

As an example of how the two types of "tinies" can be used together, consider the construction of a safari scene inside a one-gallon aquarium. At one end of the tank's floor, let a small purse mirror serve as a water hole. Trim a sheet of fine sandpaper to fit the floor of the aquarium, and cut an irregularly shaped hole that allows the mirror to show through. Build up a low hill at the opposite end of the floor space, using instant papier-mâché. While waiting for the wet mass to dry, put together a wooden fire-watcher's tower, which is one of the railroad accessories that comes in kit form. Paint the surface of the still-moist papier-mâché brown, and press the ends of the tower's pole supports down into the damp mass. Then surround the tower with a grove of tall jungle trees—made of sponges—the tips of plastic ferns, and lacy evergreens. Add two or three tiny workmen in coveralls, so positioned on the platform of the tower that they turn into big-game hunters on camera safari watching the water hole. Now place panorama animals from a made-in-Hong Kong plastic zoo set—elephants, giraffes, lions, zebras, and a rhinoceros—near the water and cement the gorilla from the zoo set in a tree near the water tower. Close the aquarium with a transparent cover of glass or plastic and present it to a friend who longs to travel in Africa.

Cake covers with colored plates and clear-plastic domes cost very little at variety stores and offer ready-made protective covering to tiny scenes built on their trays. On the green tray of such a cake carrier, railroad accessory animals and a Wild West set of molded-plastic miniatures might tell the story of a pioneer settlement. Like one frame cut from a motion picture, this scene would arrest a single moment of a continuing action. Its focal point must be a log cabin, and fortunately miniature cabins of precisely the right size are sold in mountain resort areas (with pine perfumed pellets) as incense burners. Cement the cabin near the center of the tray and cover the area in front of it with a cornpatch. Make this plowed field of wallpaper cleaner, spread thin over a coating of white glue, and grooved with the tines of a fork. Paint the moist cleaner brown and, as soon as the paint is dry, prick tiny straight bits of green plastic cedar in rows along the raised cornhills made by the fork. A pioneer home often huddled at the base of a steep hill that afforded protection from the prevailing wind, so build a hill of piled rocks behind your miniature cabin, anchoring the stones to each other and to the tray with epoxy cement. Cement a few evergreen trees in the deeper crevices of the rocky mount. Near the base of the hill, close beside the cabin, a spring bubbling out from between two boulders can be simulated with a trickle of clear liquid cement. Surround the cabin with as many necessities of pioneer life as you can possibly devise: a wash kettle on a toothpick tripod by the spring; a cow and calf in a milking pen; a pig pen placed downwind, on the far side of the hill; an outhouse behind the cabin; and firewood stacked against a side wall.

Now for the action. On level land toward the rear of the hill, where "new ground" is being cleared, one settler guides the team of horses that is hauling away a felled tree. Unseen by him, a pioneer mother clutches her baby and races for the safety of the cabin door—with a gray timber wolf in hot pursuit. At the edge of the cornpatch, a second settler has dropped his hoe and raised his pistol to draw a careful bead on the marauding animal.

Using railroad accessories only, a placid farm scene can be constructed on a light blue cake tray. At one side of the plate, cement a farmhouse atop a papier-mâché hill that has been covered with light green felt. In front of the house, place a curving strip of beige sandpaper to look like a graveled country road. Across the road, a second hill can become an orchard, with rows of small trees (made of plastic cedar tips) climbing up its sides. Cement a barn vignette, with its animals and tools, near the edge of the tray opposite the house. Between the house and the barn, cover the level tray with light green felt for a pasture, but cut an S-curved slit from one edge of the tray to another. The exposed blue surface of the platter will look like a meandering brook. Enclose the pasture and the barn-yard with HO-scale sections of white picket fencing or with ½″ strips of plastic window screening cemented to matchstick fence posts. Add horses and/or cows to the pasture, and plant a clump of HO-scale trees beside the stream. Cement some shade trees near the house and run a line of stepping stones from the front porch to the road by cutting out rounds of sandpaper with a punch press.

By itself, the farmhouse will fit inside the sort of clear-plastic photo-cube that holds six square snapshots, one on each side. Obtain the cube where cameras are sold. Slide out its one removable side, and take out the block of foam rubber that would hold the pictures in place. Build a low knoll of papier-mâché inside the hollow cube, cover it with green felt when it is dry, and encircle the base of the hill with sections of OO-scale white picket fence. Cement the house, several trees, a round bed of flowers, and a path of stepping stones to the felt before replacing the clear-plastic side in its slot. Because this vignette, in its inexpensive protective case, would take up little room on a bedside table, it would be much appreciated by a hospital patient.

Ceramic coin banks shaped like little Victorian houses or alpine inns are sold in toyshops and bookstores, and either type of bank could be the *pièce de résistance* of a gift-scene with a message. For the basis of such a scene, use a small green plastic lazy-Susan from a variety store.

Center the Victorian house on its round green lawn and surround the raised rim of the turntable with sections of snap-together white picket fencing. Make a gravel path from a gap in the fence to the door of the house by sprinkling table salt over white glue applied to the tray with an artist's paintbrush. Cut off the branches of small railroad-accessory flowering trees and glue them flat on the tray to form a flower bed on each side of the walkway. Add OO-scale shade trees on the lawn and use the tips of evergreens for foundation plantings. In the side yard arrange molded plastic lawn furniture beside a mirror "pool," and in the back yard place a OO-size clothesline-miniature that includes a laundry basket, a toddler, and a housewife pinning a red shirt to the line. Present this bank scene to young marrieds who are saving for a new home.

The yellow stucco inn should center a scene that reminds its recipients to save for a trip abroad. Give the bank a background of jagged rocks and evergreen trees and add a foundation planting of red-flowered tree branches. At one side of the inn, place molded plastic umbrella tables beside a beige-painted dance floor. On a flat rock overlooking this floor, arrange the members of a OO-scale brass band in Bavarian costume and fill the floor with tiny dancing couples.

England has always been famous among miniaturists for its lead soldiers proudly arrayed in the colorful uniforms of crack British military units. Recently these Horse Guards and Highlanders have been produced in a reduced scale that makes them comparable in size to HO-scale railroad accessories and plastic panorama figures. Especially for export, there now are Australian and Canadian sets, plus American Civil War soldiers of both the Union and Confederate armies.

Three sets of tiny soldiers plus one three-tiered glass snack server will equal an unusual gift for any history buff. In each clear glass bowl let one troop of men-at-arms follow the flag through an appropriate landscape. Confederate infantry might march along a tree-lined country road beside a field where thoroughbred horses graze. A detachment of Union artillery might struggle through deep snow to take shelter in a house surrounded by bare, ice-encrusted trees. Scottish Highlanders, in bonnets and kilts, could climb in single file up a steep, rocky path that skirts a tiny mirror "loch." When the bowls are stacked one above the other, and the tiered container is topped with its transparent lid, each scene will be visible "in the round" through the clear glass.

British metal miniatures also include fox hunt sets in which the mounted gentlemen in pink coats and the ladies on sidesaddles are no more than an inch and a half high, while the liver-spotted hounds measure less than half an inch from nose to tail. An amusing gift for a riding enthusiast, small enough to fit beneath a transparent cheese dome, would feature HO-scale trees brave in autumn colors, bordering a fallow field. Here the hunters have reined in behind the hounds, who have run an invisible fox to cover in a haystack.

Beautiful panorama-size miniatures, molded of metal and artistically handpainted, now are being produced in Spain. Spanish toy designers seem to specialize in elegant little sets that glorify the horse: Renaissance cavalrymen in helmets and breastplates on armored steeds, or gilt-trimmed state coaches drawn by eight caparisoned horses and flanked by outriders in plumed hats.

As a worthy setting for such a coach, prepare a table-top shadow box. Buy a 5"×7" picture frame with a broad filigree metal rim and search for a sturdy cardboard box of the same length and width that is at least 3" deep. (Check the stationery counter in a variety store for the boxes that hold twenty-five Christmas cards with envelopes.) Cover the outside of the box, including the bottom, with self-stick red felt or with red velvet applied with liquid thread. Turn the box on its longer side and paint the interior ceiling and walls sky blue; paint the floor green and glue a strip of sandpaper near the outer edge to represent a road. Now, with postcards make a three-dimensional background of castles in Spain, like the

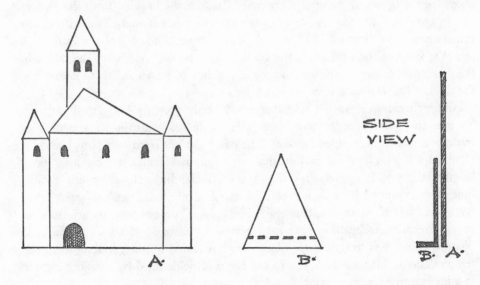

perspective views in old-fashioned peep-show eggs. Cut out a turreted castle from one card. For a stand to support it in upright position, cut a triangle of shirt-front cardboard and fold the lower side of the triangle at right angles, ¼" from the edge. Glue the cardboard to the back of the postcard castle and then glue the protruding horizontal strip to the floor of the shadow box at the base of the rear wall. From other postcards cut out hills and clumps of trees. Give them cardboard stands, and glue them in front of the castle but closer to the sides of the box. The result will be that the castle will be glimpsed at the end of a vista, as though it were seen from a great distance. Finally, cement the wheels of the coach and the hooves of the horses to the sandpaper road. Remove the backing from the picture frame, but leave the glass in place. Cover the outer edges of the box with epoxy cement and press them against the back of the frame. The edge of the frame will raise the front of the box, while the back of the box will rest upon the table; in this backward-slanting position, the scene within can be viewed with ease when the shadow box is placed upon an end table.

Although extremely small miniatures have only recently found full favor in Europe, tiny stereotyped scenes have been made for centuries in Japan. This traditional art form is called *bon-kei*. The name derives from *bon* (tray) and *kei* (landscape), and *bon-kei* is just that: a miniature landscape on an oblong lacquered tray with a narrow standing rim. Artificial and natural materials sometimes are combined in such a scene. Mountains might be made of rock or of papier-mâché; plant materials may be live lichens, mosses, and dwarf trees, or plastic greenery. Delicate bridges arch across rivers made of colored sand, and boatmen pole their fragile craft along these streams. Moon gates, houses, and temples add architectural interest to the edges of fields tilled by stooping farmers in wide-brimmed hats.

In Japan, the accessories for *bon-kei* often are treasured heirlooms, beautifully made of porcelain and artistically painted. For the export trade, inexpensive modern miniatures are mass-produced in colored plastic. Plastic *bon-kei* sets are offered in mail-order catalogues, while better-quality miniatures are sold individually in import shops, along with tiny artificial Ming trees.

For the sake of convenience, a small oblong tray might be painted dark green to serve as a grassy background for, say, a snow-capped, cone-shaped stone mountain with a pagoda-roofed temple beside a stream near its base. In *bon-kei*, the Japanese use colored sand for water, swirling blue and green artfully together to make a "deep" river appear to flow smoothly. Sometimes they use brown sand and pebbles for shallow shoals interrupted with white sand rapids. To imitate these effects, white sand bought at a pet shop may be colored with liquid dye. Spread a thin layer of sand in a baking pan protected by a liner of aluminum foil. Dilute liquid dye with boiling water and pour enough hot dye into the pan to cover the sand. Let the pan stand uncovered until all the liquid has evaporated and then lift out the foil liner to remove the dry colored sand. (To hasten the drying process, preheat the oven to 175°, insert the uncovered pan, and leave it at this temperature overnight.)

Mexico, too, has a special kind of tiny miniatures with which scenes typical of that country can be constructed. These inch-high figures are hand-molded of clay on armatures of fine wire. The set of bullfight figures that is a favorite souvenir of Mexico City has a great many colorful pieces: angry bulls with *banderillas* sticking in their shoulders; a dead bull being dragged from the ring by three horses; mounted picadors; *banderilleros* with their ribboned goads; and pig-tailed matadors in tricorne hats, brandishing red capes. Another memento of Mexico that appeals to tourists is a rectangular cigarette box with a framework of tin supporting its glass top and sides. The set of tiny figures and the see-through box can easily be combined to make a bullfight scene in a singularly suitable protective case. It is only necessary to cover the tin bottom of the box with very fine beige sandpaper, and then to attach the realistically arranged miniatures with epoxy cement.

Delightfully different tree ornaments result when panorama Christmas figures are displayed inside life-size hollow plastic fruits. The cheapest of shiny red apples and pink-cheeked yellow pears, from the dime store, are actually better for this purpose than their costlier counterparts because their shells are thinner and hence easier to cut. Dip the serrated blade of a carving knife in hot water, and slice off one side of an apple; cement narrow gold braid around the edges of the hole. Paint the cavity's curved walls gold or spray them with glue and sprinkle on diamond-dust glitter. Drip wax from a white candle into the base of the apple, dust it immediately with glitter, and while the wax is still soft set in place a tiny Santa Claus or a top-hatted snowman. The most apropos inset for the orifice of a hollow pear would, of course, be a partridge in a pear tree. Cement the tiniest of plastic pears to a little leafless twig, and add one brown-painted charm-size bird. Fill the bottom of the pear with liquid cement, and wait a few seconds before sprinkling this glue with glitter. After the cement has become thick but not hard, set the pear tree upright, and steady it with a fingertip until the glue is set. Finally, attach a loop of gold cord to the stem of the apple or pear, to serve as a hanger.

In the late nineteenth century a renowned St. Petersburg jeweler, Peter Carl Fabergé, created hundreds of fabulous Easter eggs for the Russian Imperial family. Some were solid ovoid shapes exquisitely enameled and embellished with precious or semi-precious stones; others opened to reveal such hidden treasures as a diamond-framed miniature of the Czar or a tiny golden basket of jewel-petaled flowers.

Elegant boutiques now offer, among their more costly bibelots, miniature scenes in egg-shaped containers that are decorated with gold braid and pearls in a manner reminiscent of the famous Fabergé eggs. Such an ornament makes a delightful gift and is surprisingly easy to construct. The oval container is actually a large, clear-plastic egg-shaped mold that comes apart lengthwise in the middle. (These molds, which are intended to be used in shaping stiff sugar icing into panorama eggs, are sold in confectioners' catalogues.) First, turn one half of the mold into a pair of double doors using a hacksaw with a fine-toothed blade to saw the thin plastic in two, lengthwise. Paint the inside of the three egg sections pale blue with model enamel and give the outside of each segment two coats of liquid gold leaf. Hinge each door to the uncut egg half with a small piece of adhesive tape. Then cement narrow gold braid around both the outer and the inner edges of the egg half and the curving doors; this braid will cover and secure the ends of the cloth hinges and will, at the same time, hide any irregularities caused by sawing. Surround the braid on the outside of the container with a row of prestrung seed pearls. In a hobby shop, look among the materials for decorating styrofoam Christmas balls for a large gold filigree base shaped like the bottom half of a cone and for a small gold bezel (jewel mount) to be used as a finial. Attach the large end of the painted egg to the filigree base with epoxy cement and cement the bezel in the center of the egg-half top edge; use household cement to fill the bezel with a large oval pearl-drop bead. Inside the little hollow showcase, arrange a scene composed of panorama-size miniatures and tiny evergreens; the view will be more pleasing if the figures and foliage are mounted on a lichen-covered stone or on a green-painted papier-mâché hill.

Real eggshells can be transformed into beautiful, fragile frames for panorama-size Christmas angels and Nativity figures. Remove an egg from the refrigerator and let it stand at room temperature for at least an hour; then hold it over a bowl, and tap the side of its shell sharply with the end of the handle of a table-knife. After removing the cracked bits of eggshell with a pair of tweezers, insert the point of a nutpick to break the sac of the egg yolk, and stir the yolk and white gently together. Pour the mingled contents out into a bowl to be used for scrambled eggs. Wash out the shell under a thin stream of cool water, and then enlarge the hole with manicure scissors to form a neat oval. To strengthen the shell, paint the inside of it azure blue, or coat it with pale pink nail polish sprinkled with gold glitter. Its outer surface could be painted or merely brushed with clear opalescent nail polish. Make a hanger-loop of thin gold cord, and attach its ends to the top of the egg with a generous coin-dot of epoxy cement. To cover the loop ends and bond them securely to the shell, press a circlet of seed pearls down on the still-damp cement. Outline the edges of the oval hole with prestrung pearls. Cover the bottom of the shell cavity with dripped white candle wax, dust it with gold glitter, and add a tiny angel with outspread wings, a 1"-high Madonna, or a Magus wearing a golden crown.

Empty eggshells also can be transmuted into little egg-head portrait busts that are enchanting gifts for Christmas, for Easter, or for special occasions throughout the year. After an egg has stood at room temperature for an hour, pierce the

center of its large end with the sharp point of a serrated paring knife. Twist the knife slowly and carefully to enlarge the hole—with luck, you can obtain an opening ½" in diameter without cracking the shell. Lower a nutpick into the hole and break the yolk sac; stir and turn the egg over to shake out mingled yolk and white. Rinse out the shell with cool water and let it dry overnight. Brown eggshells already have the color of sun-tanned skin, but they should be strengthened with a coat of colorless nail polish. To improve the appearance of a white eggshell and increase its durability, brush it with flesh-colored plastic-model enamel.

The egghead should now be poised upright on a neck and shoulders of appropriate size. Most brightly colored plastic Easter eggs come apart at the equator so that they can be filled with candies; half of such an egg, open end down, can serve as shoulders. White plastic curtain rings one inch in diameter are sold fourteen to the package wherever cottage curtains are on display. Three or four of

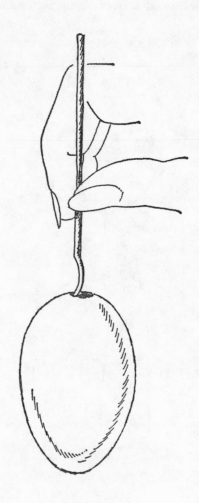

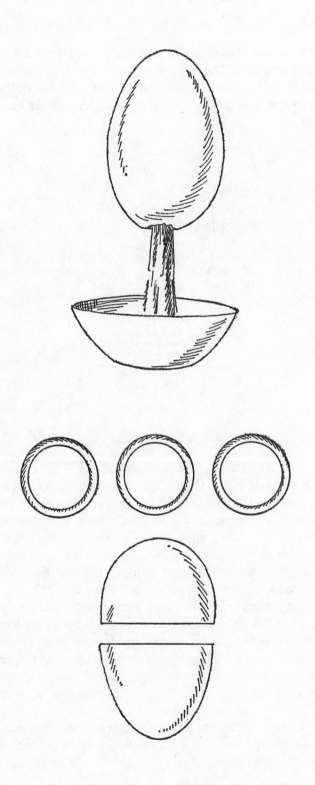

these rings, stacked one above another and bonded together with plastic cement, will be the egghead's neck. Cement the stack on top of the inverted plastic egg half; then coat the top ring with plastic cement and settle one end of the eggshell upon it. Since the neck is hollow, the curved shell end will fit down into it and balance perfectly.

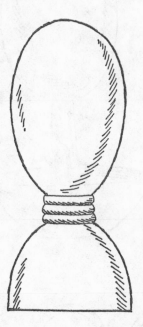

Obviously, the end of the egg that rests upon the neck has become the chin of the egghead. If the large end of the egg is cemented to the stacked rings, the hole made to empty the shell will automatically disappear, but the egghead will have heavy jowls and plump cheeks. Cementing the small end of the shell to the ring neck will produce an egghead with a slender face and pointed chin. The hole in the crown of the head could of course be covered with a Barbie-doll wig bought at a toyshop, but hair can be simulated with any number of everyday materials. First close the shell's hole with a small square of plastic tape. Then cement over the tape blond ringlets made of a section of a curly gold-colored metal pot cleaner or a gray fright wig made of wisps of steel wool. Smooth straight hair can be imitated with silky strands of yellow, brown, or black embroidery floss, while the makings of a gently waved coiffure can be obtained by untwisting three- or four-ply knitting worsted. A tuft of sterilized lamb's wool (from a drugstore) will be fine for silver-gray tresses, and bushy locks of any color can be counterfeited with absorbent cotton dipped in hot diluted liquid dye.

If you can capture a likeness with a paintbrush, by all means make each eggshell face a portrait-caricature of its assignee. Luckily, even those of us who can draw nothing more exciting than a deep breath will be able to turn the eggheads into droll characters by giving them sequin features. Use one small red sequin, cut in half with scissors, for an upper lip: squeeze two tiny dots of white glue onto the shell and lay the sequin halves upon the glue dots side by side, with their straight-cut edges down. To form the lower lip, fit the straight-cut edge of a large red sequin half below this upper lip and glue it there. For a pair of expressive egghead eyes, cut a large brown or dark blue sequin in two and lay the half moons—mounded side up—on dots of glue. If the straight-cut edges are placed

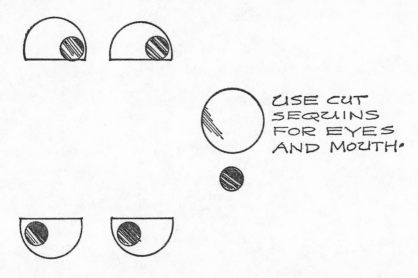

USE CUT SEQUINS FOR EYES AND MOUTH.

at the top, the eyes will appear downcast and shy; reversing the position of the sequin halves will change them into laughing eyes. Whole large light blue sequins, centered with small black sequins for pupils, will have a look of innocent amazement. Glue the small sequin pupils at the upper edges of the large blue irises, and the egghead will seem surprised; place the pupil at the outer edge of the iris, and the egghead will amuse you with a sidewise glance.

Smooth, solid china nest eggs can be used instead of brittle eggshells to make eggheads that look like little porcelain portrait busts. Predictably, nest eggs are scarcer than hen's teeth in large cities. They can, however, be ordered in wholesale quantities (at minimal cost) through a farmer's co-op or a large grain and feed store. Because these once-common objects now are rare as well as beautiful, any left over from the egghead project will be welcome gifts. (A china nest egg

has the translucency and sheen of fine white porcelain and can happily substitute for an alabaster egg on a gilded metal display stand.)

Once they have been mounted on plastic egg-half shoulders complete with curtain-ring necks, the china eggs are ready for sequin features and simulated hair. It would then be an exercise in ingenuity to dress these eggheads in period costumes by giving them hats. An oval shoe buckle made of solid-color plastic curves just enough to tilt forward over an egghead's eye like an Empress Eugenie derby; a fluffy feather borrowed from a brightly dyed duster can be angled downward like a curly ostrich plume. Little lacy plastic baskets are sold in packets of four as children's party favors. After removing its handle, turn one of these upside down to create a high-crowned Empire bonnet. Thread narrow matching ribbon through the ribs of the basket, knot the ribbon at one side, and add a nosegay of tiny plastic flowers. Cement the snap-on cap of a plastic pill vial in the center of the snap-on plastic cover of a baby food jar, and you will have devised a flat sailor hat of the eighteen-nineties. Add a band and streamers of satin baby ribbon, or a tailored hatband of narrow *soutache* braid. To complete the costume of a period egghead, one might add a veil of nylon net, a collar of narrow lace, a fur boa made of a mink tail, a plastic mesh pot cleaner for a portrait scarf, or a lacy shawl cut from a plastic mesh apple bag.

As a gift for a bride of the Christmas season, mount a china nest egg on a white plastic egg half. Pin a triangular lace veil to the egghead's hair, and give her a necklace of prestrung seed pearls. As a finishing touch, tie a sheaf of miniature lilies with white-satin baby ribbon and cement the bouquet near the base of the white egg-half bridal gown. For a recent graduate, dress a china egghead in a cap and gown of black felt. Use a circle of felt 6″ in diameter for the robe and cut a hole 1″ in diameter in the center of it. Glue the robe to the supporting egg half, centering the hole on its rounded top; then fit the lower ring of the stacked neck inside the hole, cementing it to the plastic below. To make the mortarboard, begin with a 2″ circle of felt. Cut two ½″ slashes in the felt on opposite sides of the circle. Overlap the edges of these slashes and glue them, to form a shallow cap that will fit the egghead's coiffure. Sandwich a 2″ square of cardboard between two slightly larger squares of black felt. Sew a tassel made of black embroidery thread to the center of the square, anchoring it with a black bead, and cement the flat top of the mortarboard on the crown of the cap. Then roll a 2″ square of white typewriter paper into a cylinder, tie it with embroidery thread in the college colors, and sew the diploma to the black felt gown.

Last and smallest of the miniature gift ideas—but one of the best—is a lapel-pin Christmas wreath. A dark green cord-covered ring pull (found at the windowshade display in a variety store) will form the backing for the wreath. Cut off the long loop of cord just above the knot at the edge of the pull and sew the spine of a small safety pin below the knot on the back of the ring. Using dark green thread, stitch 1″ tips of plastic cedar on the front of the wreath, overlapping the sprigs so that all their stems are hidden. To give this pin the traditional Christmas colors, hide the knot at the top of the wreath by tacking to it a little tailored bow of red-satin baby ribbon and trim the greenery by sewing on a few red beads. For a distinctive, wear-with-everything pin, use a flat bow of narrow gold braid and tiny shining balls in rainbow hues—red, pink, green, gold, silver, and bright blue. Make these by rolling up foil candy wrappers between thumb and fingers, and sew them on.

Now that all the little gifts are in readiness, reward yourself with a formal della Robbia wreath in miniature. Fashion it as before on a shade pull, sewing a safety pin behind the knot. This time, cover the front of the wreath with dark green oval leaves cut from a spray of artificial boxwood. Stitch the leaves in pairs, angling one inward very slightly and permitting its mate to extend beyond the outer edge of the cord-covered ring. Overlap the successive pairs of leaves to hide the stitches. Then select the smallest of dark red apples, sage-green pears, and bright yellow lemons. If these were part of a piece of costume jewelry, their stems will have handy holes for sewing them in place with dark green thread. If they

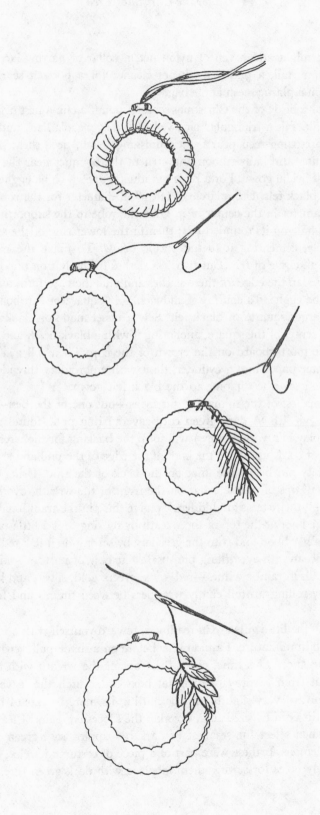

came on wire stems, the shortened wires can be pushed under the leaves of the wreath and secured by overstitching. If they were half-round fruits of the sort sold in needlework shops as sew-on trims, each one will have two holes, near opposite edges, for easy attachment. A pair of pineapple halves placed at the top of the wreath will hide the knot at the edge of the shade pull and no bow of ribbon will be required. Sew the remaining fruits in clusters around the circlet. Lacking the flat-backed pineapples, finish the wreath with a bow of $\frac{1}{4}''$-wide red-velvet ribbon.

Pin on the diminutive della Robbia wreath at once and wear it with pride—as your badge of membership in the growing guild of miniaturists.

Sources of Supply

Handmade reproductions of fine furniture and accessories:

Chestnut Hill Studio, Box 38, Churchville, New York 14428 (Cat. $1.50).

The Miniature Mart, 883 39th Street, San Francisco, California (Cat. $1.50).

Miniature Silver, 317 South Prospect Avenue, Park Ridge, Illinois 60068 (Brochure 50¢).

Southern Crafts, Middleton Plantation, Charleston, South Carolina (Cat. $1.25).

American and imported furniture and accessories, reasonably priced:

Federal Smallwares, 366 Fifth Avenue, New York, New York 10001.

Good-quality American and imported furniture and accessories, in general catalogues:

Clymer's of Bucks County, Point Pleasant, Pennsylvania 18950.

Downs, 1014 Davis Street, Evanston, Illinois 60204.

Miles Kimball, Oshkosh, Wisconsin 54901.

Rombins' Nest Farm, Fairfield, Pennsylvania 17320.

Windfall, Sharon Springs, New York 13459 (Colombian imports).

Yield House, North Conway, New Hampshire 03860.

Jewelry findings, Christmas trims:

Lee Ward's, Elgin, Illinois 60120.

Panorama figures, cake separators:

Maid of Scandinavia Company, 3245 Raleigh Avenue, Minneapolis, Minnesota 55416.

Excellent model-railroad accessories are made by these companies. Ask for them in hobby shops:

Preiser, West Germany.

Bachman Bros., Philadelphia (most of this line now is made in Hong Kong).

Atlas Tool Company, Hillside, New Jersey (good molded plastic miniatures).

Selected Bibliography

Creekmore, Betsey B. *Traditional American Crafts*. New York: Hearthside Press, 1968.

Dubois, M. J. *Curtains and Draperies*. New York: Viking Press, 1964.

Earle, Alice Morse. *Home Life in Colonial Days*. New York: The Macmillan Company (1898) 1954.

Gröber, Karl. *Children's Toys of Bygone Days* (trans. by Philip Hereford). London: B. T. Batsford, Ltd., 1928.

Hillier, Mary. *Pageant of Toys*. New York: Taplinger Publishing Company, Inc., 1966.

Jacobs, Flora Gill. *A History of Dolls' Houses*. New York: Charles Scribner's Sons, 1965.

Kornfeld, Albert. *The Doubleday Book of Interior Decorating and Encyclopedia of Styles*. Garden City: Doubleday & Company, Inc., 1965.

Marcus, Margaret Fairbanks. *Period Flower Arrangement*. New York: M. Barrows and Company, 1952.

Moore, Colleen. *Colleen Moore's Doll House*. Garden City: Doubleday & Company, Inc., 1971.

Musgrave, Clifford, OBE. *Queen Mary's Dolls' House*. London: Pitkin Pictorials, Ltd., 1969.

Pepis, Betty. *Interior Decoration, A to Z*. Garden City: Doubleday & Company, Inc., 1965.

Ramsey, Natalie Allen (Ed.). *The Decorator Digest*. Rutland: Charles E. Tuttle Company, 1965.

Savage, George. *A Concise History of Interior Decoration*. London: Thames and Hudson, 1966.

Tunis, Edwin. *Colonial Living*. Cleveland: World Publishing Company, 1957.

————. *Frontier Living*. Cleveland: World Publishing Company, 1961.

Von Wilckens, Leonie. *Tageslauf im Puppenhaus*. Munich: Prestel Verlag, 1956.

Whiton, Sherrill, Jr. *Elements of Interior Design and Decoration*. Philadelphia: J. B. Lippincott Company, 1963.

Williams, Guy R. *The World of Model Trains*. New York: G. P. Putnam's Sons, 1970.

Wilson, Jose and Leaman, Arthur. *Decoration, U.S.A.* New York: The Macmillan Company, 1965.

MUSEUM PUBLICATIONS:

ART INSTITUTE OF CHICAGO:
American Rooms in Miniature by Mrs. James Ward Thorne. Text by Meyric B. Rogers. Chicago, 1962.
European Rooms in Miniature by Mrs. James Ward Thorne. Text by Meyric B. Rogers. Chicago, 1962.

DULIN GALLERY OF ART:
The Thorne Miniature Rooms at the Dulin Gallery of Art. Text by Betsey B. Creekmore. Knoxville, 1972.

GERMANISCHES NATIONALMUSEUM:
Das Kleine Nurnberger Zeughaus. Text by Ernest Königer. Nuremberg, 1970.

HAAGS GEMEENTEMUSEUM:
A Guide to the Dolls' House. The Hague, 1970.

THE PHOENIX ART MUSEUM:
Miniature Rooms by Mrs. James Ward Thorne. Phoenix, 1963.

RIJKSMUSEUM:
Poppenhuizen/Dolls' Houses. Amsterdam, 1967.

VICTORIA AND ALBERT MUSEUM:
Dolls. London, 1968.

Index

Acacia, 91, 126
Accessories, 62, 64, 66, 76, 80–81, 82–83,
     86–87, 158, 160, 162, 169, 170
   Panorama figures (tinies), 182
Adam manner, 104
   dining room, 69, 70
   mantel, 38
Advent star, 14
Advertising, portable exhibits for, 153
Age of Aquarius, 150
Albert, Prince, 2, 176
Albert Memorial (London), 2
Albrecht V, Duke of Bavaria, 14, 25
Alexander III, of Russia, 4
American farm kitchen, 179–80
American Federal Period, 179
   mirror, 83
American history
   pioneer settlement, 183
   Thorne Rooms depicting, 22, 68, 69–70
   toy soldiers, 184–85
Animals
   carved wooden, 9, 10, 13
   for conservation exhibit, 152
   glass and porcelain, 4
   for miniature garden, 135
   pet, 87–88
   for pet shop, 159, 160
   plastic zoo sets, 182
   in Thorne Rooms, 88
   wooden, 9
   for woodland scene, 180
Anne, Queen of England, 18
Antique reproduction miniatures, 75,
     155–56, 162
Appalachia, 169, 171
Appel, Jacob, 17
Apple pyramid, 109–10
Aquarium, 113, 159
Architecture
   development of, in Thorne Rooms, 21,
     22, 68–69
   English baby house designs, 18
   garden models, 117
   working models, 1, 3
Arms and armament
   miniature soldiers, 4, 184–85
   working models, 3
Art, 4, 149–50
   op, 149
   pre-Columbian, 150
   See also paintings

Art Institute of Chicago, Thorne Rooms
     display, 21, 22, 68, 70
Augsburg, 25
   toymaking in, 9, 14

Baby's breath, 91, 126, 136, 181
Bakery, 162
Balcony, 57–58
Balsa wood, 34–35
Baroque Period, 101, 102, 106, 109
Basel, toymaking in, 9
Bathrooms, 66
   in Queen Mary's Dolls' House, 46
Bavarian Alps, 169–70
Bedding, 56
Beet seeds, 92, 127
Berry boxes, 33, 36, 37
Bethlehem, in Old Salem miniature scene,
     14
Bethnal Green Museum
   Martin Luther and first Christmas tree
     display, 11
   toy collection, 19
   See also Victoria and Albert Museum
Bible
   miniature scenes from, 10, 142
   in Queen Mary's Dolls' House, 18
Binnenhof (The Hague), 25, 160
Bird feeder, 152, 157
Bon-kei, 186–87
Bon-seki, 170–72
Book of Hours, 4, 86
Book of Kells, 141
Bookcases
   for displaying miniature collections,
     28–35
   Globe-Wernicke, 30, 32
Books, 4, 18, 62, 86, 141
Bookshelf wall, 61–62
Bookstore, 162
Boughpots, 104
Bouma, S. J., 23
Box-in-a-box construction, 20, 33, 35, 72–73
Brandt, Petronella Oortman, cabinet house
     of, 17–18
Brants, Christoffel van, 17
Bread box, 147, 155
Britain, 173
British crown jewels, 19
Brokaw, Anne, 142
Buddha, 2
Bullfight, 187

Burnett, Frances Hodgson, 5, 27
Buxom bouquets, 104
Byzantine Era, 8
Byzantium, 104, 106
  flower and fruit mosaics, 100

Cabinet houses. *See* Dutch cabinet houses
Cabinetmaking
  apprentices' miniatures, 3, 75
  for Dutch cabinet houses, 15
  portable fairs, rooms and shops, 10
  sample miniatures, 3, 75
Candles and candleholders, 21, 63–64, 76–
    77, 79–80, 82
Cape Cod cottage, 70
Cardboard theater, 153
Carpeting, 40–41, 58
Cartoons, 2–3
Castle and coach scene, 185–86
Ceilings, 42–43
Cellini, Benvenuto, 8
Celosia, 92, 126, 181
Centerpiece gardens, 135–36
Centraal Museum (Utrecht, Holland),
    cabinet house display, 15
Century of Progress Exposition (Chicago),
    Thorne Rooms display, 21
Chestnut Hill Studio, 76
Children's hospital, miniature playground
    for waiting room, 147–48
Chimney flowers, 101
China
  porcelain from, 16, 103
  pottery from, 101
Christmas crèche, 2, 12, 173–74
Christmas decorations, 177–80, 187–88
Christmas gifts, 180–97
Christmas *putz*, Old Salem, N.C., 12–14,
    174–75, 176, 177
Christmas tree, 12, 13, 173, 174, 176
  Martin Luther miniature scene, 11–12
  ornaments for, 187–88
Christopher, Saint, 2
Chrysnbon accessories, 76
Churchill, Winston, 149
Classic Revival Period, 104, 106, 110
  mantel, 82
Colleen Moore's Doll House, 140–42, 147
Colleen Moore's Doll House (Moore), 141
Community service projects, portable
    exhibits for, 147–54
Community theater advertising, 153
Conservation, portable exhibit for, 148,
    150–52
Cooking utensils, 10, 11
Coppersmiths, 10
Costume jewelry, for making
  accessories, 77, 87
  epergnes, 108
  miniature flower arrangements, 92–93, 96
  wall sconces, 79–80

Country store, 155
Craft guilds, 3, 10

Dark Ages, 3
Découpage, 4
Delft pottery, 101
  for Dutch cabinet houses, 15
Denver Art Museum, miniature room and
    shop displays, 11
Dining rooms
  Adams, 69, 70
  Louis XVI, 69
Display cabinets
  bookcases as, 28–35
  for miniature collections, 25–45
Doctor's office, 155, 156
Dollhouses
  accessories for, 10, 11, 66, 76, 160, 162
  Albrecht V, of Bavaria, 14, 25
  American, 88
  antique reproductions for, 75, 155, 162
  Colleen Moore's, 140–42, 147
  first record of, 14
  furniture for, 47, 52, 75–76
  German, 30
  lighting for, 32
  Queen Mary's, 18–20, 46, 75, 88, 112–13,
    141
  See also Miniature rooms
Dolls, 4–5, 88–90, 148, 159
  American, 88
  clothespeg, 88
  Dutch, 88
  English peddler, 10–11
  fashion display, 3, 11
  hickory-nut, 88
  Queen Victoria's, 88
Doors, 33, 35
Dormants, 107
Draperies, 37, 58–59, 75
Drugstore, 162
Druids, 173
Dulin Gallery of Art (Knoxville, Tenn.),
    Thorne Rooms display, 22, 70
Dutch cabinet houses, 14–18, 25, 27–28,
    35, 46–47, 52, 75, 88
  gardens for, 115
Dutch Hussars, 23

Early American miniature furniture, 47
Easter eggs, 190
  Fabergé, 188
Egg-head portrait busts, 189–93
Eggs and eggshells, 188–95
  China, 194–95
  for nativity scene, 188–89
Egypt, 106, 165
  floral bouquets in tomb paintings, 100
  miniatures in tomb furnishings, 2, 114–15
Eisenhower, Dwight D., 149
Elizabeth I, Queen of England, 101

Empire Period, 75, 104, 106
Engineering working models, 4
England, 176
  Tudor flower and herb arrangements, 101
Entrance halls
  Hermitage (Andrew Jackson's home), 22
  Pierce mansion (Portsmouth, N.H.), 70
Environmental protection agency, portable
    conservation exhibit, 148, 150–52
Epergnes, 107–9, 110

Fabergé, Peter Carl, 188
Fairs, 10, 11, 154
Fairy tales, illustrated in Colleen Moore's
    doll house, 147
Farm scene, 183–84
Fashion display, 10, 11
  eighteenth-century dolls, 3
Feverfew, 136
Fireplaces and mantels, 38–40, 41, 74, 80
  accessories for, 80–81, 82–83
  for weaver's house, 144–45
Flax wheel, 145
Floors, 41–42, 74
Flower shop, 181
Flower show exhibit, 148, 150–52
Folding screens, 84–86
France, Christmas crèches of, 12, 173
Francis of Assisi, Saint, 12, 173, 180
Freulich, Henry, 140
Fruits, miniature, for centerpiece, 107
Furniture, 47, 75–76
  alterations for, 47–50
  antique reproductions, 75, 155, 162
  apprentice cabinetmakers' miniatures, 3,
    75
  contemporary, 47
  dollhouse, 52, 75–76
  for Dutch cabinet houses, 14
  early American, 47
  garden, 135
  metal, 52
  molded plastic, 51, 52
  reupholstering, 52–55
  sample miniatures, 3, 75
  Victorian. *See* Victorian Era
  weaver's house, 145–46

Garden club
  miniature garden advertising plant sale,
    154
  miniature garden as luncheon table
    centerpiece, 139
Gemeentemuseum (The Hague), Ploos
    van Amstel cabinet house, 15–16, 31,
    115
Georgian Period, 103
Germanisches Museum (Nuremberg)
  miniature kitchen and shop displays, 10
  seventeenth-century houses in, 30

Germany, seventeenth-century portable
    scenes, 9–12, 142
Gibbons, Grinling, 38, 46
Globe-Wernicke bookcases, 30, 32
Godey's Lady's Book, 176
Golden Gate International Exposition (San
    Francisco), Thorne Rooms display, 21
Goldsmiths, 8
Gothic churches
  carved stone flowers and fruits, 100
  working models, 3
Grandmother Stover dollhouse accessories,
    76, 162
Grass, for miniature garden, 118
Great Smoky Mountains, 169
Greece, flower and fruit arrangements, 100,
    104, 109
Gregory Thaumaturgus, Saint, 12
Grieve, Harold, 140
Grote Kerk (Middleburg, Holland), 24
Gustavus Adolphus, King of Sweden, 25

Hainhofer, Philip, 142
Hall Company, 47
Heather, 92, 126, 136, 181
Herculaneum, 104
Hermitage (Andrew Jackson's home),
    Thorne miniature of entrance hall, 22
Hermitage Museum (Leningrad), miniature
    room displays, 17
Historiches Museum der Stadt Wien
    (Vienna), miniature shop and room
    displays, 10
History
  miniature scenes from, 10, 142
  Thorne Rooms, 22
  toy soldiers, 4, 184–85
History of England, miniature copy, 18
Hitler, Adolf, 23
Hoffmann, Heinrich, 11
Hogarth curve, 106
Holland
  cabinet houses, 14–18, 25, 27–28, 35
  Golden Century of, 15, 18
  miniature city (Madurodam), 23–24
Holly, 173
House museums, 68, 71, 75, 174, 176
Hunting scenes, 9, 185

Illuminated manuscripts, 3–4
Indians, 158
Indian weaving, 146–47
Industrial Revolution, 3, 143
Interior design, development of, 21, 68
International Business Machines Corporation
    (IBM), 21, 69
Italy, Christmas crèches of, 12, 14, 173

Jackson, Andrew, 22
Jackson, Horace, 140
Jamnitzer, Wentzel, 8

Japan
  bon-kei, 186–87
  bon-seki, 170–72
Jekyll, Gertrude, 112, 113
John Chrysostom, Saint, 12
Jordaan Quarter (Amsterdam), 24

Kennedy, John F., 165
Kensington Palace, 2
King Nutcracker and Poor Reinhold
  (Hoffman), 11
Kitchens, 66
  American farm, 179–80
  best, 17, 18
  in Brandt cabinet house, 17–18
  cooking utensils for, 10, 11
  in Governor's mansion, Williamsburg, 70
  New England, 70
  Nuremberg, 9–10, 11, 40, 73, 142
  plastic sets for, 66
  in Queen Mary's Dolls' House, 18, 46
  Thorne Rooms, 70, 88
Kunsthistorisches Museum (Vienna), semi-
  precious stone mountain collection, 9

Lambeth Palace, 142
Lamps, 62–63
Lange Jan Tower (Middleburg, Holland),
  24
Lawyer's office, 155–56
Legend, miniature scenes from, 10
Lighting, 30–35, 56
Lighting devices, 59–61, 62–63, 76–80
Linde company, 32, 47
Liquid thread, 55, 74, 86
London Museum, 2
  Queen Victoria's dollhouse and Dutch
    dolls in, 88
London Times, miniature copy, 22
Loom, 146
Louis XV libraries, 69
Louis XVI dining rooms and salons, 69
Lowell, James Russell, 180
Luce, Clare Booth, 142
Luke, Saint, 14
Lunaria, 104
Luther, Martin, 11–12, 173
Lutheran settlements, 174
Lutyens, Edwin, 19
Lying-in room, 16

Madonna, 2
Maduro, George, 23, 24
Maduro, Mr. and Mrs. J. M. L., 23, 24
Madurodam, miniature Dutch city, 23–24,
  160
Marionette theater, 153
Mary, Queen (wife of George V of
  England), Dolls' House gift to, 18–20,
  46, 75, 88, 112–13, 141

Maximilian Museum (Augsburg)
  miniature arms and armaments exhibits, 3
  miniature kitchen and shop exhibits, 10
Meket-Re, walled garden in tomb
  furnishings, 114–15
Metropolitan Museum of Art (New York
  City)
  miniature room and shop exhibits, 11
  walled garden of Meket-Re, 114–15
Mexico, 187
Middle Ages, 3, 4, 74, 100, 107
Miller's house, 70
Milliners' shops, 11
Minerals
  for Christmas gifts, 180
  for miniature mountains, 165, 166
  semi-precious stone mountains, 8–9
Miniature flower arrangements, 91–111
  air-dried materials, 91–92, 94, 104, 125–
    26, 136, 181
  artificial materials, 94
  beet seeds, 92, 127
  chimney flowers, 101
  containers for, 95–99, 101–4
  costume jewelry used for, 92–93
  Japanese style, 106
  period centerpieces, 107–11
  for period rooms, 100–6
  sequins used for, 94
  tussie-mussies, 101, 106
Miniature furniture. *See* Furniture
Miniature gardens, 112–39
  advertising garden club plant sale, 154
  animals in, 135
  in aquarium, 113
  as centerpiece, 135–36
  containers for, 113–14, 116
  espaliers for, 124–25
  fences for, 116–17
  flower bed planters for, 139
  flowers for, 125–29
  fountain for, 132
  freestanding, 114
  furniture for, 135
  grass for, 118
  knot garden, 116
  paths for, 117–18
  Ploos van Amstel cabinet house, 115
  pools and brooks for, 129–31
  portable, 114–15, 154
  potted plants for, 133–34
  Queen Mary's Dolls' House, 112–13
  tools for, 135
  trees for, 118–23, 137–39
  vines for, 123–24
  walls for, 116
  wild life for, 135
Miniature manufacturing
  antique reproductions, 75, 155, 162
  contemporary, 47, 52, 76
  tinies (panorama figures), 182

Miniature mountains, 165–72
  bon-seki, 170–72
  ornaments for, 166
  of semi-precious stones, 8–9, 167
  stands for, 167
Miniature rooms, 5, 7, 10
  accessories, 22, 64, 66, 76, 80–81, 82–83,
    86–87, 158, 160, 162, 169, 170
  American series, Thorne Rooms, 22, 68,
    69–70
  balcony, 57–58
  bathrooms, 66
  bedding, 56
  best kitchen, 17, 18
  bookcases for display, 28–35
  books, 4, 18, 62, 86, 141
  bookshelf wall, 61–62
  box-in-a-box construction, 20, 33, 35,
    72–73
  candles and candleholders, 21, 63–64, 76–
    77, 79–80, 82
  carpeting, 40–41, 58
  ceilings, 42–43
  Christmas decorations, 177–80, 187–88
  doors, 33, 35
  draperies, 37, 58–59, 75
  European (English and French) series,
    Thorne Rooms, 21, 69–70
  fireplaces and mantels, 38–40, 41, 74,
    80–81, 82–83
  floors, 41–42, 74
  flower arrangements, 91–106
  folding screens, 84–86
  freestanding, 73–74
  furniture. *See* Furniture
  kitchens. *See* Kitchens
  lighting, 30–35, 56
  lighting devices, 59–61, 62–63, 76–80
  lying-in room, 16
  mirrors, 65, 83–84
  oriental (Chinese and Japanese), Thorne
    Rooms, 22
  painting, 19, 44, 74
  paintings, 4, 64–65, 150
  period, 5, 68–90
  period centerpieces, 107–11
  picture windows, 56–57
  portable. *See* Portable scenes
  preserving the present, 46–67
  proportions, 28–29
  research for, 20, 71
  rugs, 21, 74–75
  table lamps, 62–63
  Thorne Rooms, 20–23, 33, 35, 68–70
  toys, 87, 88, 155, 156–57
  venetian blinds, 59
  Victorian. *See* Victorian Era
  wall coverings, 44, 74
  wall paneling, 43
  windows, 33–37, 56–57, 145–46
  See also Dollhouses

Miniature scenes (fairs, shops), portable.
    See Portable scenes
Mirrors, 65, 83–84
  for garden pools, 129–30
  for plateau centerpiece, 110
  for windows, 145–46
Mistletoe, 173
Model cars, 19
Model trains, 4, 142
  accessories for, 123, 169, 170, 182
Money plant, 104
Moore, Clement Clark
  A Visit from St. Nicholas by, 179
Moore, Colleen, 140
  Colleen Moore's Doll House by, 141
  dollhouse, 140–42, 147
Moravian Church, 13–14
Moucheron, Frederik de, 15
Mount Vernon, Thorne miniature of west
    parlor, 22
Museums, 75–76
  Dutch cabinet houses in, 15–18
  house, 68, 71, 75, 174, 176
  membership drive display, 153–54
  miniature collections in, 7, 10–11, 17
  sidewalk art show miniature for, 148,
    149–50, 159
  Thorne Rooms in, 21, 22, 68, 69
  Weber antique toys, 10
Museum of Science and Industry (Chicago),
    Colleen Moore's Doll House in, 141

Nanking pottery, 101
Napoleon, 4, 104
National Museum (Munich)
  Gothic church scale model displays, 3
  miniature room and shop displays, 10
  seventeenth-century houses in, 30
Nativity scene, 188–89
  Italian, 14
  Old Salem, 12, 13, 14
Navaho Indians, 146–47
Needlework Guild of Chicago, 21
Neighborhood improvement association,
    pocket-park display for, 148, 149
New England kitchen, 70
New York World's Fair (1940), Thorne
    Rooms display, 21
Nigeria, 142
Nikolaas, Saint, 173
Noak's Ark, 9
Nordiska Museet (Stockholm), miniature
    room and shop displays in, 10
Nuremberg, toymaking in, 9, 14
Nuremberg kitchens, 9–10, 11, 40, 73, 142
Nutcracker ballet, 11

Oasis, 136
Oh, Little Town of Bethlehem, 14
Old Salem, Inc., 13–14

Old Salem Christmas *putz*, 12–14
Op Art, 149

Painting, 44, 74
    for Queen Mary's Dolls' House, 19
Paintings, 65
    miniature portraits, 4
    miniature reproductions, 64–65, 150
Pampas grass, 105
Panorama figures, 182
Patent applications, 1
Peacock feathers, 105
Pennsylvania, 174
Pennsylvania Dutch miller's house, 70
Peppergrass, 104
Peruvian starflowers, 91, 126, 136, 181
Peter the Great, 17
Pets, 87–88
Pet shop, 159–60
Phoenix Art Museum, Thorne rooms
        display, 22, 69, 70
Picture windows, 56–57
Piemont, Nicolaas, 17
Pioneer settlement, 183
Pius IX, Pope, 142
Planning commission, mini-park display,
        148, 149
Plastics Period, 51
Plateau centerpiece, 110
Ploos van Amstel, Sara, 16
    cabinet house, 15–16, 31, 47, 115
Pocket-park miniature, 148, 149
Polygonum, 92, 126
Pompeii, 104
Porcelain, Chinese, 16, 103
Portable scenes (fairs, rooms, shops), 7,
        9–12, 140–64
    American farm kitchen, 179–80
    bakery, 162
    bird feeder for, 152, 157
    bon-kei, 186–87
    bon-seki, 170–72
    bookstore, 162
    castle and coach scene, 185–86
    for children's hospital waiting room,
        147–48
    for Christmas gifts, 180–97
    for community service projects, 147–54
    for community theater promotion, 153
    conservation exhibits, 148, 150–52
    country store, 155
    doctor's office, 155, 156
    drugstore, 162
    farm scene, 183–84
    flower shop, 181
    flower show conservation exhibit, 148,
        150–52
    folding, 156
    freestanding, 73–74
    for garden club plant sale, 154
    German, 9–12, 142

    hunting scenes, 9, 185
    lawyer's office, 155–56
    for museum advertising and promotion,
        148, 149–50, 153–54, 159
    Nuremberg kitchens, 9–10, 11, 40, 73,
        142
    pet shop, 159–60
    pioneer settlement, 183
    planning commission mini-park scene, 148,
        149
    poultry yard, 9
    regional displays, 167–69
    safari scene, 182
    shopping center, 161–64
    sidewalk art show, 148–49, 150, 159
    silversmith's shop, 155
    street fairs, 10, 11, 154
    toy shop, 156–57
    unique boutique, 157–58
    Victorian house and grounds, 184
    wig shop, 158–59
    woodland scene, 180
Portrait painters, 4
Pottery, 10
    Chinese, 101
    Delft, 15, 101
    for Dutch cabinet houses, 15
    Nanking, 101
    Wedgwood, 104
Poultry yards, 9
Putz figures, 12, 176. *See also* Christmas
    putz

Queen Anne's lace, 126
Queen Mary's Dolls' House, 18–20, 46, 75,
        88, 141
    garden, 112–13

Railroad trains. *See* Model trains
Reformation, 174
Regency folding screen, 85
Regional displays, 167–69
Religious symbols, 2, 100
    in Colleen Moore's dollhouse, 141
Renaissance, 8, 71, 74, 86, 107, 108, 165
    cartoons for frescoes, 2
    floral decorations, 100, 101, 106
    England, 101
    Germany, 101
    Italy, 100
Reupholstering, 52–55
Rijksmuseum (Amsterdam), 15
    Brandt cabinet house display, 17–18
Robbia, Andrea della, 100, 179
Rocky Mountains, 168
    minerals from, 167
Rococo style, 102
Rome, 173
    flower and fruit arrangements, 100, 104,
        106
Roosevelt, Mrs. James, 141

Roosevelt, Theodore, 22
Rosaries, 100
Roses, 105
Royal Academicians, 19
Rugs, 21, 74–75
Russia
    Alexander III, glass and porcelain animal
        collection, 4
    Fabergé, Easter eggs, 188
    Peter the Great, cabinet house, 17

Safari scene, 182
St. Peter's penny, 104
Salem College for Women, 13
Saltcellers, 107
Santa Claus, 173
Saturn, feast of (Saturnalia), 173
Scallop shells, as flower containers, 102–3
Schwarz, F.A.O., 75
Schweitzerisches Museum für Volkskunde
        (Basel)
    shop and street fair exhibits, 10, 11
    storybook scene exhibits, 10, 11
Sculptures, 154
Seascape, 171
Semi-precious stone mountains, 8–9
Sequins, 94, 127
Shackman company, 47
Shadow box, 56
Shaker communal home, 70
Sharp, Ann, 18
Shingles, 160–61
Ship models, 4
Shopping center, 161–64
Show window displays, 160
Sidewalk art show, 148, 149–50, 159
Silhouettes, 4
Silversmiths, 15, 17
    model shop, 155
Skating scene, 176
Smithsonian Institution, room and shop
        displays, 11
Snow, directions for simulating, 170, 176
Snuff boxes, 4
Social comment, 147
Social history, 158
Southern Craft Shop, 76
Southwest
    desert scene, 168
    mining scene, 180–81
    Thorne adobe house, 70
Spain, toy manufacturing in, 185
Spinning wheel, 146
Starflowers, Peruvian, 91, 126, 136, 181
Statice, 91, 126, 136, 181
Storybook scenes, 10, 11
Stover, Grandmother, accessories, 76, 162
Street fairs, 10, 11, 154

Teaching toys, 9, 142
Theater, 153

"This Is Your Life," 181
Thorne, Mrs. James Ward, 20
Thorne miniature period rooms, 20–23, 33,
        35, 68–70
    American series, 22, 68, 69–70
    Chinese, 22
    English, 21, 68
    European series, 21, 69–70
    French, 21, 68
    Japanese, 22
Tiffany jewelers, 165
Tinies, 182
Tinsmiths, 10
Tootsie Toys, 52
Toy manufacturing, 9–12, 14, 75–76, 156
    antique reproductions, 75, 155, 162
    folding shop, 156
    Spanish, 185
    tinies (panorama figures), 182
Toys, 87, 88, 155, 156–57
    Bethnal Green Museum collection, 19
    carved wooden, 9, 10, 13
    teaching, 9, 142
Toyshop, 156–57
Toy soldiers, 4, 184–85
Trees, for miniature garden, 118–23, 137–39
Tudor flower and herb arrangements, 101
Tussie-mussies, 101, 106

Ulm, toymaking in, 9, 14
Unique boutique, 157–58
University of Leyden, 23, 24, 160
University of Uppsala, 25
Urban planners, mini-park display, 148
Utrecht cabinet house, 15

Vatican, flower and fruit mosaics, 100
Veneering
    for furniture construction, 50–51
    for parquetry floors, 41–42
Venetian blinds, 59
Victoria, Queen, 2, 88, 176
Victoria and Albert Museum (London), 10
    Queen Mary's gifts to, 18, 19
    See also Bethnal Green Museum
Victorian Era, 106, 110, 176, 177
    bedroom, 82
    Christmas, 179
    drawing room, 22–23
    fireplaces and accessories, 80–81, 82, 105
    flowers and arrangements, 105
    garden furniture, 135
    gazebo, 133
    house and grounds, 184
    library, 157
    parlor, 22, 23, 83, 86, 87
    skating scene, 176
    Thorne Rooms, 10, 22
Visit from St. Nicholas, A (Moore), 179
Voorhout, Jan, 17

Waarenburg, Christiaan, 17
Walking wheel, 146
Wall coverings, 44, 74
Wall paneling, 43
Wallpaper cleaner, 128
Warhol, Andy, 150
Waterfall, 171
Weaver's house, 143–46
Weaving
  cartoons for, 3
  Navaho Indians, 146–47
  weaver's house, 143–46
Weber, Franz Carl, toy manufacturing
    company, 10, 156
  antique toys museum, 10
Wedgwood pottery, 104
Wig shop, 158–59
William, Duke of Bavaria, 142
Williamsburg, kitchen of governor's
    mansion, 70

Windows, 33–37, 56–57
  for weaver's house, 145–46
Windsor Castle, 20, 112, 176
Winston-Salem, 13
  Old Salem Christmas *putz,* 12–14
Wood carving, 10, 13
  animals, 9
  Thuringian, 10, 13
Woodland scene, 180
Working model miniatures, 1, 3, 4, 117
World War II, 23, 24
Wyeth, Andrew, 150

Yarrow, 91, 126, 136
Yule log, 173

Zoo, 159–60
  plastic animal sets, 182
Zurich, toymaking in, 9